W9-BYZ-574

Formation

Formation

a woman's memoir of
stepping out of line

Ryan Leigh Dostie

GRAND CENTRAL
PUBLISHING

NEW YORK   BOSTON

Copyright © 2019 by Ryan Leigh Dostie

Cover design by Elizabeth Connor. Cover image by Brian Levy.
Cover copyright © 2019 by Hachette Book Group, Inc.

Grand Central Publishing

Hachette Book Group

1290 Avenue of the Americas, New York, NY 10104

grandcentralpublishing.com

twitter.com/grandcentralpub

First Edition: June 2019

Grand Central Publishing is a division of Hachette Book Group, Inc. The Grand Central Publishing name and logo is a trademark of Hachette Book Group, Inc.

The publisher is not responsible for websites (or their content) that are not owned by the publisher.

The Hachette Speakers Bureau provides a wide range of authors for speaking events. To find out more, go to www.hachettespeakersbureau.com or call (866) 376-6591.

Library of Congress Cataloging-in-Publication Data has been applied for.

ISBNs: 978-1-5387-3153-6 (hardcover), 978-1-5387-3151-2 (ebook)

Printed in the United States of America

LSC-C

10 9 8 7 6 5 4 3 2 1

To my daughter, Adeline Sophia:
You are the wild that always calls me back home.
To my sons, Elias Jacob and Kilian Alexander:
I wish you were here to be wild with her.

Contents

Violation

A FEW HOURS BEFORE I am raped, two officers in a bar try to corner me and steal my panties. Locke and I are hovering by a standing table when they approach, standing so close that I have to crane my head back to see their faces. Despite my heels, they're taller than me.

"Want a drink?" asks the one closer to me. His dark hair is so neatly shorn that his skin looks blue. It gives him away. I point to his head.

"Enlisted or officer?"

He grins, all teeth, and leans forward, splashing me with the scent of whiskey sour mix. He's uneasy on his feet, leaning to one side, a meaty hand resting on the table for balance. "Officers. You military?"

Locke's jaw works impatiently and she ignores the men, instead looking around the bar for something better to do. She doesn't suffer boredom well and she likes her men prettier than this. "Enlisted."

"Aww," pouts the other, trying to get Locke's attention.

"You're too pretty to be in the Army," says the officer nearer to me, and I can't help but smile. I never quite understand the phrase, whether it's meant to be a compliment or insult, but I like being called pretty, even if the praise is buried in subtext. I don't have Locke's tall, toned body or her steely confidence. I still blush and preen under male approval. He likes the reaction and moves closer. He presses his shoulder against mine. "Let's get a drink."

The two men are older than us by at least a decade, and the age gap feels significant somehow. I shift my weight to the other foot to buy myself some space. "I don't know. I feel like that's fraternization." I laugh to lighten the rejection.

"I won't tell if you don't." He winks one watery eye. For as much experience as I've had keeping men at bay, I suddenly don't know how to untangle myself from this situation. Locke looks bored but shrugs. She won't turn down a free drink but I prefer to buy my own. Too many unspoken obligations tie a girl to a bought drink.

"I know." I perk up. "How about a bet? If I can take a shot better than you can, then you pay for our drinks." Locke grins. She knows this party trick and I'm damn good at it.

The officer snorts. "You think you can handle your liquor better than me?"

"For one shot I can."

"And if I win?" he asks. He's grinning. He thinks he's already won.

"You leave us alone," Locke shoots and I'm both uncomfortable and relieved by her brusqueness. I long for that kind of grit.

The officer shakes his head. "That's not a reward. How about I get your panties."

"My what?"

"Your underwear. If I win, you have to give me your panties."

Locke looks aghast and I wear a similar expression. "Why would you want my underwear?"

Locke lays a hand on my shoulder and shakes her head. Her whiskey shots are kicking in. "Don't ask questions you don't want the answer to. Fine. Deal. Whatever. Get us some shots." *Please don't gamble with my underwear*, I want to say, but I know they can't be serious.

I'm certainly not serious. It wasn't a real bet, just something said in jest.

The officer jabs his friend with his elbow. "Go get us some whiskey."

"Don't be a bitch," I counter, gathering my confidence because, though I only started drinking a few months ago when I turned twenty-one, good Christian girl turned a little bad by legality, *this* I know how to do. "Everclear," I add, naming my 190-proof corn spirit of choice. If you want a shot to knock someone back on their heels, Everclear is the only way to do it.

The officer grimaces, which is the exact reaction I was hoping for, but he doesn't back down. When the Everclear arrives, it glistens in a tall, plastic cup. It's a double shot.

"You first." Locke's hand hovers by her own drink—whiskey already purchased by one of the officers.

The officer stares tentatively at the drink, the cup dwarfed in his palm. I hope he backs down. He doesn't. He throws the drink back, swallows in one gulp, careful to keep his face composed. He blinks rapidly but doesn't cough or grimace. He carefully places the cup on the table before clearing his throat. "Your turn." The other officer slaps him on the back and congratulates his fortitude.

I scowl in annoyance. I usually win this game before I even take the shot. I hold the glass out, careful not to get a whiff of its potent stench, then breathe in and hold it. I down the drink, feeling it burn its way down my throat and pound its way into my stomach, and breathe out slowly, careful to keep my nose closed off so I can't taste the alcohol. I grin as the last of my breath escapes between tightly clamped teeth. Easy peasy.

The two officers narrow their eyes, staring, waiting for me to shiver, cough, and gag. I tip the glass victoriously before returning it to the table.

"We win," Locke says, then downs her shot, throws the cup onto the table, and grabs my arm. "Bye bye." She tugs me away from the table.

"I don't think so." The smaller officer's hand shoots out and captures my wrist. "We win. He did better."

"Did not," I protest, but the corn ethanol is working its way through my system. My feet are suddenly large and cumbersome. I grip Locke's elbow tighter.

"Yeah, I was way better." The officer makes a come-hither gesture with his hand. "Give up the panties."

"Nope." Locke pulls me hard enough that my wrist slides out of his grasp.

"Hey! A bet's a bet!" he yells after us as we make our retreat through the crowd.

"Freaks," Locke says, pushing me up against the bar. The air is suddenly hot. I tug at my dress's collar.

"Is it hot in here?"

"Here." She pushes a vodka shot into my hand.

"Nooo," I mutter to myself, eyeing my archnemesis. Everclear I could do, but vodka and I aren't very good friends. "I'm not supposed to be drinking," I suddenly remember, thinking of the doctor a few weeks back who handed me a nine-month supply of isoniazid for a positive tuberculosis PPD test, stressing, "You can't drink *at all* while taking this," and then pressing another bottle of vitamin B12 into the other hand to counter the "acute liver failure side effects" of the first drug. But possible liver disease seems a minor complication to a twenty-one-year-old and I shrug, taking the shot. Really, it's only a few drinks this one time. What's the worst that can happen?

There is dancing and more shots. I know I can handle a dozen without a problem, but I stop counting somewhere around drink ten. Locke's body weaves intricate symbols on the dance floor, her cheeks vermilion red. I sway to the music, fascinated by the drops of light that waver and splash across my skin. Maybe it's the medication, but the alcohol hits me harder than usual, faster, more violently, and I try to keep to my normal drinking pace but I've outrun my sobriety. I skirt to the outside of the dance floor and lean into a corner. I rest my head back, legs braced apart, using the hard angles of the corner walls to hold me up.

"Hey you," says a familiar voice, and I crack open one eye. The dim lights burn.

"Hi?" My voice crackles. The officer leans against the wall beside me. "I won our bet from earlier, you know," he says.

"Meh." I don't have the will to argue and I close my eyes. Sight makes me wobbly.

"I believe these are mine," he says and suddenly there is a warm hand on the inside of my thighs.

I gasp and slam my knees together, pinning his hand in place. "What are you doing?" But the protest comes out breathy and weak.

He grins, his face so close to mine. He's tall and I'm not standing upright, making his upper body loom over me. "It's all in good fun," he tries to assure me, wiggling his hand upward.

I laugh because I'm nervous and drunk. "Stop." I catch his wrist and try to push it down. "Come on, you lost the bet." The other officer is there to my left and my spine is pressed into the corner, locking me in place. His fingers slide up my skirt, up against the outside of my hip, and loop around the material of my underwear. He tugs and the fabric slides down. "Seriously, stop," I laugh, swallowing hard, knees shaking, and I use my other hand to grip my underwear, trying to hold them up. But it's four hands against two and they're winning. I feel tiny, as if I've shrunk and they're giants, black shadows bent over me, blocking out the rest of the club.

"Hey!" Locke breaks through between them, a vengeful spirit, all wild dark hair and crimson cheeks. "Fuck off!" she snarls, so tall, so muscular, jabbing one of the officers in the ribs and pulling me out from beneath them. I stumble after her, quickly trying to straighten my underwear with one hand.

"Jesus Christ, Dostie, learn to punch someone in the face," Locke throws over her shoulder at me. I stare up at the strong line of her shoulders, the muscles that contort and roll beneath her black tank top, the exposed white skin that defies the December night cold, and feel shamed.

Outside, I embrace the sharpness of the cold against my skin. I shiver, as if I can physically shake off the feeling of rough palms searching between my legs. Andres is there, materializing as if summoned, and I lean against him, dropping my head onto his shoulder. He and Diaz had been at another part of the bar, placing as much space between them and the dance floor as physically possible. I cuddle against Andres's safety and warmth. I have a sometimes-lover at another post, so my relationship with Andres has been platonic, though not strictly so, with tentative flirtations of possibly more. I trust his inherent instinct to protect me, as if I'm a wobbly fawn in constant need of tending. "I need to go home," I say, to him, to Locke, probably to myself.

"No, come on. It's too early." Locke pouts. She complains. She begs for reconsideration but I've had too much and I sprawl out in the backseat of Diaz's car, glad to have a sober friend, our faithful designated driver. I keep one hand on the hem of my skirt, as if retroactively keeping it in place.

Diaz drops us off at the barracks parking lot. Locke has convinced him to take her back into town and they encourage Andres to join them. The night is too early and I've ruined it too quickly. But Andres waves them off and I feel bad, but mostly thankful. I eye the long path to the barracks building warily. I'm not sure I can navigate it alone. I concentrate on placing one foot in front of the other, like it's some complex physics formula that needs all my attention. Mere steps from the main door, my foot catches on nothing and I plop down onto the pavement. Andres grabs my elbow but I shake my head. "Nope. Just leave me here." Drunk me doesn't want to dare the stairs.

There's a short laugh. "Looks like someone had a good time," says a guy from our Military Intelligence unit. He sits on the cement benches outside the main door. He has a thick, white v-shaped scar that covers the back of his head. It's his only distinguishing mark. Otherwise he's nondescript: short, stout, and with lazily buzzed brown hair. I don't know much about him, since he's in a different platoon. I think he's an intelligence analyst, and I'm a Persian-Farsi/Japanese linguist; we barely overlap.

"Yeah, she's going to bed," Andres says above me as he tries to pull me up.

"To bed!" I cheer loudly, because that's exactly where I want to be. My sheets are calling me.

The guy says something else; there is an exchange that is literally over my head, and when Andres guides me toward the stairwell, the analyst grabs my other elbow, balancing me out. I smile in gratitude, feeling protected between fellow unit members, my sentinels.

At my room door, I sway before the electronic combination lock. Our barracks don't have keys. Instead each door is fitted with a box that has four simple punch buttons, each lock needing a specific series of numbers stamped in a particular order. I punch in my number and try the handle. It rattles in hand. "Shit," I hiss and punch the number again. The handle refuses to move. "Shit fuck." I jab the combination, one hand braced against the doorframe. Third time is a charm and the door swings open. I sprint on foal legs to my bed, curling up around the sheets, nuzzling my pillow.

The bed shifts and someone sits by my feet. I have to sit up for someone to sit on the other side of me. There is masculine laughter, a conversation that I'm not quite part of but I smile and nod. A wine bottle passes in front of me, from one man to the other, and I don't know where it came from. It's pink wine. It's definitely not Andres's. The bottle is pressed into my hand and I wrap my fingers around the neck. I take a gulp because it's there, because I feel the intense need to keep up, to prove that I can. I start to pull the bottle away from my lips and the analyst grabs the bottom of the bottle, tipping it up so that I take another mouthful. "Drink," he says, and I chug another two gulps. It's too much. I shove the bottle into Andres's hands and crumble to the side, wrapping my arms around my pillow. I drift between awake and asleep, startling now and again at a particularly loud punch in the conversation.

"She's definitely had enough," Andres concludes and I hum in response. Andres herds out the analyst and I hear the shuffle of their feet as they leave, the comforting click of the door locking behind them. I slip off to sleep in the cool darkness, still fully dressed, still wearing the underwear that has made it this far, but will make it no farther.

how it happened

I WAKE WITH MY CHEEK pressed into my bare mattress. I don't know why it's bare. I had a sheet on it when I fell asleep. Something happened and I missed it. There is a black, gaping hole in my memory and I'm trying to piece myself around it, remembering the door closing shut, that warm, safe click of the lock, but now I'm on my stomach, face smashed into the faded blue-and-white-striped mattress. I turn my head, rearing back slightly, and there is a man behind me, kneeling, weight back on his heels, hands on my waist, gripping tight to the flesh, ramming himself into me, again and again, and I don't know how I got here. I'm simply confused at first, for a second trying to follow the bread crumbs of my memory but stumbling into the void, the missing parts, and I say, "I don't know what's going on," because I don't and it seems the most reasonable thing to say. "I don't understand what's happening."

He ignores me, pulling at my hips to hitch them up higher, to give him better access. "I don't know who you are," I say, and it's the start of my protest, my way of saying I'm not okay with this, because I don't know him, and that's important to me. I don't have sex with men I don't know. I don't have sex with anyone at all, save for the on-and-off-again lover stationed some hundred miles away. This isn't supposed to be happening. I plant my knees, trying to push up, to low-crawl away, but he bears down, pressing his weight onto my back, pinning me in place. "I don't know who you are," I say again, louder this time.

"Yes, you do," he grunts between thrusts. "I'm Kevin. Kevin Hale. You know me."

I know the name, vaguely, like a dim recollection, some analyst in another platoon but it's reaching, stretching for a memory. "I don't know you." My upper arms hurt, but I don't know why; the back of my skull hurts, and I don't know why. There's a short flash of a memory, of my head bouncing off the white brick wall, of hands digging into my arms, but it's too fast, too inexact, and instead I try to squirm, shift my hips away. "What the hell are you doing?" I ask, or at least I mean to ask in English, though it probably comes out in Japanese, because I'm drunk still and quick, easily accessible emotions always translate better in Japanese when I'm drunk. Senseless words tumble out because nothing makes sense anyway. もうやめて, I demand, said angrily, said loudly, said more than once, and he's getting angry now. His body stretches over mine, sweaty, naked flesh rubbing against my back, and I cringe, wanting to swipe away the sweat, the touch of his skin, but I can't get up, can't get my limbs to coordinate, to cooperate. "¡Cállate!" he hisses into my ear, lips pressed against the lobe, hot breath ruffling my hair. "¡Cállate! ¡Cállate! See, I can speak another language, too."

Then there is another trip into the black hole, moments sliced out of my brain, gone, and the next thing I see he's pulling out of me, climbing off the bed, not looking at me, seemingly disinterested. I scramble to the far side of the bed, clutching a pillow to my chest, fingers digging into the fabric, using it as a shield against my nakedness. There is a silence as he dresses and I watch warily from my corner. "It's okay," I say, for some reason trying to normalize the moment. "It's not like I don't know what rape is."

He looks up from fixing his belt, flashing a half grin. "I'm sorry you feel that way."

My mouth is wired shut. I want him gone—out of my room, no longer in my space. I pull the pillow tight against me, as if I can drag it into my body and erase the places he has been inside me. He's dressing too slowly, moving too leisurely. I just want him *gone*.

"Call me if you want to do this again sometime," he casually adds as he grabs his jacket.

I stare back dumbly. I don't know who this woman is. I should scream, rage, throw the pillow at him, grab the books off my desk and hurl them one by one at his head, grab the chair by its back and swing it into his chest. But instead I cower, heart pounding painfully against my rib cage as he leaves, hearing the click of the door lock in a way that will never be warm and comforting again.

I wait. One minute. Two minutes. Until I can't wait any longer and I scramble off the bed, grabbing wildly at the clothes on the floor, yanking on an oversize black T-shirt, hands shaking. I crack open the door, staring into the empty hallway. The light against the wall flickers and I hesitate, ensnared in the doorway, staring intently at the stairs he had to have used to leave the floor. I stare hard, waiting to hear boots on the steps, a shadow across the wall, so hard that I forget to breathe and I finally suck in air, a loud, wet sound in the emptiness. When I'm certain he's left, that he's not coming back, I dash across the hall. I slap my palms against Andres's door, my throat too tight to scream and my knees too weak to hold my weight.

The door next to mine cracks open and I twist quickly, flattening against the door, hands clutching at the doorknob that won't turn. Sergeant Rivera stands in his doorway, dressed in sweatpants and a PT shirt. He regards me softly, saying nothing, his forehead pinned together in sympathy, his eyes telling me he knows. He must know, yet he stands there, doing nothing. How can he know, yet do nothing? I'd spit if I could find the rage in me to do it, but it's all fled, leaving me trembling on bare legs, knees pressed firmly together.

Andres's door opens and I spill into the dark room, arms wrapped around my chest. I can't form any words; I huddle, head bent down. I rush to his bed, grabbing blankets like shields, rolling them round and round me until I'm a bump under thick linen, knees, thighs, body clenched shut.

"What happened? What's wrong?" Andres stands by his bed, asking again and again, but I can't say it.

"Kevin Hale just left her room," Rivera says, standing in the door. "I was afraid this was going to happen." He shakes his head.

His girlfriend peeks out from behind him, watching me with sad, dark eyes. A small, elfin girl, she is a military police officer and she's the one who suggests, "Do you want me to call the MPs?"

"Wait, he went back there after I left?" Andres asks, fuming. "After I kicked him out?" There is the rage: His teeth are clenched tight; his chest rises and falls rapidly. I hope it's contagious. I want it to be contagious, but I can't feel it. I just tremble and snivel. "That fucker," he snarls, clenching his fists. "I'll fucking kill him."

I only groan, wishing I could disappear, digging down further in the blankets. I don't want them to look at me. I already hate the lilt in their voices—pity intermingled with outrage. I want to ask why Rivera did nothing to stop it, if he knew. I want to ask why he waited until I burst out of the room.

It's Rivera's girlfriend who actually calls the police. I don't know if I said yes, if I said I want to report it. I can't stop shaking; I can't lift my head. It doesn't seem real and I want to peel off my skin, turn it inside out and scrape apart my insides, anywhere he touched, ball it up and throw it in the trash. Maybe burn it for good measure.

If I had been a bit more rational, maybe I would've rested a hand on hers, said, "No, don't call." Maybe I would've just cried it out, scrubbed it away. Maybe it would've been okay and I would've gotten over it and moved on. But that's not the way it happened, and which is worse? To be raped—one singular act done and then over with, or to be raped and turn to your command, to your lines of authority, your father figures, your abstract constructs of justice and integrity, to innocently curl up against them, whispering, "Save me; believe me," and have them stare back at you, stone-faced? To have them hold you at arm's length and announce, in a joint, resounding voice, "No"?

I don't act like a rape victim, they say. I'm not sure how a rape victim is supposed to act, but apparently I'm not doing it right. They write that in the report—that I don't act like a rape victim. The MP demands we conduct the interview in my barracks room. I hesitate at the door, loath to cross the tainted threshold. I pad into the room with bare feet and borrowed sweats. The room is a mess. I see it from an outsider's eyes—the clothes strewn across the floor, the bottles of makeup scattered on the desk, the shoes that spill out from the open lock closet. It looks disheveled and irresponsible.

The woman writes that in the report.

Someone has placed my desk chair in the middle of the room and it's startlingly out of place. Fingers clutching the bottom of the chair, my bare feet twisting on the tile floor, I stare down into my lap as the officer sits in a chair across from me. I can't look her in the eye. She is rigid and terse in her black suit. I can't hear her questions over the buzzing in my head. I ask again to leave the room—the air chokes me. But it's seemingly important we linger here, facing each other in the midst of the dirty room and soiled sheets.

I hang my head, muttering responses, not really hearing, not really responding. Maybe it appears suspicious, this inability to uncurl from myself, the unwillingness to engage with the officer, but I don't realize I'm already being scrutinized and questioned and mistrusted. I don't realize it starts this early.

An MP offers to take me to the criminal investigation department office and I'm relieved to escape the room. I scuttle out the door, shoulders slumped forward, feet shoved into shower shoes. This MP is animated and playful. He grins and assures me everything will be fine. He has a big smile and he makes small talk and I respond because I need to fill the space with white noise. I need it to distract me. I'm grateful for that small talk but it's the wrong thing to do. "She didn't act like a rape victim," they'll say.

They'll write that in the report.

I don't cry. I don't know why that is. I should cry. That's what rape victims do. They cry but I don't and I don't know why. They write that in the report, too.

They take me to a medical clinic where no one is happy to be woken up at three in the morning.

I inconvenience everyone.

They put my feet in cold, metal stirrups. I've lost my underwear somewhere. I only realize this when they ask me to pull down my sweatpants. I contemplate that lost article of clothing. How had I gone from my barracks room, into the police car, and to the medic station to only now realize I've lost my underwear? Somewhere. I hope they don't notice, as I place my heels onto the cold metal. If they did, would they think I'm one of *those girls*, someone who doesn't wear underwear when she goes out, who doesn't understand the propriety or necessity? I want my underwear back.

I squeeze my eyes shut as they probe inside my body with cold instruments. From over my kneecaps, I see the top of an older man's head and he fingers my vagina with stiff hands. It reeks of violation and I grit my teeth, gripping the plastic sides of the table, wanting to slam my knees shut, wanting to close myself off, close them out, because they've cracked me open with metal devices, left me exposed, with my legs flopped open like cold, clammy chicken wings.

"I don't see any semen," the doctor accuses, calling out from the cavern of my body, and I don't know what that means. He touches the cut at the edge of my vagina, noting the tear in the skin. It stings and I cringe. He pulls out the speculum, the long clamp sliding out with all the breath I am holding, released with a hiss, and I can finally press my thighs tightly together. If I could bind them in place I would.

They give me shots for STDs, sticking needles in the meaty section of my arms. I sit on the edge of the examination table, shivering in a paper gown. All frowning faces are turned away. No one really looks at me.

"Do you want the morning-after pill?" someone asks. She pours a handful of white pills into my palm before I answer. "They're birth control pills but if you take a week's worth, they do the same thing as the morning-after pill." This seems sketchy to me. I stare at the pills sitting in my hand, trying to access a clear thought through the fog in my brain. I have the feeling that if I could go back to my teenage self, just scant years before, in the midst of all my Christian upbringing, someone would tell me this is abortion. Everyone would tell me this is wrong, this is murder, and then I drink them down, not dwelling on the moral implications, maybe because I'm still a little drunk or maybe because I just don't care.

One woman smiles lightly at me, patting my arm. I don't know where she came from, this woman who, despite the late hour, is dressed in a pink button-down shirt and crisp brown skirt. She slips me a card. "No one can go through this without help," she says softly. "You can come here and talk anytime you want. Anytime, okay?" She stresses this, making eye contact, holding my gaze with warm brown eyes. "Don't let your command stop you." She's the only friendly face I see. She's the only face I remember.

They let me put my clothes back on and I still can't look at the people around me. They're passing shadows of sterile white and camo green. I wish the woman in the pink shirt would come back, but she's gone and the military police drive me to their office.

I move in a haze. Time and space have no meaning. I'm working on autopilot, like a little windup toy that moves this way or that, only as directed. They go into another room to do...something. I'm left alone in a bare room with only one cold lightbulb and a wooden bench for company. I curl up on the bench, pulling my knees to my chest, twisting my hands under my head. I close my eyes and I sleep to escape, huddled in that cold, empty room.

I drag my eyes open when I feel a shadow looming overhead. A shape I recognize as First Sergeant Bell leans over me, bowed at the waist, staring down. He blinks dull eyes, hastily dressed in his uniform, and his white hair pokes out in odd directions. He says nothing. He offers me no consolation; he doesn't ask what happened. I wish they had sent me someone I knew better, or at least someone who knew me at all.

I turn my head away, tightening my fetal position and squeezing my
eyes closed again. I notice Captain Wells isn't here. He sent his First
Sergeant instead, couldn't be bothered to come down himself. I don't
know if he's supposed to be here, if there's some military etiquette he's
failing to uphold. Not that he would make me feel any better, with his
cold formality. Tonight I suspect he's just being lazy, sending an under-
ling in his place because he has no intention of rousing in the middle of
the night for one of those female soldiers he never wanted in his units
in the first place. A former tanker commander, he prefers his units sans
women and greets us with both confusion and indifference. Perhaps I
should have known then, but I am still naive and hopeful.

"We'll do another interview in a week," says a gruff CID officer,
startling me awake. He stands in the doorway, fists planted on his hips.
He looks unhappy. "When she's sober," he adds. He stares at me on the
bench then waves me away. I'm relieved to be released.

It's already day, the sun just starting to peek out between the old brick
barracks. I crawl into the back of the police vehicle. I have no small
talk now. I just want . . . I realize I can't have what I want. I can't curl up
in my bed to sleep—that desecrated haven holds no appeal to me. As I
stare at my barracks, the windows all black and filled with slumbering
soldiers, I realize I have nowhere to go. Simply by habit I drag myself
up the stairs, simply by habit I reach my floor. But the door to my room
might as well have been made of napalm and fire. I sway in front of
it, lost, without a home, and realize I am going to have to sleep on the
frigid tile floor in the common area.

Andres, good, faithful Andres, must have been waiting for me. He
must have stood for hours by his door, checking the peephole each
time someone stumbled into the common room, because he opens his
door when he see me standing there—listless and without purpose. He
doesn't bathe me with sympathy or pity. There is a type of cold fury in
him that I appreciate. I want to wrap it around me, like a blanket, in
the hope that it will wake me up from this fog. But I'm too numb to
grasp on to it.

"Locke said you can sleep in her room," he says, knocking on Locke's door. I think he must be reading my mind. I want to say thank you but I say nothing.

"I took care of him," Andres says suddenly. I blink dumbly at him.

"I went to his room and broke a beer bottle over his head."

"You did what?" A hint of...something pierces through the haze in my head. "When?"

"Right after you told me. I got there before the police did. When he opened the door, I smashed the bottle over his head. He fell on his ass and stared at me like a fucking dumb-ass. I said, 'If you ever come near Dostie again, I'll cut you.'"

I almost smile. "Way to *be* the stereotype." I like that I sound normal when I say this. I like that he did it, that my protective, macho friend had risked the police seeing him standing over a bleeding rapist, weapon in hand.

Locke opens her door and her dark eyes are too curious, too bright. She wants to know what happened, how it went down, giving me that signature half smile. It seems too eager. I'm rude. I don't answer her questions; I sidestep them and use the shower instead. I stand in the white tiled stall, clothes rolled in a ball in the corner. In the movies, the girl always scrubs hysterically, sobbing to herself. I don't have it in me to do it. Instead I turn the water as hot as possible. My skin burns red and still I stand under the stream. I imagine the skin boiling away, peeling off and falling in wet clumps around my bare feet. I don't cry. I don't scream. My body slumps forward, an invisible weight resting on my shoulders, pulling me down, pooling into my fingertips and the bottoms of my feet. I don't have the energy to cry. I don't even have the energy to push the scalding water out of my eyes. Even here I'm still not acting like a rape victim.

Andres brings me clothes from my room and I huddle in an oversize sweatshirt and flannel pants. Everyone's awake but all I want to do is sleep. I crawl up to the extra bunk, press my spine against the wall, pull the blanket over my head, and escape into sleep.

I never go back into that barracks room. Every time I try, I stand at the threshold, balk, squirm, refuse. Andres, Diaz, and Locke team up to scrub the room clean, pouring bleach over the tiles, tossing the soiled sheets where I had thrown up at some point that night, straightening the shoes and uniforms, washing away any remaining suggestion, but I still won't go in that room. Andres and Diaz offer their shared room, and sometimes Andres gives me his bed, but more often than not I sleep in the tiny space on the floor between the bed and the metal wall locker. The width is too small for my sleeping bag to fully unfurrow, but I don't mind the tight space. Sometimes the cold metal against my back is reassuring. From the bed above me, the steady in and out of Andres's soft breathing comforts me when the room is too black and I can't fall asleep.

If the command knows anything of this sleep arrangement, they say nothing, not even to suggest I sleep in Locke's room instead, where she has a spare bed with no roommate. This suits me just fine. Ever since that first night Locke and I have been doing an uncomfortable dance, circling each other in a sort of silent civility as we briefly greet each other but say nothing real. An ugly word, a word now *mine*, fills the space between us, pushing us ever farther apart. It won't be until we're planted in the dirt of Iraq that our friendship will have a chance to bloom again, when, with the arrival of new commanders and the urgency of war, I will pretend to put all this rape business aside. When I am new again, the chasm between us can be bridged by normalcy.

My platoon sergeant, Staff Sergeant Pelton, offers me periodic use of his couch after he learns of my bed on Andres's floor. "Yeah, anytime," he says, his cherub face bright from the sun, but brighter still with the smile that rounds his cheeks and makes his blue eyes glow. He gets it. I love that he gets it.

I sleep there mostly during the day, the late afternoons after work, to nap after I've been worn thin by a long night on hard tile floors. He lives on base housing, in a small house of creams and beiges. His couch is soft, I sink into it, face pressed into the cushions, and it's safe. I take up everyone's space, having none of my own, switching from person to person in order to give each a break from me. Sergeant Pelton lets me come and go as I please, gathering myself onto the couch even when he's not yet home, as if he's taken in a refugee. His pregnant wife lays out the sheets and fluffs couch pillows, smoothing the makeshift bed with hands that remind me of my mother. She often offers me tea and leftover meals.

Sergeant Pelton is a good man with a quick, generous laugh, one he still offers to me in kindness. He moves quickly, in the sharp, sudden movements of someone who has too much energy. He crackles, like a bonfire on a cold night. He is handsome and kind, a Christian, which is important to me when I'm Christian and less so later, when I'm not. I like him instantly, and his initial refusal to push me aside gives me legs and helps raise me off the floor each morning.

First Sergeant Michael Bell is less accommodating than Sergeant Pelton. There is nothing lost between us after the rape, because there was nothing to begin with. I know him in the cursory manner one knows a disliked higher-up—as a peripheral, to be greeted but never sought out. What little I know of First Sergeant Bell isn't promising. He's a tall, gawky man who breaks forward a little when he stands, shoulders sloped downward, long neck sticking out as if he's waiting for the sword that will inevitably drop and sever head from body. His perpetual grin is neither smart nor funny but instead planted there dumbly, uncomfortably, impossible to move. It's said that First Sergeant Bell is a pathological liar. Once, as he boasted about the time he rescued children from a burning forest, crossing a river with child after child raised over his head to keep them dry, Specialist King whispered, "Isn't that a scene from *Rambo*?" Another day Sergeant Bell pulls up a chair to sit with the Persian-Farsi linguists as they study, confiding that he had, on his own, broken open a spying operation at the US embassy in Tehran where the Iranians were attaching listening devices to live cockroaches. There is no US embassy in Tehran.

The First Sergeant is Top—usually a term of endearment referring to the top of the line, the trainer of professionals. It was a term of respect for First Sergeant Cole, who stood in front of his unit and commanded their attention, who was rumored to mix whiskey in his morning coffee and who, one morning, swayed in front of his formation so he could explain where the term *to freeze the balls off a brass monkey* came from. I don't know if he actually drank or not, but we didn't care either way, because he's First Sergeant Cole and that meant he could do whatever the fuck he wanted. This Top who was loved, who fell off the side of a five-ton truck and broke his hand: This Top could no longer lead his troops into Iraq, so First Sergeant Michael Bell took over. But Bell will never be called Top.

Eventually First Sergeant Bell tries to lure me back into my old barracks room, standing in front of the door and demanding I go in. "We can't give you another room," he says. "There are none." It's a blatant lie. From over his shoulder I can see the open door of Rivera's room, which is empty and cleaned out, now that he's moved on to another assignment in another post.

"First Sergeant, I can't stay here. I won't. I'm just . . . I'm not. I'm not staying in there." He sighs, his head hanging forward in that awkward, droopy posture of his. Had it been First Sergeant Cole, I would've been humiliated and properly cowed by his disappointment, but this is Bell, whom I neither know nor respect. His displeasure means nothing to me.

"What if we have the combination changed? Would that make you feel better?"

As if that's the only reason I won't enter that violated space. He doesn't get it and I don't know how to say it.

"I will *not* stay in there." I'm firm.

"You're being difficult." He wants me to be easy, and I'm noncompliant.

I have nothing to say in response to that. The standoff continues and I sleep on the cold, hard tiles of Andres's floor.

At the start and end of the workday, my rapist and I stand in formation together. This is a certainty but at least in formation I know where he is. I see him; I mark his space and its distance from mine, a mental measuring tape that I try to stretch as far as allowed. It's the times in between those forced encounters that terrorize me, though, when I'm not sure of his whereabouts and when I see him everywhere, especially where he's not.

I'm not allowed any time off work, so the days keep clicking by, moving forward like some unstoppable iron freight train, and I learn to adapt, to clock out when my body remains present. I eat, a lot, finding comfort and oblivion in cakes and chocolate. I sleep wherever I find a place to rest. Reality becomes simple snippets between long hours of black. Getting out of bed takes hours. It physically hurts, this act of being awake. When awake I dream of sleeping, when asleep I dream of nothing. There is this quiet, white place inside my skull I flee to, my own personal winter wonderland where there are wide, rolling expanses of nothing. My favorite place to be.

The oblivion is addicting. I simply slip away—in the chow line, while in formation, standing in the motor pool where I'm supposed to be working, in the car, like the time I forget I'm driving and the Subaru bounces off the road, rolls down a ditch, and crunches to a halt on the gravel and dead grass at the bottom of the slope. The sudden stop causes my head to snap forward. My forehead bounces off the steering wheel. I don't feel the pain. My hands drop from the wheel, falling languidly into my lap, fingers curled upward. I stay there, head resting against the leather, staring at nothing, hearing only the click, click, click of an errant blinker light. I know I've crashed my car but I can't dredge up the energy to care.

I probably should've hit the ditch harder. If I wanted to do anything, I should have hit the gas just a tiny bit harder. But I don't want to die. I just don't want to live, either.

what they want

THE INVESTIGATOR from the criminal investigation department waits a week to call for an official statement. I don't know what takes them so long, but I'm still surprised when I get the phone call. It's the middle of the workday and our platoon has been ordered to decorate the hall for the upcoming officers' Christmas party.

"Specialist Dostie, can you come down to the office for your interview now?" the lead investigator asks without preamble.

It's too abrupt, a sudden, disorienting turn from Christmas music, paper snowflakes, and dangling lights. "What? Right now?" I swing around in a circle, looking for Sergeant Pelton. He stands on a chair, hanging green paper leaves over a doorway. "Hold on," I say to the investigator. I shuffle up close to Sergeant Pelton. By now the reality of the investigation has begun penetrating the ranks, and I feel an uneasiness between Sergeant Pelton and me that has never been there before. There's a stiffness around his eyes now. "The CID wants me to come down for an interview," I whisper. Other soldiers are around, close enough to hear, close enough to peer my way, eager to add a new piece of rumor to the mill.

"Right now?" Sergeant Pelton asks, annoyance heavy in his voice. He's stressed; Captain Wells shoved this assignment on him suddenly and expectations are high. He's pressed for time and can't spare another soldier. "I really need you here, Dostie," he says and turns back to his paper leaves.

I can push him. I can say that he has to let me go, that he has no right to hold me here, but it's not something I'm willing to do. I don't want to burn bridges, not realizing they've already sunk. I step away and place the phone back to my ear. "Is there a way I can reschedule?"

There is a pause that haunts me. I hear a thousand words in that hesitation. "That's fine. I'll call back to reschedule." He doesn't bother with anything more and the line goes dead.

I feel it instantly; a cold knot fills my stomach. I replay all the unsaid words that saturate the short conversation. I hear him say I'm not taking this seriously, so it must not be serious. I hear him say that clearly I'm fine, not consumed, not broken, and I realize I'm doing this all wrong. The phone is a hot iron in my hand and I'm sweating, standing outside in the December air, compelled to dial back. "I changed my mind." The words tumble from my mouth the moment he answers, breathlessly. "I want to come in now."

"I'm sorry," he says shortly, but he doesn't sound sorry. "After I talked to you, I let everyone go home early for the day."

It isn't more than five minutes since he called. Less, only enough time for me to walk outside onto the porch of the building we are decorating. I press my lips together. "So there's no way I can come down now?"

"Well, no. You said you didn't want to do the interview now so I let everyone go." He reiterates the situation, stressing my role, my lack of desire. "We can reschedule for next week."

Tears burn my eyes and frustration closes my throat. "Fine, okay." My voice is strained.

"Next week."

I have to live with the dread over the weekend. I can't shake it off; I can't bury it. Those things left unsaid worm their way through my brain, burrowing holes, leaving me in a panic. I choke on fear, huddled on Andres's floor under a sleeping bag, cold but not numb.

It's another week with my rapist standing smugly in formation. Another week of whispers, sideways glances. "Fucking bitch," one of his friends hisses in my direction, narrowing her eyes at me. She passes on the rumor that I'm a lying whore.

It's another week on edge, seeing him here, there, and cracking just a little more with each encounter.

I'm still waiting for that call that doesn't come in a week's time, and I stand rigid by the cement block wall of the barracks, spine fused to the bricks, neck craned as I peer around the foyer corner, examining the gaggle of soldiers just outside my barracks building. Sweat trickles down my back but I'm not hot. December in Louisiana is mild compared with New England's wintry bluster, but I still shiver in my Gore-Tex coat. Morning formation is in ten minutes but there are soldiers blocking the path and I have to know who is in that group.

I dissect the men, trying to piece together features in the sea of camo green. Their faces are split open in grins, milling around in the dead, prickly grass. One of them has a familiar slump in his shoulders, a nearly identical overgrown buzz cut, that short, stout silhouette, and I'm sure it's him. My brain fills in the missing pieces until I'm certain it *is* him there blocking my path, barricading me inside my building, and I shrink down, wondering how I'm going to make it to formation on time. My rib cage aches and I realize Captain Wells is going to narrow his watery, round eyes at me in further disgust when I am late. Another strike against my character. Dostie, the shitbag soldier who cried rape.

The soldier turns slightly to the side, exposing his profile and the back of his neck. His nose is sharp and strong and he boasts a cut chin. His head is clean—no v-shaped scar engraved into the skull—and I unfurrow like a banner released. My knees still shake, though, as I dart down the barracks path, past the group, feeling the weight of stares and sudden silence, either because I'm a woman who was raped, or a woman who reported rape, or simply because I'm a woman.

I trot over the brown grass, up the hill, over the broken and cracked pavement of the basketball court. I check over my shoulder once, twice, expecting someone or anyone to materialize. There's no respite when the path is empty.

When I arrive the platoon is relaxed, idly talking in the bright sunlight. I halt at the edge, inspecting the bodies until I'm sure he's not one of them. It's both a relief and a fear.

I seek shelter again, slipping into the company building, thankful for the shadows. It's stuffy, filled with the familiar scent of metal, oil, dirt, and wet concrete. I find my corner, the one I have begun to know so well because it allows me to see both the front and back doors. If anything, rape has made me a far more observant soldier.

A loud, masculine voice shouts inaudibly and a vague formation starts outside the open double doors but I stretch the minutes, waiting until the very last moment so that everyone will be in position, boots rooted to their spots where I can mentally mark each of their places.

"Dostie, get outside," Captain Wells snaps, appearing in the doorway. He doesn't smile at me, because he doesn't like me. I represent all the problems that come with a woman in the military. He glares, jaw working over a wad of chew, his eyes somewhat hooded by a low-hanging forehead, the wide expanse of white skin that scrolls upward into an equally pale dome head. Captain Wells started his officer career in a tanking unit and would have stayed there, among his companies of men, but, as rumor would have it, one day during a training exercise, he popped his head out of his tank and a tree branch smacked him upside the back of his skull. It was decided that he was too stupid to be a tank commander, or so the rumor continues, and he was sent to where he could do less harm, a Military Intelligence unit, which is how we ended up with a commander who wanted nothing to do with the women under his command, or their feminine issues. If he could have swiped me off the map, he would have.

Even in the face of Captain Wells's impatience, I sigh and linger at the door for just a moment more, buying myself those extra few seconds because I'm never quite ready to be in that formation again, where I can see that white, distinct scar just a few ranks over to the left. But then there's the order, "Fall in!" and I'm out of time.

I go to my squad, spine so rigid it could snap.

Sergeant Pelton narrows his eyes at me. "Dostie, what are you doing? You're not in this platoon anymore." He points to the platoon on the right. "You're in EW2."

I blink dumbly. "What? Since when?"

"Just go." He flashes his hand in a quick, impatient gesture of dismissal.

Baffled, I step out of formation and start toward EW2 but I don't know which squad to fall in with so I slip into the last rank.

At the front of that squad fearsome Staff Sergeant Daniels holds up both his hands in dramatic frustration. "What the hell are you doing? You're not in my platoon. You're EW1."

"Sergeant Pelton just told me I'm in your platoon now," I reply, trying not to let the intimidation seep into my tone. Sergeant Daniels is alpha badass of this unit.

"Well, you're not. Get back over there."

The First Sergeant is getting into place and time is running out as I rush back toward EW1, thoroughly flustered.

"What the fu—Dostie! What did I just tell you?" Sergeant Pelton hisses. Captain Wells strides up to the front of the formation and Sergeant Pelton can't finish his sentence, instead gesturing for me to get out of his platoon formation as he spins on his heel, falling to attention.

I have nowhere to go. I flutter between the two platoons, a soldier without a home, a literal Army of One. Sergeant Pelton is trying to pawn off the trouble girl on Sergeant Daniels and Sergeant Daniels is having none of it. This is my punishment and penance for reporting rape, I realize. I wish someone had let me in on the secret sooner—never report, never tell, swallow it whole and let it fester at the bottom of your stomach, because rotten insides are better than public ostracism.

I fall in at attention in my one-woman platoon at the back of the unit formation, next to platoon leader Lieutenant Davis, who regards me with curiosity but doesn't offer any guidance. I don't cry but I want to. I want to scream but it'll just be another black tally mark against me.

Look at that psycho girl. Crazy, crazy Dostie. So crazy, you just know she must have made it all up.

I try to push out the dull drone of Captain Wells's voice—that slow, insipid drawl, just like the man, and my lip starts to curl in anger, as it always does around Captain Wells, at the commander who has said nothing, done nothing, who steadfastly ignores the girl who reported rape, perhaps hoping that in doing so she would simply disappear. Just as I start to feel a slow, building burn of rage, I catch a sight at the corner of my eye.

Kevin Hale is there. And just like I always look for him, he looks for me, too. He finds my new ousting oh-so-amusing. I can't look at him directly, I never will be able to, but I can see his grin. He elbows his friend, jerking his chin in my direction. The other soldier lets out a sharp bark of laughter and passes on the information, jab, point, stare, laugh, rolling down the line until an informed group stares back at me with narrowed, slit eyes, snickering hard enough that their shoulders shake with the effort of silence.

I dig my nails into my palms, breaking the skin, but the pain does little to relieve the weight against my chest. I labor for air, leaning slightly to the side, as if the minute inches will somehow save me. I don't move my feet, won't leave formation, can't leave; I raise my chin to breathe, shaking with the effort not to let out a loud, wet sob, a sound that would roll over the formation, snake round and round all those male heads, settle between male ears, and sound so very feminine, so terribly weak. I fight not to scream. Not to run. I am trapped in a formation of me, myself, and I.

I contemplate running. Really running. Ducking out of formation and sprinting, stripping off camo, Gore-Tex, boots, to my green Subaru and putting miles between me and this place. Long, heavy miles where Fort Polk would become smaller and smaller in the mirror. I could go up to Maine, to my father's place right on the Canadian border. It would be nice up there under the shade of tall trees. Quiet. No people, no questions, just snow and pine. I fantasize solitude until I remember my security clearance and that this is a time of war. The FBI would be notified within twenty-four hours of my absence. I wouldn't be given the regular thirty days and it would be a federal offense, made all the more criminal because of the hundreds of thousands of dollars the government wasted on training me as a linguist.

AWOL isn't a viable option. Not unless I want to end up in a small, black prison in God knows where. I hear him and his group laugh, though, and for a moment I pause and wonder if a distant prison cell would really be all that bad.

The investigator finally reschedules our interview. He sits me down in an interrogation chair. It feels like an interrogation chair. His dark wooden desk is huge. He sits calmly behind it, papers meticulously stacked in front of him. A tape recorder whirls between us, loud in the tense silence. I am huddled in the hard wooden chair, arms wrapped around my knees. I look like a child, I know, fists clenched around my uniform pants. I feel like a child, tiny and fragile, staring up at him as he stacks the papers and begins.

The first few questions are easy enough. Where had I been; how had I known the analyst; how much did I drink. Then things take a turn for the darker and without looking up, with no real warning, the investigator asks, "Do you feel he raped you?"

I cringe at the word. It hangs in my mouth, heavy and taking up space. I can say all your four-letter words—shit, fuck, cunt—just don't make me say the R word. I hate saying it out loud, to people in power, who judge me for the word used and resent me for making them face its implications. I swallow the word instead and say, "Yes."

He finally looks up and I see the first breath of fight in him. "So you said no." It's not a question but an assertion, a natural ending to his sentence.

My brow furrows slightly. "I said I didn't know who he was, and that I didn't understand what was happening. I told him to stop, but

I…sometimes when I drink I get confused and maybe I said it in Japanese." I watch his face darken and I rush to add, "Because, like in Japanese you can say whole sentences in a few words, do you know what I mean? It's…hard to explain but I just switch over sometimes. If I've had too much to drink. Sometimes." My Japanese had triggered his Spanish; the snarling of *"cállate"* into my ear is suddenly loud and persistent in the back of my skull. I shudder and look down at my hands, feeling like I have been punched in the gut.

"But you didn't say 'no,'" he pushes.

"I don't know if I said 'no' exactly, but I did say 'stop.' I said I didn't know what was going on." I pause, mouth dry, trying to figure out why my heart is racing suddenly, and add, "I pushed at him. Like pushed him away. Or I tried to."

"So you think he raped you."

"Yes."

"Are you sure?"

"Yes!"

"But you didn't say no."

"It was very clear that I didn't want…" Again my stomach clenches tight and I'm running out of words. "I didn't want what happened."

The investigator leans back, face closed, mouth slightly pursed. "You understand that in order for sex to be rape, you have to have said no."

I'm angry now. My knuckles are white against my knees, boots planted on the floor. "So you're saying that if someone has sex with a sleeping person or someone who's unconscious, that's not rape because they didn't say no?"

He glares at me now, as if I'm being a difficult child who refuses to understand reason. "There are different rules for that sort of thing. You weren't asleep or unconscious."

"I might have been! I don't know how he got in the room and I wasn't able to…I wasn't…" Frustration closes off my throat and I turn my face away, ashamed.

"How did he get in your room?"

"I said I don't know." I want to scream it, but it came out as a harsh whisper.

"Did you let him in?"

"No. I mean...I don't think so."

"But it's possible that you did."

"I don't know. I don't think so?" I glance up, wanting him to agree with me, to say that it's true, I probably didn't open the door, that I had had too much to drink, how would I have made that walk from my bed to the door, how had I woken from my drunken slumber from someone knocking, how could I have said, *Sure, come in,* knowing these things didn't seem possible or like me at all, and yet his jaw is set. He shows me nothing. "But even if I did..." I close my eyes with those words, not wanting to ever imagine them to be true, the thought makes me sick. "Even if I did, that doesn't mean I wanted to have sex with him."

I hate the whirl, whirl, whirl of the tape recorder as it fills the silence and he takes his time, scratching his pen onto paper. "Did he rape you?" he asks again.

I fucking hate that word. That dirty, soiled, shameful word. Don't make me say it. "Yes."

"But you don't remember saying no?"

I drop my head into my hands. We're chasing our tails, going round and round. It's getting all muddled in my head. How could it not be rape? I know how I feel; I know I hadn't wanted...that. That thing that happened. How could that not be rape? "I'm not making this up," I say, desperate, so desperate to be heard.

"Did he rape you?" he asks again. And again. Round and round we go.

I'm lost, so thoroughly turned around that I've given up trying to orient myself. I can't find north. I break. "I don't know what it was, but I know what he did was wrong."

He writes clear and hard onto the paper, and funny how that sentence is the only thing that makes it into the official report.

The investigators want me to be a whore. They're looking for some sordid sexual past, interviewing anyone there that night, as well as some of my fellow platoon members. They want me to have spread my legs quickly and often. Two CID officers lean against the doorpost of Sergeant Forst's barracks door, my current squad leader, grinning down at her. They laugh, loudly, so pleased to be talking to her, with her pink, cherub cheeks and wispy pixie blond hair. They look like wolves to me, all teeth, tall to her short, towering—looming really—but no one seems to share my newfound fear of men. Sergeant Forst's cheeks are flushed; she laughs with them and I know I'm the irrational one. I can't hear them but it can hardly be official business. I sneak up the stairs to my floor, not wanting them to see me.

Sergeant Forst fills me in later, that between flirting they asked about my sexual past. Did I have many lovers? Was I promiscuous? How disappointed were they when she told them I had no lovers, that in my six months at the post, I had yet to fall into a single bed? Did they have a box to check about fundamentalist Christian upbringings that preached against premarital sex? How much had that messed up their report then, that I had believed sex was sacred, shared only in love, cherished and hallowed? Not much, in the end. They shifted tactics, countering with, "So she could be protecting her reputation, then. She doesn't want anyone to know she slept with him."

The report will eventually say that Rivera's girlfriend tells them I would never sleep with the likes of Kevin Hale. "So she's embarrassed," they reason, an angle they'll type hard into white paper, a suggestion that I'm "covering it up" to spare myself the shame.

I would have been damned had I been a slut, but I was just as damned for not having been one.

exodus

ANDRES AND I HAD a flirtatious friendship before, but it had never been physical. He's a handsome Mexican American, short but broad in the shoulders, with a strong, L-shaped jaw and a slight cleft chin, which is somehow endearing. His barracks room is across from mine, meaning that when I initially arrived at the unit, the first morning when I had to be at formation, he led the way, and then every day since. I lean on him and his friendship because I like having someone to turn to before formation, or during lunch, or after the workday is done. He doesn't seem to mind me hanging out at his barracks room, sitting on the tile floor as he introduces me to Gael García Bernal, Rage Against the Machine, and Ayn Rand. He's younger than I am but jaded. He reads older than his age, as if he's accumulated decades under his young features. And yet, ironically, his only life goal is to be a good father and husband. He wants a big family. He doesn't tell me why he left Chicago and joined the Army, although he's adamant it was a mistake. He never seemed interested in anything physical between us, which works for me, because I'm still a little hung up on Jonathan, an ex-boyfriend stationed three states away, whom I occasionally visit on four-day weekends, making the twelve-hour car trek alone, speeding down highways as fast as my Subaru will go because I miss him, yes, but also because this was the only sex I was comfortable with. I learned to justify this premarital sex, to find a way to align it with my Christian upbringing, because this was done in love and something done in love is still beautiful and blessed. Back then, I didn't know how to make this jump to another man, a different man, especially someone I wasn't sure I loved yet. It seems less important now.

So I don't remember the first kiss with Andres. I don't remember how it happened, or how we got here, two weeks after I was attacked. Exodus starts tomorrow—most of the unit leaves for Christmas break and I'm getting on a plane in the morning, fleeing for two weeks, but here we are pressed against each other on his bed, one of his hands tucked under the back of my shirt and his palm pressed hard against my spine. *I shouldn't be enjoying this*, I think. My sleeping bag is spread out on the floor below, and one of my legs is tucked under the other, pointed downward, and if I can just touch the bag with my toe, perhaps I'll be transported there and untangled from here. And even still, despite my mind racing for an out, a safe way to unravel limbs and tongues and intentions, there is a spark of arousal that starts small at the base of my stomach, tiny but building steadily. I resent it. I don't want to be enjoying this. I pull back and notice a red mark on his neck from earlier. I stare at it and grow increasingly uncomfortable. "If anyone asks, make sure you don't tell them that's from me," I say.

He rubs the mark, slightly smirking. "I'm not stupid. I'm not going to tell anyone," he promises, but it does nothing to elevate the sudden intense anxiety. I want to check the door to make sure it's locked, to stare out the peephole and see who's in the common area. Who saw me come into the room? It feels different now that we're kissing, now that I'm no longer just sleeping on the floor. I feel like they'll all see it branded across our faces somehow.

It never occurs to me that they all probably thought we were sleeping together this whole time. Instead I obsess. I wonder if they'll even believe him when he says it's not Dostie, never Dostie. My stomach tightens, knots, and he kisses me again, and I kiss him back, but not really. My body does, but the rest of me races forward, imagining already the knowing smirk of Captain Wells, who will see and say, "That was fast."

This is fast.

I arrive home with New England's Christmas spirit in full swing. The lampposts are dressed in faux-green finery, little white lights wrapped around posts and down the streets. The air is cold, "Carol of the Bells" blasts through speakers, and it's pretty, and fine, and I pass through it all in a haze. I remember snow, but maybe that's wishful thinking.

My mom asks, more than once, "What's wrong with you?".

"Nothing," I say. "I'm fine." I intend never to tell her.

It should feel good and safe here, away from Kevin Hale and the post and the investigation and the stares and the whispers, but it doesn't; it doesn't feel very different at all. I'm dragging along a heavy pack that's strapped down around me, following me wherever I go, and everyone keeps asking, "What's wrong? What's the matter?" because they can see the dust it stirs up.

I look in the mirror one day, as my leave narrows to an end, trying to see what they see. I look the same. Same pale skin, dark hair. Same hazel eyes, oval face. There must be a mark there, somewhere, and I'm just not seeing it because I look the same to me, and yet everyone keeps asking, "What's wrong with you?"

I don't worry that my family will find out. There is my life there and my life here and they're very separate. I can hide this, bury it, and no one here will ever have to know. I look at my mom and her brow is pinched together in concern. She tilts her head, stares at my face, as if she hopes to read something just below the surface there, but I'm closed and don't say a word. It's not because she wouldn't care—she would. Abundantly so. It's not because I worry she wouldn't believe me. She would, with more fervor and righteous rage than a legion of angels. But I don't know how to broach the topic, how to bring a conversation around to it, or even what to say.

How do I look my mother in the eyes, stand before her, open and raw, and inform her that her little girl has been raped. How do I stand there then, and watch her cry, and wrap an arm around her, as she bows forward, broken over, and how do I say, *It's okay, I'm okay*, when I'm not. But she'd be crying and someone has to stand solid, resolute. I can't cry when she cries. Our tears have always been allocated between us two, rationed to one or the other but never both simultaneously. At least it feels that way for me, because I don't cry in tandem.

So I don't tell her. Instead, I tell my brother, in a very roundabout way.

"Mom's worried about you," he says. It is just after New Year's, the night before I leave for Fort Polk, and we're driving to our aunt's so that I can say goodbye to the family. I sit back in the passenger seat and stare out the window. It's night and I can't see much. I'm tired of having to avoid people's questions. I'm tired in general. I shrug one shoulder.

"Some guy broke into my barracks room." That's all I say; that's how I tell him. I shrug again.

He continues to drive, staring out the dark windshield. He sits there for a moment, as if he hasn't heard, and I turn back to the window, glaring at the darkness. The unsaid sits between us and takes up too much space.

"Can I tell Mom?" he finally asks.

"No," I say, shortly. It's a bit unfair, I realize. Unloading this kind of information on him then not letting him do anything with it. I don't know why I've told him. I'm surprised I said anything at all, as if the declaration had grown a will of its own and popped out of its own accord. I sit rigidly, defiant, ready to say it's not a big deal, dry-eyed, but the conversation doesn't go anywhere and all my resilience is wasted.

But when we arrive at my aunt's, he herds her into the kitchen, sits her down. The room is warm, both in temperature and feeling, with its burnt-amber walls and saffron hanging lights. "Tell her what you told me," he says. It's not an order, exactly, more of a suggestion.

"Tell me what?" Aunty Carol asks, glancing from my brother to me, curious but not alarmed. Nothing seems alarming; no one is crying, or frantic. This is a very ordinary kind of conversation.

"That some guy broke into my barracks room." I say it flatly, again shrugging it off. There is a very big divide between what I'm saying and what I'm implying, and I stand in the space in between, able to make light of what is being said simply because everything else is left unsaid. I want to avoid the drama of the moment, the emotions behind these sentences. But this time I add, "I called the military police and they're doing an investigation."

"You have to tell your mother," she finally says, softly, but she proves just as resilient as me. She doesn't cry and I'm grateful.

"It's just going to upset her, it's not like she can do anything."

"But she should still know. She already knows something's not right."

"Well, I'm not telling her." I say it a little too loudly, pressing the palm of my hand against my chest. "*You* can tell her, if you want."

Aunty Carol nods. "Okay, I'll tell her."

"After I leave," I specify. "Don't tell her until I leave." She can tell my mom once I'm gone, so that I can ignore her phone calls when she's desperate for more information, to know what happened and who was it and where is he now and how did it happen, and I'm not interested in answering any of that so I don't. For days afterward I'll glance down at my phone when it rings, see her name, and click DECLINE, then drop the cell into my pocket. I only let her approach when I'm ready, months later, and even then the information I give her is patchy at best.

I never ask how my aunt told my mom or how that conversation went. I don't know how my mom handled the information, how she processed it, or how long she waited to call me the first time, or the second time. Or the third. I don't know who else she told or who she leaned on for support. I didn't ask then; I don't ask still.

I arrive back in the barracks at night. Andres waits for me in his room, where I still sleep. I still have no room of my own. I drop my bags at the foot of his bed, glancing at his neck. The marks are gone, the skin clean and fresh. "Did anyone say anything?" I ask in greeting.

He looks up, for a moment confused, having to drag himself backward into before we left. "Sergeant Pelton noticed. He had this stupid smirk on his face and he was like, 'That from Dostie?' like a fucking creeper. I told him it was from some girl up in Lake Charles. I should've told him it was none of his fucking business."

"And?" Captain Wells might think the worst of me and there's nothing I can do about that, but please, not Sergeant Pelton, too. Anyone but him.

"And he just said, 'Yeah right.'" Andres shrugs because he couldn't care less if Sergeant Pelton believes him. "I don't know why you care what he fucking thinks. He's a scumbag." But everyone with any kind of rank is a scumbag to Andres. Andres hates them all.

If I had any relief from leave, it's washed away in a sudden surge of panic. The anxiety presses against my chest, a toothy demon sitting there and grinning, *Remember me?* I crouch on my sleeping bag, palms sweaty. What did Sergeant Pelton think? Did he tell anyone? Was there a good laugh passed between men, a mental slap on the back for Andres? Will this, too, go in the report? I know they're looking for a reason to disbelieve me, their goal unmistakable from the questions they've been asking the others around me, always looking for a crack in the wall. I can't be messing it up like this. I can't give them more reason to doubt.

I unfold onto my sleeping bag, and when Andres says, quietly, "You can sleep up here," I pretend not to hear.

Welcome back to Polk.

quarters

SERGEANT PELTON IS STILL letting me sleep on his couch, despite everything, even though I'm now settled into Sergeant Daniels's platoon, even though no one is speaking to me the way they once did. I am still grateful for the couch, for the feeling of home, for his wife who reminds me of my mother.

She stands in the kitchen by the open refrigerator door one afternoon, holding out a carefully manicured sandwich, crusts sliced off, cut diagonally, and I take it from her outstretched hand. She cranes her neck to see her two-year-old daughter playing on the living room carpet, then checks the rest of the space, as if gauging where her husband is. "It's not your fault," she says suddenly, urgently, taking me by surprise. I don't know what she knows, how much was said, and I drop my gaze, fumbling with the white bread. My fingers leave deep imprints in the sandwich, ruining the aesthetic. I quickly cover the bruised sandwich with my other hand so that she won't see. "Everyone drinks," she adds, softly, the refrigerator door cutting off the rest of the room and creating a small, private space just for us.

I don't respond because I don't know what to say. No one has said this to me yet.

She tilts her head in the direction of Sergeant Pelton. "Even Flynn's come home plenty of nights and passed out on the bed dead drunk."

I can breathe for a brief moment, shoulders rising with a full chest of locked air, and I blink rapidly so that I don't cry.

"And I heard—" She lowers her voice and leans in toward me. I lean in, too. "—that one time, at an officers' party, Captain Wells got stupid drunk and he grabbed one of the poles, like the metal structure ones? He starts swinging around it, round and round, singing 'I'm a pony! I'm a pony!'" She grins and I do, too, imagining Captain Wells's fleshy face sweaty and red, stumbling over his own boots, and there is a certain satisfaction in the image. "Everyone drinks," she reiterates, closing the refrigerator door. I can now see Sergeant Pelton in the living room, kneeling on the carpet, rolling a ball to his daughter, both of them giggling wildly in delight. My chest tightens. "So it's not your fault," she says again, soft, quick-spoken words, and then she's making her way across the kitchen, sitting down with her family, holding out another sandwich square to her daughter.

Sergeant Pelton's wife is the only adult who tells me this, just once in passing, and I try to internalize the words, to engrain them on the inside of my body, but they slide away when men who get drunk blame me for drinking.

Then, some weeks after the investigation starts, Sergeant Pelton calls me into his office to ask me if I'm sure I was raped. *Office* is a generous title for the room—it's nothing more than a box made up of plywood walls and a threadbare door. Pelton sits behind the desk, glancing up when I walk in. "Leave the door open a little," he tells me, and I do. He looks anxious. His brow is pulled together, crumbling his forehead, his small hands fluttering over papers. "I was reading the report," he says of a report I haven't received, that I still haven't seen, and I'm not sure how he's read it before me. "And you really had a lot of shots that night, didn't you."

I misunderstand him. I think he's commenting on all the needles they poked into my arms to protect against STDs. I arch my eyebrows. "Yeah, they gave me all kinds of shots, for things I haven't even heard of." I try to laugh it off, to be light and airy and Pelton stares at me oddly, as if I've said something very off. I halt mid-sentence, trying to place the emotion on his face. Uncertainty. Doubt. He suddenly seems very uncomfortable, shifting in his chair, eyes darting toward the door, which probably doesn't seem open enough for him, as if he's suddenly found himself caged with a very dangerous creature. I get it then, but I don't want to. I've never been *that* girl before.

"I . . . you mean, drinks?" Not Sergeant Pelton. He's not supposed to look at me like that.

He's always been there, constant, unwavering. He's not supposed to be one of them.

"It says you had *fourteen* shots." He stresses the number, draws out the syllables, as if it somehow has a deeper significance.

I half shrug one shoulder, because fourteen sounds about right. A tad high but it isn't even a drinking night until I've downed eight shots, my partying minimum. There's sober and drunk; I was new to drinking so I hadn't learned to navigate the land of moderation yet.

He stares at me, head tilted just so, and perhaps innocently, maybe sincerely, he asks, "Are you sure?" There is a heavy pause. "It's just that . . . you had an awful lot to drink. *Are you sure?*" As if I had simply misplaced my keys. Are you sure you left them here? Are you sure he shoved his dick inside you, are you sure you feel dirty, ruined, violated, savaged? Are you sure you're soldier enough, you who can't protect yourself never mind her country? Are you sure you're man enough for that uniform?

I grasp for words, for some kind of coherent response, but I have nothing. I see a line in the sand, one that separates me from them. I trusted him. He let me play with his daughter, gave me food from his refrigerator, took me in and let me rest. I feel his betrayal more acutely when he becomes one of them.

But I don't quite grasp the depth until a few days later, when I arrive at his base housing like normal, like nothing has changed, and he stands at the door, one hand braced against the frame, barring my entrance.

I balk slightly and stand awkwardly on the stone stoop. I check over his shoulder for his wife.

"Sandra's pregnant and I'm not sure if you're contagious," he's saying, and I'm wrapping one arm around my middle, trying to fill the hollowed sensation. He points to my arm, where the PPD test for tuberculosis had come back positive, the one I was taking medication for, the medication that fucked up my tolerance that night at the bar. But that was months ago, the tuberculosis is not new information, and I don't understand why he's so concerned about it now.

"I don't think I'm contagious," I say.

"We just can't take that risk because you could get the baby sick."

That's the last thing I want so I nod, I say I understand, and he doesn't slam the door in my face. He closes it gently, but I hear the final click, a sound that rings like struck cast iron, a sound that reverberates up one side of the street, down the other, as if a thousand doors have suddenly been slammed shut, locked, and I stand on the stoop for a moment, trying to figure out where to go.

They eventually give me my own room, but not without a last bit of resistance. First Sergeant Bell is back in front of that door again, but this time with one of the new soldiers who have just been attached to the company. I stand to the side, trying not to be awkward and failing. "You'll be roommates with Specialist Starre," he's saying, gesturing to the small, very pretty, and very hardcore soldier next to him. She's a Farsi linguist, just like me. We were at Defense Language Institute together, and I had always liked her.

"I'm not staying in that room." It's a mantra, often repeated yet consistently ignored.

Starre looks up at me with vibrant hazel eyes. She's small, somewhere under five feet, but she has an unwavering gaze. "You really don't want to room with me?" She doesn't sound hurt, just direct.

"No, no, it's not you," I stutter quickly.

Starre pulls full lips into a firm line. She doesn't believe me.

"That's fine," First Sergeant Bell interrupts, grimly pointing to the room next to my old one. "I guess you can have Sergeant Rivera's old room. Start moving your stuff over so Specialist Starre can move into her room."

I don't thank him. He leaves and Starre starts to back into her new room. "It's really not you," I say quickly.

She tilts her head at me, watching me with that strange, direct gaze.

"I was..." I fumble for a moment, glancing over her shoulder into my room, which still houses my stuff, the bathroom still littered with my bottles and creams and makeup jars. "Assaulted in there." I don't say *sexually* and I most certainly don't say *rape*. I say as little as possible.

She blinks in surprise. "I'm sorry to hear that."

I'm not quite sure she gets what I'm saying and I'm sort of happy for that. "So I just don't want to be in there."

She shrugs. "I get it." She doesn't.

I retreat to Rivera's old room, a new place given to me at last, and I walk the empty space. It's barren and stark. In one corner lies an old construction sledgehammer. I don't know where Sergeant Rivera got it from, or why he left it behind, but I palm the wooden handle. It's heavy. I bring it over to the bed and place it by the head of the frame. I scoot the nightstand over to make room for it.

I like it there, even though it's too heavy to be an effective weapon. Later, I'll often wake at night, not startled or alarmed but half pulled from my sleep, and I'll see a dark shadow looming over me, standing by the edge of the bed. I'll reach out and touch the sledgehammer handle, grind my fingers around the wood until it creaks. Eventually I'll tuck a flimsy steak knife I'll lift from the DFAC under my pillow, the kind with the plastic handle and the cheap, thin metal, but nothing comforts me quite like that sledgehammer.

Andres and Diaz move my stuff from one room to the other. They do it quietly, without telling me, a silent kind of support as they fill the lock closet with my uniforms, stand boots and shoes neatly side by side on the floor, fill drawers with clothes. I return to the room one day and it's fully stocked, all complete, lacking only a bright-red bow. They make it so that I never have to step back into that room and I stand at the threshold of my new room, eyes burning, blinking back tears, and I breathe once, twice, collecting the emotions carefully because they spill too easily these days. "Thank you," I mumble over my shoulder at them, inarticulate and insufficient.

I have no roommate, just my sledgehammer, and Andres begins to spend more time here in this room, quiet hours of just him and me behind closed doors. Sometimes I keep the door ajar, just to prove that nothing is happening. Sometimes I don't.

And holed up between these four walls, I begin to eat. I drink strawberry and vanilla milkshakes from the convenience store—sometimes several bottles a day. I don't even have to leave the barracks to get them. I simply ask Andres and he'll leave on the spot, drive to get whatever I want, whenever I want, because I think that's his version of comforting me. He's not the type to hold me while I cry; he bears it in silence and offers no words of relief. He'd much rather do something, hand me anything, his quick compliance a cover for the fact that we don't overtly talk about the rape at all. In fact, he tells me one day, "Stop talking about it," when I bring it up yet again to someone new. I flush, instantly mortified, not realizing I've been saying so much, that I was stretching that hard to find validation even from people who don't know me or the situation. So instead I fill my mouth with chocolate bars, even though I don't much care for chocolate. I eat cheese on my fries, anything fried, loading my plate well beyond what is necessary. I eat to shut up, I eat out of anger, I eat to give myself something else to think about, because at least I have food to look forward to. I gain weight. A lot of it. And fat is not something the Army abides. In this insular community, where there are no physical disabilities, no deformities, no elderly, no sick, nothing but youth and mandatory fitness, no one is more of a *shitbag soldier* than the one who is fat. I become not just the girl who cried rape, but the fat, repulsive soldier who can't do PT *and* who cried rape. "She'd have to get raped just to get laid," someone snickers, and I tighten my grip around the flesh on my arms, pretending I can't hear.

I hate who I've become. I keep saying I'll stop, and that I'll start a new diet and lose the weight. Tomorrow. "You probably should start today," mutters one of the Sergeants, the side of his mouth lifted ever so slightly in disgust.

I can't do push-ups; I fail my two-mile run. I huff and cough and carry my disgrace around the middle, my uniform fitting too tight. They threaten to kick me out but it's weak intimidation—no one is getting kicked out right before deployment. I wear my shame physically, the hatred of myself reflected in the bulge of my hips, the width of my thighs. In trying to disappear, I've only made myself bigger.

As a young Christian, I was raised on a staunch diet of abstinence. I took the edict of "no sex before marriage" very literally, though. I internalized the idea of "this much but no further" so that there was a Rubicon River I would not cross, but right up to the bank was fair play. So aside from Jonathan, with whom I crossed the river both willingly and eagerly, I have years of experience of holding other boys at bay, of successfully slamming knees together to avoid the wandering hand, or twisting hips to tilt away access, of giving this much of my body but not *that* much. I know how to placate boys, how to allow hands to tightly grasp bare breasts so that I can keep them away from the hem of my skirt. I know how to twist out from under the weight of a body when he's half naked and I'm completely bare, how to make it out of the room even then, how to be so *nice* while saying no. I know how to push my own discomfort to the side so that I'm not rude, allowing access to parts of me while contemplating how best to whisper soft apologies, underwear still firmly in place. I know how to swallow dread and anxiety, to give just a little more when they plead, wet lips brushing against my ear, begging for that last drop, that tiny, final distance that I'm so proficient at denying. Coercion and persuasion can only get so much from me.

Usually. Usually I'm so good at this, deflecting, parrying, just barely getting away, but something is off tonight. This time I sigh in annoyance, not so *nice* while Andres presses his lips against my neck. He doesn't care that I've gained weight—perhaps because he played a part in it. Or maybe because he genuinely likes me, although I can't understand why, then. I recline my head back, elongating the line for him, but stare at the ceiling. I clench my jaw, irritated that we're here again, the movie blaring in the background, flooding my dark bedroom with erratic flashes of white. I twist away after giving him a moment. I'm not in the mood.

Sometimes I am. Sometimes I don't mind his kisses, his direct, dark stare, drinking in my every gesture, taut with need. Sometimes it feels good to be wanted, especially when I don't even want this body myself. And sometimes it doesn't, like now, when I know I'll ruminate over every little touch, running an invisible tally in my head of how much we've done and how that's not okay for a rape victim to do. That's one too many touches, one too many kisses. I'm confused by my own desire, betrayed by a body that wants. It should be more broken than this. Right? I have an impression of what a rape victim should be and I'm not aligning up correctly, a realization that makes me sick.

Andres has a trump card he never plays. He could remind me that after formations are released, I stand off to one side, one step away from the inside. He could mention that I wait there for him because he's the only one there who joins me. It would be a very easy thing to whisper—a casual reminder that there are polite smiles from others in my direction, greetings made in passing, but there's nothing deeper to warm me should he stroll away in the opposite direction. Andres never says this. He's not that kind of man, but I'm acutely aware of these facts, too.

"Please," he murmurs against my skin, brushing his palm up my shirt, wiggling awkwardly under the sports bra. He sighs, resting his hot forehead against my shoulder, squeezing lightly. Even this little delights him. But, like all of them, he wants more. "Come on, Dostie. Please?"

He pushes me slightly and I let him, lying back on the hard barracks mattress.

And I'm so tired. My shoulders sag, my body sags, my knees sag in something like defeat. I've become so proficient at deflecting actual sex that I'm doing it out of habit. My jeans peel off. My shirt gets tossed off the bed and rolls under the desk. It occurs to me there is no sacredness here. This is a bodily function, as elegant and necessary as an early-morning shit. I wrap my arms around his neck and I'm tired. I have the sense that I've been worn down. Coercion and persuasion may not have worked, but persistence did.

I'll always resent you for this, I think as he eases into me, a bumbling affair as we try to figure out each other's parts, the way we fit together, the measure and rhythm of our bodies. I'm being unfair, I'll realize much later. I could say no. I always could say no with Andres. But I want someone to blame, at least at the start, for why I tumbled so quickly into this. I poison what we could have had with this single thought, this lasting grudge.

I feel shame like a jab in the gut as he thrusts against me, the sound of bare skin slapping echoing across the room, overpowering the hiss of TV static. A part of me wants to pull away from this, to wrap around myself and protect my middle, the softness, the most vulnerable spot of me. But another part of me enjoys it. My body flushes, warms, skin turning pink, my legs wrapping firmly behind his back, hooking ankles together, and I enjoy it.

It's just a body, just meat and bones and skin. I feel it here for the first time, that savage epiphany, that brilliant flood of power as I crack open my eyes, watch his abandon, watch him lose himself in me, and wonder why I never noticed this before. I no longer care about this body, and there is something savagely powerful in that.

classical conditioning

SOMEONE LET THE CAT out of the bag and told my father I
was raped. That's not something I want him to know. Daddy's little girl
doesn't get raped—that's not something my princess books prepared me
for while growing up. In my mind there was no reason he should know.
If anything the Army gives me physical space from home so that I can
firmly live in two separate worlds, and they needn't intersect unless I
allow it. There's something to be said for having an entire sustainable
existence that operates separate from one's family. When my mother
found out, it didn't occur to me that she'd tell my father. He just calls
one day and knows.

There isn't a big conversation about it. It's succinct and brutal.

"Just say the word, and your uncle and I will be on the next plane," he
says. I'm pacing the room, barefoot, anxiously twisting the fingers of one
hand around my loose hair. I don't want to be having this discussion.

"I'll break both his legs," my father swears.

I envision him stomping down the metal steps of a puddle jumper on
Leesville's tarmac, my tall uncle just behind him, a wooden bat slung
over each of their shoulders. I don't doubt him. It's an honest and earnest
offer and for that very reason, I decline. I don't think he'd get away with
it. But he volunteered, I refused, and never is the subject broached
again, not for over a decade, for so long that I think he forgets.

It's not the only offer I receive. A semi-friend, more of an old party acquaintance from another unit, a medic with a less-than-pristine reputation, makes a far more gruesome proposal. "Do you want me to kill him?" he asks.

"Kill him?" I awkwardly laugh. I haven't told him but that's how rumors work around here. Everyone knows about the MI girl who was raped, even if they don't know her by name or face.

"Yeah, kill him," says the medic. "I'll get rid of him for you." He says it with a casual flick of his shoulder. He's leaning over a table, rolling what, at the time, I thought was tobacco into a thin, white paper.

"And going to jail doesn't make you want to rethink that?"

He snorts, bringing the unlit, makeshift cigarette up to his mouth. "I know how to do it without getting caught," he reassures me.

It's a bizarre conversation and feels wholly rhetorical. "Yeah? How?"

He leans back in his couch and rests one ankle over his knee. "There's the draining of the body, you know, the whole upside-down thing in the shower thing, and the sawing off of the limbs and putting them in different plastic bags, the basic shit everyone knows. That's nothing new. The real issue is hiding the parts without them ever being found. For that, you need a deer."

"A deer."

"A dead deer. You dig a hole on the far side of the post, put the body in there, fill it partway, throw a dead deer on top of that, and, boom, when the search dogs find the spot, police will only dig until they find the deer and assume that's what's got the dogs all riled up."

"That's a terribly specific plan." I laugh it off. I think he's not serious. I hold my hand out and he hands me the quarters slip I came for, pre-signed by some doctor at the aid station. It'll get me out of work for the day, at least.

"Want any prescriptions?" he asks, thumbing through a different booklet.

"Nah, I'm good." Taking a forged quarters slip seems a lot less illegal than drugs, but it's semantics, really.

"Let me know if you want anything," he says pointedly, sounding a lot like one of Andres's cartel movies, and it's funny, until a few days before we roll out for Iraq when he and his roommate get busted for large-scale drug dealing, supposedly holding several kilos of cocaine in their barracks room, as well as a few illegal firearms, and pads and pads of doctor's prescription booklets. So who knows?

My mother is far less violent than the men, and far more efficient. She wants something done and done now. If that means calling her congresswoman, then so be it. If that means threatening to descend on Fort Polk and kick in doors, she'll do it. My mom would've rattled the bars of this post until someone or something fell out, but the problem for her is that I won't let her do it.

"What is your commander saying?" "Have you gone to JAG?" "What are the MPs doing?" She has a question for every time she calls me. "I can get Channel 8 News," she says. "Congresswoman Rosa DeLauro called me back, she wants to talk with you," she adds.

The more she pushes, the more I back away. These lives aren't supposed to overlap; my family isn't supposed to be within my Army sphere. And it's not that I don't want to talk about it, but I don't want to talk about it to *them*, my mother and father. That my Fort Polk life has now infiltrated the other half of my world feels egregious. I want it done with.

"Stop asking, Mom," I tell her shortly, using the excuse of formation to hang up.

"I don't want to talk about it," I say the next time and the time after that, except she's not listening because she's a mother and she just wants to uphold her maternal right to protect her baby, but I'm too young and angry to understand that then.

"If you keep talking about it every time you call, I'm not going to answer anymore," I promise her.

She accidentally calls my bluff, more of a slipup really, when she asks, too intently, how I'm *feeling*, and that's enough for me. When she calls next, I glance at the cell phone and drop it in my cargo pocket. She calls, and calls, and then calls again, and so when I finally answer, two weeks later, she's trained like Pavlov's dog, no longer breathing a word about the subject.

spoliation of evidence

I DON'T KNOW WHAT *unsubstantiated* means. I've never heard the word before; it isn't part of my vocabulary. So when Captain Wells says it in front of the entire company, heads swiveling in my direction, I don't know what he means or why it's so significant.

The investigation has been going on for months, long weeks where I hear nothing from the case, almost like everyone has forgotten all about it. Now we're sitting in an Equal Opportunity briefing; the company sprawled out across the small theater, seated in heavily worn blue thread seats. Andres reclines his head back in boredom, staring up at the ceiling, and I glance at his dark profile. "This is so fucking pointless," he groans, not quietly enough. I know it's pointless, but for entirely different reasons. Andres's squad leader hisses at him and Andres grumbles as he shifts in the seat, sitting up. Captain Wells is in front of the company, standing on the wooden stage, halfheartedly preaching about the necessity to speak out if one feels threatened or sexually offended.

Captain Wells scans the crowd and his eyes linger on me slightly as he nears the end of his speech. He hesitates, showing me the tiniest lift of his lip in a sneer, then turns away. "Now, everyone knows about the sexual assault case going on in the company right now."

I go cold, my heart sputtering in shock. Captain Wells stares back at the upturned faces of his company and says, "And that case has been found unsubstantiated. So guys, if a girl accuses you of something you didn't do, don't worry. You won't get in trouble unless you actually did something wrong."

"Is he talking about what I think he's talking about?" Andres's face is dark with anger, his mouth open, aghast.

I sit rooted in place, incredulous, thinking he can't be talking about *my* case, he's not talking about *me*. I can feel the eyes of the company turn toward me, drinking in my reaction, and I wonder how many minds are made up in this moment.

"What does unsubstantiated mean?" I ask no one.

The briefing is over and I jump up from my seat, pushing through bodies, forcing my way to Sergeant Pelton. Everything has slowed; a buzzing in my ears dulls the noise of the crowd. "Was he talking about me?" I blurt out to him and grasp his elbow, forcing him to face me. It's aggressive and inappropriate but I do it anyway, as if having him pinned in my hand will force him to take me seriously. Sergeant Pelton freezes, his normally bright eyes jumping to the side, looking for an exit plan. "He couldn't have been talking about me, right?" I persist.

Sergeant Pelton sighs. He doesn't want to be here. "Captain Wells just told me today. The case was found unsubstantiated."

"I don't know what that means." I rest my palm against the wall to hold myself up.

Sergeant Pelton's eyes flutter shut, as if asking for strength. He doesn't want to be the one to do this. He shouldn't have to. Captain Wells should have—his absence, as usual, is telling. "It means that they can't rule one way or the other. It's your word against his."

The words fall like physical blows. I'm still holding his elbow, my grip tightening. "And this is how he tells me? This is how I find out?" Sergeant Pelton says nothing. "But what about the photos?" I shake him, trying to knock loose all the answers I need to hear. I remember the MPs calling me back into a small side office, asking me to strip, standing half naked in a stark, cold room while a female officer held a camera up to my skin, capturing the bruises that lined my arms and rib cage, her nose inches from my flesh, the bare lightbulb swinging on its cord overhead as she examined me. "Don't those prove anything?"

"I'm sorry," is all he says, and I drop his elbow. How sorry can he be? It's not like he believes me anyway.

They give me a blank manila folder with the report in it. Someone at the company places it in my hands and I walk out of the building with it tucked under my arm, smashed against the side of my chest. It's non-descript but it still feels like everyone knows what I'm carrying. I soldier out into the sunlight, into the warm spring air, and find an empty picnic table. I sit on the tabletop, boots resting on the bench, folder resting on my knees. I eye it warily, unsure I want to know. I already know the case was found unsubstantiated; I already know Sergeant Pelton read it and hesitated. That it made him look at me differently.

The report is thinner than I expect it to be. I expected it to be heavier somehow. I unpeel it from the folder, flipping through the pages, reading but not. There are witness statements, short little paragraphs and each a punch, a swift, steady jab to the gut. In the clear, bright sunlight I feel myself splinter.

"He said he was going to 'that Dostie-chick's room because she's crazy drunk,'" says a friend of Kevin Hale, about how Hale crowed and swaggered before his conquest, and how he later returned, gleefully victorious.

The pictures are surprisingly absent but allude to photos that once were, like the descriptions of angry, red scratches across Kevin Hale's body, but I don't remember scratching him. There are descriptions of the bruises on my upper arms and back, but I don't remember exactly how I got them. It's like there was an entire hidden scene performed, an act played out for an audience of none, and the void where the memory should be terrifies me. Had I fought back? Had there been some epic struggle and did it even matter if I can't remember it?

They reason it away. "A wrestling match" with his friends caused the scratches. My bruises are evidence of a drunken night. They have an explanation for it all, carefully sectioned-out words that set out to prove the very opposite of what really happened. They're trying too hard.

I jerk my chin away, flipping the pages. "Dostie never would sleep with the likes of Kevin Hale," says Sergeant Rivera's girlfriend, the MP who had been there that night. "She wouldn't want anyone to know if she slept with him," she continues. I had already heard this from her, when she explained her interview to me in person, but the report makes different connections and the insinuation burns. In the unsaid details it suggests I worried about my reputation, that I would do horrible things to protect a reputation I didn't even know I had. I squint at the pages, blinking rapidly to see through tears, trying to understand why she would say such a thing, why would she even suggest such a horrid thing, and it doesn't occur to me until years later, when it's too late to ever ask, that the investigator might have poked her, too, prodded her the same way he did me, twisted and turned her words into an artful statement that suited them just fine.

My testimony is there, too. A small, tiny space, it's short—dreadfully, deceptively short. Black, round letters stare back at me: *I don't know, but I know what he did was wrong.*

I stand suddenly, gripping the report, crumpling stark pages, and it's only a few steps to a wire trash bin. I drop the report into the pail, letting it fall on top of spent coffee cups, a box of half-eaten pizza, and bottles filled with tobacco dip. I never finish reading it and I never look back, leaving it to rot out there in the open.

shock and awe

AROUND THIS TIME, in March 2003, they tell us we're deploying but no one believes them. There is a perpetual sense of denial, maybe because we're going, then we're not going, then we're going again, back and forth, military-orders badminton, until it doesn't make sense to stress over anything because nothing is permanent or certain. Rumor has it that our squadron commander, Colonel Fox, wants to go, to drag our unit into the desert because he needs that combat patch to make rank, to join his family connections in the Pentagon. We don't need to be there, the rumors say, but he's pushing hard to make it happen.

We all figure it'll be Afghanistan. We prepare for Afghanistan. "I hear it's really quite beautiful there," I say to female King, a fellow Farsi linguist from my platoon, trying to make a silver lining of the possibility of war and Taliban. "The mountains, I mean. I hear the mountains are really pretty. Like Iran." Iraq is shiny and newly invaded, an abstract idea, not yet a reality. No real Army soldiers have been there yet, just Marines. And so I'm not nervous yet. It's not really happening, we all say. They'll pull the orders, we all agree.

But a few days later there's Captain Wells in front of the company formation saying "Iraq" and we all sort of stand there, stunned. The Farsi linguists look at the French linguists, the French linguists stare back at the Farsi linguists, and we all say "What?" in our respective languages.

Captain Wells pulls Sergeant Pelton aside after the formation, gripping him by the elbow and leaning in. "If I give you guys all the books, can you learn Arabic over the weekend?"

Sergeant Pelton blinks in stunned horror. "No, sir. No, we cannot," he just manages to get out. Captain Wells grits his teeth. He's displeased.

"He *does* know Farsi and Arabic are two totally different languages, right?" male King, female King's husband, mumbles to the group of us linguists, who stand huddled to the side. "He's not that stupid, right?"

"I think he's that stupid," I say.

"But, I mean, he's had Farsi linguists in his company forever now. He has to know what language it is," fellow Farsi linguist Sergeant Baum objects, but I'm not that surprised. Captain Wells has never shown a particular interest in the linguists, he never visits us at the language center when we're studying or questions us on our DLPT scores. He doesn't care until he has to care because now we're going to Iraq in four weeks and no one speaks the language.

And so there is the prep for war. There's a surprising amount of paperwork. Inventory becomes a four-letter word. Connex boxes have to be packed and we stand in the motor pool, stocking the dark metal storage vans with gear. Sweat drips down my spine and off my chin. It's not exactly hot, just muggy. The wet air gets trapped inside the connex and catches in my lungs. Ever since I got a tick-borne fever during a field training exercise and almost died, I have to use an asthma inhaler to breathe. I heave a green duffel bag onto a pile of plastic bins, shoving it against the metal walls. I don't think any of us thinks deeply enough, in the moment, to register a fear of war. I move, I lift, I shove, I fill checklists and do it all again, functioning on a setting of disbelief. There is an undercurrent of anxiety in the motor pool, but it's covered by gallows humor and a pure, uncomplicated frustration at the bureaucratic dysfunction.

One of the supply sergeants stalks up to the connex, clipboard in hand, white-knuckling the papers. "Take it out," he yells as he nears, gesturing wildly with one arm over his head. "Take it all out."

"Are you kidding me?" Sergeant Holt spins around, flushed and huffing from the heat. He's new to the unit and my TC, the navigator for my driving. He seems like a decent TC so far, even sticking thick black letters onto our Humvee window shield, labeling it A HORSE WITH NO NAME, but he's not yet accustomed to the fuckery that is Fort Polk. He faces off against the supply sergeant.

"It needs to be inventoried."

"We already inventoried it all!"

"It needs to be inventoried again."

Sergeant Holt abruptly kicks a semi-empty bag, sending it skidding across the cement. "The fuck!" He turns back to us, the Specialists, the Privates, the lower rungs, and angrily points to the full connex. "Take it out."

"We literally just finished," a Specialist complains.

Sergeant Holt's face is blood red. He grabs a bag closest to him, drags it from the storage van, and dumps the entire thing out onto the pavement. "Move it all out!"

Grumbles, swears, the connex unpacked, only for another Staff Sergeant to replace the last, swearing at the sprawled-out gear. "Why is this unpacked? Put it all back!"

"We were told it needs to be inventoried."

"It's already been inventoried. Put it all back." He stalks away and Holt holds both hands up over his head in outrage.

"Does anyone know what's going on? Doesn't anyone have any fucking clue what's going on right now?"

No one does.

Rinse and repeat.

I spend most of my time in the motor pool, moving gear from one pile to the next, and sometimes back again. The entire regiment is up in a storm. Now that our deployment country is announced, things are moving rapidly. Units are smashed together, sharing mechanic bays, connex boxes, storage units. Some units sneak up to our vehicles to steal brackets, doors, or mirrors, some of us sneak over to theirs to steal them back. Everyone wants their inventory perfect but there's not enough gear to go around.

"I don't care how you get it as long as you have it," Sergeant Daniels repeats as he collects inventory sheets. As the saying goes, there's only one thief in the Army. Everyone else is just trying to get their shit back.

The intermingling fills the motor pool with unfamiliar men. Everything feels just a little bit unsafe to me. I look from side to side, to indistinguishable faces in uniform, and think *I don't know you. I don't know any of you.* I notice Starre jumping off the back of a deuce and a half, helping unload the vehicle with four other guys from some other unit. They crowd around the edge of the vehicle, handing down stuffed duffel bags. I've never seen them before. I gesture her over, standing a bit away from the vehicle. She trots up to me, all petite and beautiful and happy.

"Do you know those guys?" I ask, glancing over her shoulder at them. She looks back and shrugs. "No."

"You have to be careful," I hiss, leaning forward, heart pounding. My palms itch. I'm cold despite the early-spring heat. "You can't just get in vehicles with random guys."

She looks up at me, brilliant hazel eyes fringed with long, dark lashes. She's confused. She tilts her head slightly. "What are you talking about? It's fine," she says with ease. Never suspicious, not uncomfortable. I realize with a sudden start that she's not scared of them. I realize, in the same moment, that I am. But of course her behavior is normal. How many times had I been surrounded by men before, and never given it a second thought? With the male-to-female ratio in the Army so drastically skewed, and made even worse in Fort Polk, there was no avoiding it. How often had I mingled and mixed and been perfectly fine with it all? I rub the heel of my palm against my chest, trying to physically ease the anxiety. The men watch us from the back of the deuce and a half, probably innocently, probably curiously, certainly more interested in her than me, who has grown too fat in comparison, but all I see is dark eyes, mouths slashed into downturned lines, large hands resting on bent knees. I see height and strength and numbers and I don't want to. I blink hard, trying to fight tears, suddenly embarrassed. I flush hot red.

"Never mind," I mumble. "It's nothing." I want to reiterate that she needs to be careful. That she's the kind of beauty men pause to look at. That she has smooth, pale skin with just a splash of freckles, enough to make her look sweet and harmless. I want her to know that she looks very pretty and very small but she somehow doesn't see that and I don't know if I should ruin that bliss for her. I don't know if I should contaminate her, too.

I leave her, my stomach tight with dread, trying not to make a mountain out of a molehill. I have my own molehill to deal with.

In this new mashup of platoons and units, everything is topsy-turvy, everyone is thrown together. Even still, I didn't expect to see him. First Sergeant Bell had told me not to worry. They already moved him, Bell assured me, somewhere else, somewhere not here, and that was fine with me. So I don't look for him anymore. I don't scan the backs of heads or faces. And because of that, he sees me first.

I don't know how long he's been watching before I turn my head and realize he's there, staring. I had believed them; I had learned to breathe again. My rib cage had unhinged, my shoulders risen, and I had thought *I can do this.* So while I sit in the regiment motor pool during deployment prep, cross-legged on a five-ton spare tire, waiting for my vehicle to be cleared by the mechanics, I don't expect to turn and see him standing there, frowning in my direction. I freeze. He breaks away first, gaze sliding to the side, feigning indifference. I'm hunched forward on the tire, realizing he never left, he has been here the whole time, and my mind races, collecting slips of memories when I hadn't checked to see if he was around, hadn't searched for engraved white scars at the backs of heads, hadn't scanned the street or the company or my barracks building for his silhouette, and I wonder how many times he'd been there. How many times had he seen me first?

I scramble off the tire. I run out of the bay, a mechanic shouting after me because I'm not supposed to leave my vehicle unattended and I don't care. I race up the hill, over the grassy slope, boots sliding on loose gravel, and I don't check the double-lane street for traffic before I dash out into the road. I run with one goal in mind, faster than I've ever run for PT, lungs burning, calves aching, and burst into the company building. I look for Sergeant Pelton. I shouldn't. He's not my platoon sergeant anymore. He's handed me off to Sergeant Daniels ever since that first, awful day when I was stranded between the two of them. But Sergeant Daniels and I never had this conversation, I don't even know what he knows, if he read the report, or if either Captain Wells or maybe even Sergeant Pelton had leaned forward and whispered evil in his ear. I can't come to him blubbering in uniform, in the middle of the workday, so I run back to Sergeant Pelton instead. He might not believe me but at least he knows. I swing the thin door open into his office, sobbing, red-faced, and he stares up from his long desk, pen frozen in his hand.

"Dostie?"

"Hell no," I say, and realize I've been saying it over and over, a type of chant, and I can't break its rhythm. "Hell no, hell no," as I drop down and crawl under the edge of his desk. I'm unprofessional and unreasonable. I press my back into the wall, curled under the wood, and I cry, harshly, loudly, into my knees, tightening myself into a ball, as if I can fuse all my skin and limbs together, never to be unrolled.

Sergeant Baum comes to the door to watch; he saw my flight from the motor pool. They stand awkwardly by the doorway, shuffling boots against the concrete floor, unsure what to do with me. Then they look away and begin to talk over and around me, as if I'm not there, balled under a desk like a schoolkid waiting for the hydrogen bomb. It's near the end of the workday and they leave me, not abandoning me exactly, simply turning a blind eye, which I'm grateful for. I'd rather be invisible, than this stain on the uniform. Formation is eventually called and I peel myself away from my corner, drained and humiliated, and too tired to be afraid.

I wish Kevin Hale had beaten me that night. I wish he had broken all the bones in my face and smashed the back of my skull harder against the brick walls. I wish it had left a red smear on the cement blocks because maybe then they would believe me. Maybe then I could believe myself. Because violent rape is the only thing they understand, the only thing that releases me from my blame and my part in it. I reimagine it always, re-create it in my head, and in my fantasies there's an epic struggle, a battle of fists that he wins—he always wins eventually, as if even in my own re-creations I can't escape that reality—but at least I would have fought, would have raged and screamed and stood defiant and at least they could have seen my broken parts and believed me. But he didn't, I didn't, and I wonder even if it went down that way, if the barracks room had been an empty battlefield of smashed furniture, shattered glass, and blood, would it have been any different?

I'm learning to survive on rage alone. I want to make it into a weapon, a stone-ball club with a wood and rawhide handle, the kind that slams into a skull and leaves a sunken, round indent into the hard bone. I want to scream, not the cry of a girl terrified, but of a creature enraged.

Since I was deemed "unsubstantiated," I've begun to hate Wells. We were never close, and rape has spoiled any ground between us. The emotional depth is perhaps unfairly projected, but anytime I encounter Kevin Hale I feel only an inconsolable terror, no room for anything else, and so I move my crosshairs a little to the left, to something safer. It's that self-righteous kind of hatred, directed toward someone who was supposed to protect me but failed. It fills in all the holes, plugs up any places that should hold fear or worry, and it is now I realize rage is my strongest ally. She gives me feet. She holds me steady. She burns with an intensity that promises to take the whole world down with us. I should be frightened by her, by the way she pours into my hands and jaw and shoulders, slowly cinching each muscle tight, whispering lullabies of release through sweet violence, but she doesn't scare me. I embrace her. I'd rather rage than cry.

One Friday Captain Wells addresses his unit, his dull eyes scanning the formation. He gives the weekend safety briefing, the basics of don't be stupid. Don't drink and drive. Don't do drugs. His gaze settles on me. We stare at each other for a year or two, or maybe just a few seconds, and his fleshy lips pull into a slanted smirk. He lingers to let me know what's coming. Then he turns back to his formation and adds, "And don't drink and have sex, then regret it in the morning and call it rape."

He gets his desired effect—I suck in a short, hard breath, and for one blind second I want to scream, to stand on the brick wall behind me as a red-hot brand in front of the entire unit formation, and to point one finger at his white, fleshy face, shouting that he knows that isn't what happened. That "in the morning" I had already spent long hours curled up on a wooden bench in a military police station, torn figuratively, torn literally. I had been waiting for Captain Wells to storm in and tell me everything would be okay, that he had my six, but he never even bothered to show up at all.

It's clear to me he likes playing this card; he likes the half-hidden chuckles and the sideways glances thrust in my direction. But in the end I can only stand in my squad, fists clenched behind my back, lips pressed together, because I have already learned the consequences having a voice. If you're sexually offended, never show it. If you're sexually harassed, never say it. If you're sexually assaulted, never, ever report it. The truth burns in my chest and I wish I had learned this lesson before. I wish someone had leaned forward and whispered into my ear, "When you get raped, don't tell anyone. Never tell anyone."

Captain Wells releases us and I break from formation, smoldering. My fury tastes like copper and fire. It stops me from crumbling onto the asphalt; instead it lifts me up, lengthens my spine, and I believe I can be remade in its image.

"I hate him," I hiss to Sergeant Forst, blinking hard through hot tears. "I hate him, I hate him," I repeat, wound so tight that should I release, I'd be napalm.

"I know," she says and pats my hand, but she doesn't share my anger. There is a calm acceptance in her voice; she is sympathetic but nothing more. I want others to hate him the way I do, but no one else is fucking upset enough.

That isn't to say that Captain Wells isn't spectacularly disliked, however. When a random US soldier in Kuwait purposefully throws a grenade into his commander's tent in early 2003, the report gets back to those of us in pre-deployment and First Sergeant pounds one closed fist on Captain Wells's back; with a loud laugh, he suggests our commander always wear a flak vest. Wells's greatest enemy is us, who watch him with dark, glittering eyes and waiting for any sign of weakness.

There are reasons he's hated. Rumor has it that Captain Wells hates his wife. So the whole time we're in Fort Polk he keeps his company late daily, just so he doesn't have to go home. He schedules extra weekend field exercises, even in the blistering cold, the wet frost covering bare branches and sticking to uniforms. Locke and I huddle in the back of a covered Humvee, snuggled against each other for body warmth, her breath a white fog.

"We're MI," she grumbles against the cold. "We're not supposed to be doing this shit." And we're not. I didn't spend two years in training just to babysit some 1980s-era equipment in some frozen swamp in Louisiana. Captain Wells has a cot by his Humvee and a Gore-Tex sleeping bag, so he doesn't mind.

No one likes this Captain who cares only about himself. Soldiers have a way of knowing these things—of sniffing out the frauds who are only in it for the brass and pay grade and who have no fidelity to their troops.

But no one hates him like me.

I prefer not to salute Captain Wells. Outside, in our company space, I try to see how often I can walk by without rendering him a salute. Sometimes he catches me.

"Do I get a salute?" he asks. He has his own rage, a self-righteousness I don't understand. I dramatically snap to attention.

My salute is perfect—my back straight, my hand flawlessly raised to brow. But there's nothing respectful in the way I drawl, "*Sir,*" drawing out the title sardonically. I mock him with flair and if he knows it, there's little he can do; I've completed the task to the letter. He stands with several subordinates—undoubtedly trying to show off. I am the kink in his otherwise decent unit. He leaves me there for a moment, stuck at the position of attention, before decorum demands he release me—with nothing more than a halfhearted flash of his hand no higher than his cheek. A pathetic attempt at a salute for a pathetic officer. I stalk away. His presence clings to me for hours, making it impossible to process words or details. Sergeants shout orders at me but I stand and hear nothing. Rage makes me both dumb and blind, a sort of numbness except it burns all the way through.

If I have any anticipation for our deployment at all, it's for simply this: a stray bullet, a single mortar, an IED just beneath his wheel well, all the possibilities of war that end in his death.

the last push before the end

AS THE DAYS CLICK closer to April, onward to our deployment, I sit in my barracks room, legs crossed, elbows planted on my knees, the light of the television blinding in the dark room. I watch the 2003 Air Force Academy sex scandal break. The television camera pans over the academy, showing women in uniform shuffling down stone steps, as numbers are forcefully declared: 70 percent allege they are victims of sexual harassment, 22 percent experienced pressure for "sexual favors," and 19 percent claim to be victims of sexual assault.

"Nineteen percent," I breathe, feeling a sudden affinity, a commonality with a number.

And suddenly everyone's talking about it. The media buzzes, crackles, hisses, *the leadership knew and did nothing about it.* There is outrage, a blast of moral righteousness from the public, and I hope.

"Maybe now they'll actually do something," Andres says, watching beside me, leaning back against the white brick wall. He gestures vaguely at the screen. "Some of them went to civilian lawyers," he adds, repeating the news. He shrugs one shoulder. "It can't hurt to try."

And so I look up a local lawyer, because if these girls did, why can't I? Except when someone actually answers, despite the late hour, I stumble over my words, coming out in a breathless rush: "Hi, I'm in the Army, I'm here on base, but...so I don't know if you can help me or not, because you're a civilian, but I heard in that Air Force Academy case, some girls used civilians, but I'm sorry, I'm calling to see if you can take my case. I think I was...raped."

His response is instantaneous. "You *think* you were raped?" A brutal scoff. "You would know if you were raped, honey. I can't take a case where you *think* you were raped. Call your Judge Advocate General's office." And then he hangs up, before I can counter, before I can explain that I can't just come out and say the word outright, without some kind of antecedent, that I need to dip my toe in. But he's gone and I'm not calling back.

But I do take his advice. I call JAG. "We'll call you back," they say, and then they don't.

So I stand in the JAG building, staring down at the polished floors, shuffling boots from side to side, and then corner a JAG lawyer.

He steps out of an office and I recognize the name on his uniform, the name the office keeps telling me would eventually call me back. "Sir!" I bark, a little too loudly, and dart after him. He glances once at me, over his shoulder, assessing me with one singular glare. He stands before the elevators, jabbing the button with one blunt finger. "I'm on my way to a briefing," he says, deflecting.

I parry and lunge. "I'm going upstairs, too."

The elevator dings loudly, and he steps in, not checking if I'm following. I rush in behind him, gathering my courage, my pre-prepared speech, but then the elevator doors slide shut and I'm inexplicably struck with a sudden jab of panic. He stands across from me and I back up. He's much taller, very broad, and older in a sense that is not just physical years. I suddenly feel small and young.

The elevator is small too, the space tight, but I've never been scared of elevators before. I stare at the doors, the skin on the back of my neck crawling. I say little to the officer, squandering my chance, pissing it away because I'm terrified of a pair of elevator doors and four constricting walls and I don't even know why. I mumble something about my case, so bare bones that no one would want it from my description.

The elevator doors slide open, and the officer steps out, along with all my breath. "Leave your information with the office and I'll call you so we can set up a meeting."

He never does.

Elevators have unnerved me ever since.

So I return to the criminal investigation department to push a little more, to ask a few more questions, and am met with a wall. An officer I'm not familiar with, who has never interviewed me, bars my path. He stands, arms crossed over his chest, his belly protruding and straining against his uniform top. "If it were true, why did you wait a week to report it," he asks, glaring at me like I'm a liar, the worst kind of woman, lips pursed disapprovingly.

"What are you talking about? I reported it *that night*. The MPs came right after he left." I stare aghast, watching my narrative change, becoming rewritten, and he just raises his chin a little, as if defiant. "I did the actual *interview* a week later," I stress. "Is that what you mean? Because I *did* report it. Right away." My words are clipped and hard.

He shrugs, as if he can't be bothered to actually read the report. He says instead, with a heavy sigh, "Do you really want to ruin this guy's life?"

As if I have the power to do so, as if I have any ability to inflict or inspire destruction, as if I have any power at all. But instead I'm the only one being destroyed here. I'd burn it all down with me if I could, every last rank, file, and line, but I'm screaming at the top of my lungs and no one seems to notice.

So I retreat back to my room, sitting on my bed, one hand wrapped around a chocolate milk bottle, the other dipping into the bag of barbecue chips by the pillow, eating, eating, *eating*, getting wider and wider around the middle, and again feel an affinity with a number, that 19 percent. I stare blankly at the screen, at more news updates on the Air Force sex scandal, and I wonder how they broke their story, how they got people to care. Why did justice work for them but not for me? I feel an affinity and yet a wide divide. People rally and march around them, yet I'm left standing in a barren land.

We're getting closer to deployment and somehow I know the moment my boots leave this ground, there will be no coming back to this case. If nobody cares now, how will I convince them to meet with me after a war has been wedged here in the middle? I feel the time slipping by, a pressing expiration date, and so I try to make myself unmissable. I wait uncomfortably in the inspector general's office, fists buried in my lap. I don't look up at the admin officer who sits at his desk, occasionally sneaking curious glances in my direction. He flips paper rhythmically, seemingly without order or sense, until I wonder if he's simply shifting papers back and forth to appear busy. I'm not supposed to be here. I have no appointment; I didn't tell my platoon sergeant I was coming. There was no grand plan; I didn't know I was going to leave until I left. I had stood before the company doors, hesitating in the sunlight, trying to gather the courage to go in and ask for permission, when suddenly I turned on one heel, a perfect about-face, and simply walked away. I crossed over the DO NOT CROSS grass, cutting a straight line to the inspector general's office.

The IG is the very peak of the chain of command, the highest a soldier can reach for help. It's a definitive and purposeful jump in command to approach the IG, a rocking of the boat that no command ever appreciates. I wonder what my command will say when they find out, and then I realize I don't care. If I get them in trouble, all the better. I've grown bitter.

The IG breezes into the tiny office. Her blond hair is swept into a bun and I'm surprised she's a woman. I'm secretly delighted. I state my name and my company, haltingly begin to state my case but she waves it off, swishing one pale hand in my direction as she turns to her desk, spreading out papers with the other hand, pinning them to the desk with long fingers. She knows who I am. She has been forewarned. I glance at the admin officer and wonder when he made the phone call.

She turns to me, then, and tilts her head slightly, a gesture of sympathy, but she wants me to be quick. She's short on time and patience. My story is a lot shorter than it should be. A handful of sentences and her brow pins together appropriately as I speak but there's nothing deeper behind her eyes as she watches me. She cares, but not enough, and she pats my hand. "At this point, you just need to move on with your life," she says.

I withdraw my hand, sitting back in the chair to mask the reaction. "Why should I have to move on with my life? That's not even fair. He should have to suffer, too." The statement surprises me a lot more than it does her. I didn't know I wanted vengeance. I don't feel like the vengeful type. But somehow the concept of "forgive and forget" rots at the base of my stomach.

"Nothing in this situation is fair. You'll feel better once you've moved on."

"But he's still *out* there," I say, a little too loudly. "Yesterday he was driving a truck with another female soldier." My heart pounds at the memory, the surge of fear I had for a girl I didn't know, who looked out the cab window contently, unaware, and I wanted to rush forward and fling open the door, grab her by the elbow, and jerk her out of the seat, tell her to get out, run. "She could be in danger."

The side of the IG's mouth twitches, like she's suppressing something. "I think he's more of an opportunist," she says slowly, as if she's speaking to someone very dim. "I don't think he's the type to do anything violent at work." This is said to appease me but it doesn't.

"At this point, you just need to put this behind you and move forward," she reiterates. I hear the unspoken order. Move on, that's *easier*. Easier for you, easier for me, easier for everyone involved. Less paperwork, less headache. She doesn't speak the words *Drop it*, but the message comes through loud enough. I despise how easy she makes it sound. Like I should simply unburden myself, the dropping of an old rucksack from my shoulders, then simply walk away. Because a strong soldier could do that. A real soldier moves on with his life. I hear her dismissal as a testament to my weakness. Real soldiers don't dwell. I'm not that strong and I'm not that real.

At last I do the unthinkable. I call in my mom. She flies down, along with my brother, aunt, and two cousins. I tell them they're just here to help pack me up, which they do, folding uniforms and stuffing duffel bags as we watch CNN, tanks rolling over sand dunes where I'll soon be, Geraldo Rivera getting kicked out of Iraq. I regale them with tales of Fort Polk and Leesville, like the exotic pet tiger that someone released into the wild onto the north side of the post who still lives in the swamps, or the movie theater that periodically catches fire, ruining movie date nights. They learn that in fact Super Walmart *is* the only non-X-rated thing to do in town. And between that, my mother carries out her own agenda, which I knew she would, which was why I called her, as a last resort. She storms CID, demanding to speak with the head investigator, and I watch, standing a little behind her, as my adulthood gets ripped from my hands. Captain Wells won't meet with her, he's far too busy for something like that, but she manages to book an appointment with the Sergeant Major. I pace and worry and agonize for hours before the appointment, wondering what he'll say, if he even knows, if I'll be an unpleasant surprise, and I pretend he doesn't know, that's why this has gone on for so long, surely someone up there would change things if they simply knew, but when I walk in for the appointment, my mother one step in front, it's not the Sergeant Major but First Sergeant Bell sitting there behind the desk, who first says he's sorry, the Sergeant Major had a sudden schedule shift, and "what can I do for you," only to finish with "is she sure she really wants to ruin this guy's life?"

My mother returns home baffled, astounded by their lack of urgency or care. I feel for her. I'm pretty used this all by now.

But I still go back to Sergeant Bell for one last meeting, this time alone. "I can't take it anymore," I say to First Sergeant Bell. It's days before our deployment, just over three months since my rape. I'm still dwelling. The unit is still in chaos, labels put on Humvees, scraped off, then reapplied. Inventory sheets are written, typed, lost, and inventoried again. The Army at the height of its administrative effectiveness.

I don't want to go to Iraq. When I joined the Army on something of a whim, pre-9/11, I never imagined myself in war. The thought is still abstract. I try to grasp it but it slips out of my hands and flounders about, like a bar of wet soap. I'm not Rambo. I'm neither brave nor fearless; I joined at a time when war was far from the American consciousness—an impossibility because "who would ever want to go to war with America," as my recruiter had promised so confidently. But neither am I a coward. I'm strapped to my unit; I can't cut free because that's desertion, and that's something I won't do. So I don't say to First Sergeant Bell, *I won't go*. I say instead, "I can't take it anymore," and let him decide what to do with me. My brain is scrambled and even I know someone shouldn't put a loaded rifle in my hands. I bear this awareness with both fear and shame.

First Sergeant Bell sits at his desk, elbows propped onto the wood, long fingers intertwined. He rests his fleshy chin on his hands and regards me dully. I wonder how I look to him. I know what he doesn't see: my left arm, hidden by the long sleeve of my BDU top, where the skin has been split, the edge of a blade pressed against the flesh until it parts, slicing a long, slender cut across the underside of a forearm. My arm is decorated with such lines, a judiciously hidden canvas for a very precise self-medication. It's a careful, therapeutic process—every step of the meticulous ritual soothing, from the sterilizing of the blade, to the slicing of the skin, to the keen interest of watching blood bead, dribble, and finally the deliberate bandaging. The anxiety, panic, rage seeps out with the blood, rolls out in thick, red beads, until I'm sweetly empty and tranquil in the stillness.

I've only stopped, just recently, after a small mishap, the twist of the blade that went a bit too deep and blood splashed onto the floor. I had progressed to the inside of my ankle because my left arm was packed with red, angry stripes, and the slice was too quick and deep. Surprised, I wrapped the ankle with a towel, trying to enjoy the numbness, trying to make the most of the moment, but the blood seeped through, staining the fabric, and I had to switch it out for a larger one. I realized I might have to go the hospital. I pressed down on the towel, trying to think of an excuse, a reason to tell the medics, but nothing came to mind. The bleeding slowed, though, and I wrapped it with gauze and tape.

But First Sergeant Bell simply watches me from under the heavy, white pelt of his eyebrows. "Hale's not going," he informs me.

Which infuriates me. He gets away with rape and now he doesn't have to go to war, either? A tiny, less civil part of me grumbles in frustration. A quick image of him facedown in the sand with an angry hole in the back of his head rises and then fades from possibility. Probably for the better. I probably wouldn't have gotten away with it.

"His enlistment is almost up," First Sergeant Bell is saying, refusing to read all the signs of rage I'm projecting. But he makes eye contact, a kind of slow, purposeful stare, and I wonder if he's smart enough to bait me. Is there a flash of genius in those flat, watery eyes? "You can stay here with him in rear deployment until he leaves. Or you can come with us." To war, to war.

It is a surprisingly easy decision.

And so then there is Iraq.

Conception

in the beginning

THE FIRST ELEVEN YEARS of my life, I'm raised in a cult. As far as cults go, it is a fairly good one. It's run by a Christian matriarch, her silver hair perpetually coiffed, a slightly overweight woman who appears huggable and soft, but isn't. Her eyes are black and sharp; she catches every detail when she surveys the room. She is prophetic, or at least she says she is, and speaks with a slight accent, clipping her words so that they are perfectly enunciated. She is intelligent and wise and educated, but mostly she is undisputed. When she says she knows if we children are lying, I believe her. I believe she can read minds. When I'm in a room with her, I stare at the floor, trying to think nothing, just keep my mind blank and white. She has a manner of questioning your beliefs, of forcing you to undermine your own certainty until you're standing on shifting sand and she is the only rock on which to build a foundation. She is Mother, and most call her "Mom," something that wounds my mother's mother for years.

Her right-hand man is a woman, a sweet, soft-spoken older woman who folds in over herself, slender and fragile, and never strays far from the matriarch. Her role or what she actually does I never know. She is quiet and gentle, dark-haired, and was perhaps beautiful once.

The matriarch's enforcer is a young woman with loose black hair, pale skin, and bright eyes. Her job is to report back to the matriarch, and I clip my teeth shut when she's around.

These women of my childhood are intimidating, but strong, walking

the compound with a sort of undeniable elegance, a confidence that
can't be slapped down or away. Backs straight, shoulders back. Whatever
their past was, they are now remade through power and poise.

This church is small, nothing more than an old colonial house on a
flat piece of land located at the heart of the small New England town.
A rock wall lines the periphery; an herb and vegetable garden stretches
across the entire front yard. There are no more than twenty members
at any given time. The house grows as the members work tirelessly
on building, expanding, adding rooms and space for families to live
on the compound. It's transformed into something larger, beautiful but
secretive. We do not speak to outsiders about this church, though the
small town is curious to know, leaning in, trying to see into the yard and
windows and spreading whispers and rumors, all of which are untrue.
They want to believe this is a sex cult, that the women have lovers and
trysts and affairs, because clearly anything with women in power must
be reduced to a sexual nature. Their rumors are all a lot more dramatic
and interesting than the actual truth.

I'm not aware of most of this as a child. I understand that some
secrecy must be maintained, that I am not to answer odd questions that
may come from outsiders, but beyond that it seems a normal enough
life. My mother, brother, and I don't live on the compound, though we
spend most of our free time there. I remember long summers of weeding
the garden, we children set to work because idle hands are the devil's
workshop. The hard roots cling to the earth and the plants rip at my
hands, smearing them green. It's an endless task, and I resent it. We're
bowed at the waist, the sun scorching our shoulders and the backs of
our necks. This task has ruined gardening for me forever. Once we leave
this place, I will never pick another weed again.

Between weeding, and moving this wood from here to there, and helping adults with this or that, as new walls and roofs are built, there is the
biblical learning and education. I don't mind this as much. Bible study
is inside, and the house is usually cool, primarily lit by large windows
and skylights. It's much bigger than my house at home, expansive, with

newly laid hardwood floors and carefully crafted crown molding. As a child, it never occurs to me to ask where the money came from to build such a house. I assume the Matriarch had funded it herself. (She didn't.) In Bible study, we children are sectioned off by age, a few kids to each adult, and we engage in rigorous study of verse and meaning. I read the Bible from front to back, then back to front, learning my favorite stories. I'm drawn to the excitement of the Old Testament, to First and Second Samuel, to books filled with war, the rise and fall of monarchs, the heroic warrior king David and his tragic love affair with the beautiful Bathsheba. I'm fascinated by the ancient cities of Babylon and Egypt, by pharaohs and Babylonian kings. Even as a child I was drawn to war and ancient lands, although age has tarnished these books a little for me, as I notice that King David's love affair with Bathsheba sounds a lot more like rape and the true villain in the Book of Job is God himself.

We're not allowed to watch TV or most movies, something that ostracizes me slightly from my secular, elementary school peers. I pretend to know who New Kids on the Block are, learning tune and verse from hearing everyone else sing it. But we do watch old musicals, like My Fair Lady or, my favorite, Calamity Jane, a 1950s musical about a woman sharpshooter on the frontier, a woman who so bucks the expectations of femininity that she's often mistaken for a man.

During all this, I never question that I am loved tremendously. I feel the love daily from my own mother and father, but even better I have multiple mothers, a village of women I can go to for any problem, each of whom has the voice and place and power within this community to address any issue herself. These are strong women: businesswomen, mechanics, lawyers, carpenters. They take care of their own. There is no subservience here. The concept of bowing head to husband is utterly absent from my youth. Our church is woman-heavy, home to single women, single mothers, divorced women, women in strained marriages, women in healthy marriages. There are men, too, but it's the women who shape our world. I suspect that being raised by so many women has an influence on my older brother, who is soft-spoken and kind. He has the patience of a man many times his age, slow to anger, enduring everything with a calm stillness. He's the oldest boy of the children, but he has no interest in seizing the power that could come with that role. Whether he is with the youngest children or the adults, he is always eager to please.

If being surrounded by so many women made my big brother more feminine—if such traits are to be called feminine at all—it creates the opposite in me. I'm loud and brash, opinionated and selfish. I enjoy being contrary and am invigorated by debate. Stillness bores me. Adults tell my mom that I will go on to do great things because I am wild, and I enjoy this assessment. The expectations don't stifle me but instead fill me with wonder. No one warns me away from my ambition.

You could call me a tomboy, I suppose, but I never would have. I see nothing wrong with femininity. Dresses have their place, and I enjoy them within the narrow confines of the space in which they can be enjoyed. But I also enjoy jean shorts, sneakers, and swinging my legs up into tree branches, low-crawling through dense bushes, scrambling through thorn thickets as we explore the world behind our houses. I don't mind the dirt or the mud or trekking through rivers in search of the perfect adventure, the next most outrageous story. I want to be wild. I always think this is my father's inheritance, my father who started his own white-water rafting business, who skis down double-black-diamond slopes and climbs mountain faces with only chalk on his hands. It is he who teaches me how to rappel off rocky cliffs and how to handle moguls on a snowmobile at high speeds. To my surprise, I'll learn later it was actually my mother who was the rodeo barrel racer, who rode a quarter horse who knew only two speeds: stand and gallop. She was the one who met him at age fifteen while hitchhiking on the side of the road, who encouraged my father to take that very first white-water rafting trip, the one that made him fall in love with white-capped waves, the one who inspired him to start his business. So maybe wild is my legacy from both sides.

At the church there is a clan of a dozen or so children ranging from babies to preteens and we are tight-knit, interwoven until we are like family, living what seems to us like a perfectly normal childhood. When not working or doing chores, we play hide and seek, we spend long hours outdoors, exploring plant and insect and tree. Our church is focused on education, on the arts, and we put on plays on homemade stages, with curtains made of blankets, well-choreographed reenactments of historical accounts or old poems.

There are the adult Bible studies on Thursdays that last late into the night, until one or two in the morning, and my brother and I sleep with the other kids in temporary beds until my mother comes to scoop us up, into the car, and we can finally go home. It must be hard for my mother, who works long days as a mechanic. It's always early mornings for her.

Then there are the moments that don't seem normal at all, like the November when we're kept up late into the night, sitting in the Matriarch's room, watching the 1992 presidential elections come to a close. We collectively wring our hands and I shift uncomfortably on the thick white carpet, sick with dread, staring up at the screen with little understanding of what is happening except that Ross Perot must win. He doesn't and this marks the End Times and the coming of the Antichrist.

There also is the night the Matriarch prophesized would be the final day, because the second coming of Christ is due to happen at some point during the night. We stay up praying, praying hard, and when he doesn't come I think it's a failure on my part, for not praying hard enough, not believing strongly enough (a recurring theme for all prayers unanswered). No one ever seems to question the Matriarch for this miscalculation, her prophecy unfilled. We simply wake at some point after dawn, a little relieved to see the morning sky instead of heavenly trumpets or a whirlwind of fire and air, which all sounded kind of terrifying. (The concept of the rapture will haunt me even into adulthood, still somehow a presence in my mind, so that every once in a while when I make a few phone calls and no one answers, I wonder to myself if the rapture happened and I just haven't been told yet.)

Despite these details, which only seem slightly off at the time, I embrace this religion with all the unquestioned devotion of a child raised on nothing else. At age five, I crawl into my mother's lap, pressing my temple against her shoulder. I had a nightmare, which wasn't uncommon for me. "How can I go to heaven?" I whisper. My mother thinks a moment, perhaps how to best word the salvation message for such a small child, then says, "Jesus is our savior and forgives our sins." She prays with me and I accept Jesus as my Lord and Savior and my mother gives me a tight, proud hug, burying her nose into my hair. She sighs with relief. "Now you're born again," she says, and that sounds very important. I believe what she believes and what my brother believes and what my church believes.

My father, however, does not. He never is a part of the church, never sets foot on that compound soil. He takes advantage of my mother's time away, though, and eventually leaves her for another woman, one of his mistresses, when I'm five. I don't understand because I have never seen them fight. Not a single word, never a raised voice, not once a slammed door or a broken plate. It's silent and abrupt. One day he's there, then suddenly not. The unexpectedness startles me and hunkers down in my bones. It will sit there for decades, a physical reminder that they can leave at any moment. Don't trust too much, never rely too deeply, they can leave at any time.

I blame my mother, not for his leaving, but for the financial mess he leaves us in. My mother works endlessly, tirelessly. Her long hours mean that sometimes she comes home late, but always in time for dinner—even if dinner needs to be pushed back a few hours—because we eat together as a family, a small trio bent over our chicken or spaghetti dinner. Even as a child I'm aware that she works like this to keep us here in our comfortable home, and that we could've moved elsewhere and been fine—had more clothes or better cars or things we didn't need but simply wanted—but these schools are the best in the county and she's determined to give us that. And still I blame her, unfairly, because if she hadn't depended on a man, this never would have happened.

I'll never be like you, I think, criticizing her for having once relied on my father to keep her stable. *I'll go to college*, I think, which is something my mother didn't get to finish at the time. *I'll travel the world*, I promise, which neither she nor my father ever did. *I'll make my own money*, I swear, and I internalize that oath until it's scored into my bones and I live my life dedicated to that one promise: I will rely on no one, I will be self-sufficient, no man will ever leave me desolate. This will keep me safe.

Meanwhile my mother swallows her grief whole, buries it deep down in her stomach and pushes onward. I remember only one time when she cries. At the beginning of the divorce, we live in a space of "not anymore," of small changes to our daily lives as certain things no longer happen. Daddy's not coming home anymore. When I answer the phone, I no longer need to say "North American White Water Rafting," because my father's business has followed him out the door and into another home. One morning my brother comes into my room. He recognizes my mother's sadness more than I do, maybe because he has two years on me. "It's Mom's anniversary," he says. "We should give her presents. It'll make her happy."

I don't know what an anniversary is, but I do want to make her happy so I search through the trinkets in my room, discarding this or that, until I come across one of my prized possessions. It's a glass unicorn head that sits on a wooden platform, a tiny lightbulb inside the base, filling the head with shifting colors of light. It's magical and would make anyone happy.

We softly tread down the carpeted steps. My mom's bedroom door is open a crack but the room is still dark. My brother stands by her head and holds out a letter made of construction paper. "Happy anniversary," he says faintly.

She shifts under the heavy blankets and peeks out. Her face is white in the darkness. Slowly, as if it takes great effort, she sits up in the bed, her dark hair obscuring her face. "Thank you, baby," she says, but her voice is both low and harsh.

"This is for you!" I say, my din in contrast with my brother's quiet. I thrust the unicorn head and base into her hands. She turns it over and maybe she smiles.

"Thank you," she says again. She sits there for a moment, the unicorn sinking into her lap "But we don't have to celebrate this day anymore." This is another end, another "not anymore," and while I don't understand the why, exactly, I do know it involves my father in some way, and that like many things now, this day is to be packaged up and placed to the side, best forgotten or untouched. I follow my mother's silent example; I learn to compartmentalize well, to physically move on, to follow through with the necessary motions of daily life, even when emotionally I just want to dwell.

The divorce fractures my parents, but it winds my brother and me closer to my mom. She becomes our permanent structure, the measure of authority, the home of kindness. She plays the roles of mother and father equally well. She calls our family the Three Musketeers, and it's true enough. If she rages about my father's infidelity, or the unfairness of being left to raise two children alone, she hides it well. She never once says an unkind word about my father. "He loves you the best way he knows how," she often repeats when he forgets to call that day, or doesn't end up visiting when he said he would. But after my father is gone she doubles down on church life, bringing us more often to the compound, and the women flock around her, shouldering up the extra childcare hours, the house duties. I'm surrounded by a village of women, but despite all this love here, I'm still just a little girl who wants nothing more than her dad.

Even after he leaves, however, my father remains an indomitable force in my life. He's not there for all the school meetings or the homework or the chores and the discipline, but he's there for some weekends, for hiking and white-water rafting and skiing, snowmobiling and ATVing, for mountain climbing and rappelling off the edges of rock faces, for laughing across bonfires in the dark of a cool Maine night. In my memories I am forever running after him on tiny legs, stumbling over rocks as I try to keep up, try to stick to his side, but I'm somehow continuously just a little bit behind. He talks about what he wants, directs each conversation to his preference, and I have to repeat myself, lean forward, break in, and even so I remain unheard, my voice an afterthought, white noise in the periphery.

My father is the rugged outdoorsman, the charismatic carpenter, the hard worker with large, callused hands and perpetually sun-scorched skin. I have his love but not his attention. He is more god than man, and just as unreachable.

"God is in the trees," he says one night when I'm ten, staring out at mountain landscape, his breath escaping in a hot, white cloud around his face. He holds a beer in his hand. His sweater sleeves are rolled up, despite the cold winter air. He's drunk. I don't mind. I stare out at the snow-laden trees, their branches bowing beneath the wet weight. "God's not in some church, he's out there." He gestures to the wild, to the night and the stars, rejecting my traditional deity, my mother's god. I find the concept intriguing, a small heralding of my father's Mi'kmaq Native American ancestry, and I like that very idea of pressing against my boxed version of God, of examining it from different sides and angles, even if I won't appreciate the potency of his words for decades to come.

We parry back and forth, our first real exchange, rebuilding the concept of nature gods, his normally ruddy face deepened from the beer, one work-worn palm braced against the porch banister. I don't mind that he drinks, because we have *this*, these moments when he can see me, speak to me, as if I'm a permanent fixture and I don't have to strain my voice so deeply, I don't have to yell, "Dad. Dad! *Peter!*" to get him to turn briefly in my direction.

When I'm eleven my mother leaves the cult. As a child, I don't understand why. All I know is that I'm being dragged from the compound I grew up calling home, severed from the other kids I love like family, and that it's all final and deafening. She'll tell me much later that it wasn't one single event, but instead an accumulation of things. She woke each morning sick with anxiety—dread over the long Bible studies, of striving to match the version of herself that the Matriarch demanded she be, of meeting this unobtainable status of the perfect Christian. It all leaves her stomach perpetually coiled in knots. She no longer experienced the happiness she had once found in God. She lost her joy.

The church does not want to let her go. They bring the children to my mother's door, the whole tribe standing out on the lawn as we kids cling to each other, wailing. The compound kids are homeschooled, which means our paths can't cross even at school. "You won't get to see each other again," they say. "Say goodbye," they order.

Other mothers look on with angry, accusatory eyes. "Why are you doing this to them," one of them asks my mom, who stands on our red-brick steps, one hand firmly planted on the door frame. "Why are you breaking them apart?"

I turn in the arms of one of the girls, Lizzy, who has been practically a sister to me, tears dribbling off my chin. "Why?" I keen, my voice quivering, my arms tightening around Lizzy's neck, cheek pressed against her soft brown hair.

If my mother gives an answer, I don't remember. I see her standing there, unyielding under this sudden assault, her head hung forward. She doesn't move from her stronghold at the door. I think then that it is stubbornness. It doesn't occur to me that she needs the frame to hold herself up. It takes me years to realize the strength it must have taken, to make such a stand against a church she once loved, a church that has so consumed her life that it has fractured outside friendships, weakened family bonds until she had very little outside those compound walls. Leaving must have been like another divorce. She bears it with a kind of strength and elegance that I don't recognize then, but will later. How heartrending it must have been to lose her two great loves.

There will be other churches, however. Other friends to be made between sermons and church pews. My mother remarries, to a Texan mechanic with a loud, instantaneous laugh and warm, kind eyes. Together they eventually find a new church, where I pray and study and serve.

event horizon

BY THIRTEEN I'VE GROWN restless. My nose points northward; something wild calls me, propels me forward. I'll call this the Dostie Curse, a disquiet I've inherited from my father. It vibrates under the skin, rattles inside the rib cage, an incessant need that has no name. Stillness bores. Mediocrity is terrifying. Domesticity is cancer. It's not so much an ambition as a compulsion, a consuming want to see more, do more, be there and not here, and sometimes I get it, how hard it must have been for my father, confined by the four walls of marriage in a small town in Connecticut.

So at our new church, a nondenominational sect that is wholly nondescript, I find myself volunteering to travel to Russia for a missionary trip, arm stretched high overhead when the pastor asks which teens want to go. I barely make the age requirement. I don't feel young, though: I need to move, to push out for no deeper reason than to flee normalcy. And I do, raising the money for the trip through babysitting and car washes and yard work, eventually rolling into St. Petersburg just three years after the Iron Curtain falls. In Russia I befriend other teenage churchgoers, determined to forever change the world in a way only a thirteen-year-old can imagine. At the time, I envision a spread of Christianity, a spiritual saving of humanity and my single hand in the movement, although the truth is I'm simply enthralled by the history and culture of another place, and really, deep down, in love with this feeling I'm nurturing of being different from everyone else. I need to be extraordinary.

I get my first taste of international life in Russia, my first exuberant life experience as I fall in love with a beautiful Russian man who is almost a decade my senior. I love him in that tiny, early-teen kind of love, consuming and brilliant and fast, leaving me feeling altered, like nothing will ever be the same, when really it is only a two-week encounter, where he does nothing more than linger with his lips against my cheeks, because I've been told sex is only for after marriage and never, ever for before. We write long, poetic letters to each other after I head back to the US, and then he joins the Russian army and ships out to Siberia, which I find terribly brave and foreign. I promptly forget about him when the letters stop.

The summers I am fifteen and sixteen I spend in Haiti, with yet another new church, a predominantly African American Pentecostal ministry. We build churches and pass out food and clothes to the poor, and I am intrigued by the diversity of the world yet abhor the Haitian heat, the way the sweat sticks to my body and slithers down my skin. I eat goat, and ants, and clams straight from the ocean, the flesh squirming in my mouth as I clamp my teeth down on their slippery, salty meat. I travel with my church's youth group, with my on-and-off-again boyfriend, a Will Smith look-alike with eyes so brown they appear orange in the sunlight. This love, too, feels earth-shattering; I love him with my whole teenage being, as if our love were the entire world.

We sneak kisses in church closets, in dark hallways between youth group meetings, never too much more, because he reminds me, "This is wrong," with his thumb brushing against my chin, his hand cradling the back of my head, the other wrapped around my waist. I press up against him in that tiny closet, the door slightly ajar, light peeking in from the church kitchen. My foot knocks a broom and the wood handle slides to the side with a loud clack. I startle, glancing out through the sliver of light, but no one hears us. I remind myself that this feeling is the desire of the flesh, spiritually harmful, but I am flushed, heart pounding, and I want, I want, and I'm not supposed to want. Sex is for marriage and this sort of play is sinful, detrimental to my relationship with God. I press my forehead against his chest, with a sigh trying to shut back the feelings, the pulsing from deep inside my body. I can't, not really.

I grow roots in this Pentecostal youth group. I become a worship team singer, a Prayer Warrior, a leader in the group. There's a hierarchy here but I don't mind because I'm at the top. My friendships are established here in this youth church and I take my Christianity seriously, attending youth events like Acquire the Fire, headlining See You at the Flagpole at my school, being the first to open a Bible study club at both my middle and high school. One summer I travel the coast with our youth group band, singing for churches from Connecticut to Florida. Yet none of this is strong enough to tie me to Connecticut. I'm still itching to go, to get out, even though I don't know what *out* means.

At sixteen I ask my mother if I can study abroad in Japan for a year. Thanks to a closeted obsession with anime and manga, I've fallen for the language, dazzled by its sheer distinctiveness from Spanish or French or German or Italian, the only other languages offered at our school. I attend after-school Yale University courses for it; I join two Japanese-language summer camps at Central Connecticut State University because I'm determined to become fluent. I excitedly hand my mom pamphlets and flyers, hopping from one foot to the other. She looks down at them and gives a soft, deflated sigh. She hesitates, the words heavy in her mouth. "We can't afford this, Ryan," she says. Most trips cost at least six thousand dollars, which isn't something a Subaru service manager can afford.

I keep my disappointment to myself and continue scheming. Finally an Italian-language teacher stops me in the hall at school, saying, "Didn't you want to study abroad? The Rotary Club is doing interviews right now, looking for students who want to do an exchange program." I lunge at the opportunity, and my mother manages to sneak me into a spot on the last day of interviews, where I breathlessly say that no, Haiti wasn't better than Russia and Russia isn't better than Haiti, they're just *different* and you can't compare them like that. Turns out that is the correct answer that earns me a scholarship to study my junior year in Japan.

The money taken care of, my mother never asks me not to go. Among all the things she has done for me, her greatest gift is that she never tries to clip my wings. For my part, I feel no remorse about leaving. It feels like a natural progression.

So at seventeen, I board a plane to Japan to spend my junior year abroad, attending an all-girls high school, living with host families who speak little English, whose daughters teach me to wear my sailor school uniform with the skirt rolled at the waist until the hem is just so (so short that we girls have to hold our hands against the back of our skirts, pressing the scant material over butt cheeks as we climb the train station stairs), how to glue loose socks to my calves because that is the fashion and I want to be as Japanese as possible. I join the kendo fencing club after school. I immerse myself. I have no American friends, know few English speakers, and this works for my language skill, which eventually blossoms into the stunted ability to hold a basic conversation. At times this makes for an isolating experience. I can speak enough to be friendly, to make loose connections with the girls in my school, who are all kind, but not enough to establish anything deeper. The inability to fully express oneself in language is ruthless, it fractures the confidence: I'm more than what I can't say, I want to tell everyone, but I don't know how. My voice fails me.

And yet it's also worth it, because there is the time I sit with my friends, talking about the difficulty of the Japanese language, and when I emphatically agree—"that is so true!"—one blinks at me, saying, "You just sounded so Japanese right now," and I glow. Or there's the time I climb Mount Fuji. Or when the local newspaper comes to the school to cover the story of an American who joined the kendo club, because seeing a foreigner do a traditional Japanese sport is exciting to them and I explain that I love the sport because it is fast and hard and completely different from anything I've done, and I like different. I'm slowly drawing up an internal list of all the things I've done that most others haven't, and I'm struck with the compulsive need to make that list longer. I am young, and this reckless pride passes for ambition.

In Japan I am the center of attention, all eyes on me, the white, foreign girl dressed like a local. People stop on the streets to stare, to whisper "*gaijinn*" when I pass. I grow used to the feeling of uniqueness, of being special, a point of interest simply by existing, until I come home to Connecticut and realize I'm not. Back on American streets, my averageness annoys me. I want to be more. I want to take up more space. I need to maintain my upward trajectory, to capitalize on the moment when someone takes notice of what I've done so far in my life, the places I've been, and says in shock, "And you're how old?"

I feel the need to cram more in, to keep momentum moving, so at eighteen, when I find myself staring at a handsome Army recruiter in my high school cafeteria, I'm quietly intrigued by both the promise of adventure and the unorthodoxy of it all.

"I love a man in uniform," groans Jojo, one of my high school friends, resting her chin on her palm as she openly ogles the recruiter. He's standing there in all his uniformed glory.

"Go talk to him then," I prompt, nudging her with my elbow.

"What, like I'm going to join the fucking Army?" she scoffs. "They already call me enough as it is. No thank you."

"They've never called me," I say, a little put out at being excluded. "I should go over there and ask why."

She laughs big, like she always does. "You? You want to crawl around in the dirt and play with guns?" She gives me a crooked grin. "I don't think so."

"No, I'm just going to go talk to him. He's hot."

She smirks, my co-conspirator, and gestures one hand at the recruiter, like he's a meal on a platter. "Get his number for me, then," she says.

I flash a dorky thumbs-up sign, pretending not to be intimidated, pretending I'm worldlier than I am and that after studying abroad, talking to a grown man is no big deal. That fake confidence carries me all the way to the recruiter, who reminds me of a young John Travolta. Fists on my hips and chin angled upward, I confront him flirtatiously. "You guys never call me," I accuse.

The recruiter flashes a dimpled grin, eyes bright and brilliant blue. "Give me your number now and I'll call you all the time. What are you going to be doing after high school?"

I'm not sure if we're flirting or if this has suddenly veered professional so I laugh clumsily. "It's not like I'm going to actually join the Army or anything." It has never even crossed my mind. "I was just saying, you guys have been calling everyone but me. I think it's because I was gone my junior year." I'm talking fast because I'm nervous, trying to fill the space with my voice. "That's when you guys get everyone's number, right? Junior year? I was studying abroad in Japan then." I am still a little overly pleased at my own accomplishments.

His blue eyes widen and he freezes, as if he's just discovered something terribly extraordinary. "Wait, you studied in *Japan*?" I've suddenly become the most interesting thing in the room.

"Yeah, for a year." I cross my arms over my chest, pretending to be older than I am, like we're equal adults in this conversation, even though he has a decade and some years on me.

"Do you speak Japanese?" he asks.

I shrug, pretending to be humble, but I'm not. "Yeah. I'm going to go to college to major in Japanese to get better. You know, like really fluent."

"Wait!" He throws both hands up. "We! Need! You!" he says in a dramatic rush, enunciating each word with violent gusto, and despite myself I believe him. It's hard not to. He's leaning in, vibrating with excitement. I am swept up in my sudden importance.

"We have the Defense Language Institute in Monterey, California, which teaches almost two dozen different languages." He pauses for effect. "Including Japanese." He spreads both hands wide in a why-the-hell-not gesture. "If you're going to study Japanese, why not do it at the top language institute in the world? And for free?"

He's got my attention now. I didn't make it into Bates College in Maine, where I wanted to major in Japanese, but it wasn't like we could have afforded that college anyway so maybe it had always been a pipe dream. I then contemplated going to a local college to study forensic anthropology, simply so I could one day write really accurate crime fiction, but that seemed impractical as well. And I had recently left my church's youth group, who didn't like that I was so focused on college, who felt I was spending too much time away from the group and the band, that I was "not dedicated enough." So I have nothing holding me here, not that I ever did anyway.

He sees my hesitation, sees me running the possibility through my head, and he quickly places a pad in my hand. A good recruiter knows when to strike, and he's a very good recruiter. "Here, write down your number. I'll give you a call and we can talk about it. We'll sit down with your parents and I'll bring all the information about the school." *The school* sounds nice, like I'm going to college, not really joining the Army. So I scribble down my number, my event horizon in a single flourish of the hand, and he hands me a card with his name and number, "In case you have any questions."

I slowly walk back to Jojo, a little dumbfounded, the card burning in my palm. She's wide-eyed. I flash her the card, holding it up between two fingers. "Got his number," I grin and she laughs, because she still thinks we're being outrageous, except I'm being a little serious. The truth is, I have no strong grasp of gender expectations and norms. If a woman wants to be a mechanic, she can. If a woman wants to lead a community of followers, she can. And if a woman wants to join the Army, she can do that, too. This doesn't seem that impossible, and better yet, it's unusual, a path less followed. This is my continual incline, my rise out of mediocrity, and nothing in my history tells me that I can't or, more important, that maybe I shouldn't.

suck it the fuck up, buttercup

MY HANDS SINK into the dust pit, fingers splayed open, arms shaking as I press out another push-up. I cough, choking on the dirt, teeth grinding as I move up, down, up, in counts of three. The grumble of artillery rolls in the distance, echoing across the cold Oklahoma sky, a sky so vast that it domes at the edges, the land a single dry, flat plain beneath it. Steam rolls off our bodies, curls into clouds and hovers over the platoon, a tangible mark of our torture.

"I'm going to smoke your lazy bitch asses until snot bubbles come out your nose!" Drill Sergeant B promises, strolling between the lines of Privates, hands clasped behind his back. "Up!" he orders and we're up, running in place. Sweat soaks my undershirt; my knees tremble. "Down!" And we're back in the push-up position, beads of sweat dangling off my nose and dropping with soft splatters into the dust. "Go!" We flip onto our backs, kicking up dust clouds, boots waving in flutter kicks. "Up!" Again, repeat, up, down, go, until my stomach clenches, grows rigid, and I'm going to vomit.

I'm not supposed to be here, I'm not supposed to be here: The thought runs through my head on an endless loop as muscle fatigue sets in. I drop to my knees for the push-ups.

"What in God's name are you doing, Private?" Drill Sergeant B turns like a bloodhound on a scent, pivoting on his heel, instantly right there, crouching, leaning in so that his face is inches from mine. "Are you having a hard time, Private? Is this a little too much for you?"

"Drill Sergeant, no, Drill Sergeant," I gasp.

"Are you sure, Private? Because if this is a little too much I can get you a nice cup of SUCK IT THE FUCK UP, BUTTERCUP! This ain't like your job back at home, Private. Get off your fucking knees!"

I'm not supposed to be here.

I was frightened of basic training. Somehow, I managed to hold up my right hand, swear an oath, and sign a contract all while not really considering basic training.

"You have nothing to worry about," said my recruiter, breathing easy as we jogged up and down the Yale campus, training for the upcoming training. I labored and coughed beside him, face blood red. "You're going to Relaxin' Jackson."

As the sidewalk inclined, I fumbled a few steps, head down, ignoring the sweeping stone towers of Yale. I didn't have the breath to respond.

"It'll be too easy," he promised, waving off my fear with one large hand. He's not lying. North Carolina's Fort Jackson is famously the easiest basic training assignment. Cushy, as they say: meant for the intel world, like me, but also the paper pushers, the supply lines, nicknamed Relaxin' Jackson for its less-than-severe reputation. Basic is only ten weeks, then I'll finally be shipped off to the Defense Language Institute, which is the whole reason I'm here. I try to keep my eye on the prize, on the promise of the language school perched on the California coast where I'll finally get to study more Japanese, but those ten weeks in between now loom large, obscuring my vision, and I can't see around them.

I chose the Army after some debate. I came home from school that day, still holding my recruiter's card, and said to my mother, "The Army has this language school that can teach me Japanese. And it's free! *And* they'll pay for college afterward!"

She spun to face me. There was a flash of wild panic in her eyes.

"You didn't sign anything, did you?" she asked, but it was more of a terrified yell.

I snorted. "Of course not. I just gave him my info. He said he'll come here and meet with you." After he did, and my mom realized I was serious about the opportunity for free college, she decided that if I was going to do something like this, I had to shop around. She was convinced it would be safer for me to join the Air Force. She was probably right. But there was something lacking in the Air Force recruiter, in his presentation, as if he were trying to impress upon me how much easier it would be. Easier and nicer, not so much PT, not so rough or tough, and somehow the idea of that safety bored me. I wanted to get thin and muscular and hard, made strong by gritty training. And I never quite made it into the Marine recruiter's office, pausing at the office door, staring at those stacked men with their near-skintight uniforms, precise movements, steel spines, and was a little scared. I settled for the Army, not too badass, but badass enough. I'm the Goldilocks soldier.

My brother saw me join and liked the idea. He took their tests and scored in the top 1 percent. I was envious. I wished for intelligence like his—I'd be at Yale or Harvard. I'd be out of here already. The recruiters grew excited, dropping pamphlets into his lap, promising West Point, officer schools, only the crème de la crème for their most intelligent recruit, but then he came up red-green deficient in the vision test and his job options were narrowed down to combat arms, which he did, though he'd get sick in basic, unable to finish, and they'd discharge him before they even bothered diagnosing him. I also got my ex-boyfriend, the Will Smith look-alike, to join, as well as my current boyfriend, a nice Christian boy who quit my youth group around the same time I did, so we had that to bond over. The Army gave me an extra rank for bringing in these new recruits.

But all my excitement, that foolhardy grit, was missing the day I boarded my plane for basic. I hugged my mother for a few extra seconds, clinging tight for just a moment too long, very much still only nineteen in that moment. She stood at the gate, watching me sling my bag over my shoulder, and as promised I paused in the long hallway before the plane door, waving one hand back at her, because you could do that then, pre-9/11.

And then I was standing in Columbia Metropolitan Airport, heart pounding, wiping my hot, sweaty palms on my jeans as a Sergeant from the USO pointed me toward a white, idling bus. He didn't smile; no one was friendly. But then again, no one was outright mean, either. The ride to the base was uneventful. As was getting off the bus and lining up.

"I thought they'd yell at us," I said to the girl standing next to me.

We stood at a pathetic attempt of attention and she turned her head slightly in my direction. "You're complaining about them not yelling at us?"

"No." I shrugged, watching as Army-green people bustled to and fro in front of our line of recruits. No one was really paying attention to us. "I just mean in the movies, they yell a lot more."

She shrugged back. "Relaxin' Jackson." The camp's reputation preceded it.

We were segregated by sex, but not by military occupational specialty, a conglomerate of various jobs and futures, placed in reception, a sort of holding tank as we waited to in-process, a waiting period before the waiting period before actual training. "Hurry up and wait," I heard for the first time, and that's exactly what we did. Hurry from one place to another to simply wait, hours crawling into days, then weeks. Almost three weeks passed as they pushed our all-female platoon around, squeezing us into ill-fitted PT uniforms of black shorts and gray T-shirts. North Carolina was hot even for September and we sat in our bays most of the day to avoid the heat, reading fat books that had been left behind by past troops.

And then came the night when we were ordered from our beds and out into the hot, sticky night, dragging our bags behind us. Thunder rumbled through the heavy clouds; a late-summer electrical storm was brewing. Floodlights brightened a stage, and our reception drill sergeant climbed on top as we fell into formation. She stared down at us, oddly quiet, mouth turned down in a grimace. "We're at capacity," she said out over us, projecting her voice as only a drill sergeant can. "Fort Jackson has no more space for recruits."

I blinked, tugging at the sweaty collar of my PT shirt. Girls around me turned their heads, glancing at each other in confusion. There was no murmur of questions because we already knew better.

"So..." Drill Sergeant hesitated. "So we're going to have to send you to another base."

Fear instantly clutched my stomach. Somewhere other than Relaxin' Jackson? We were going somewhere other than here?

"You're flying out tonight," she continued. "And going to Fort Sill." Lightning ripped through the night sky, followed by a loud clack of thunder, a perfectly timed premonition. "I'm sorry," she finished softly, softer than I had ever heard her voice before, and she sounded terribly human.

It was so clichéd, the lightning, the thunder, the impending rainstorm, the regret in her voice, and I seared it into my memory because it was too surreal, reading like fiction. This couldn't actually be happening. Not Fort Sill. But we had already signed away our self-agency and our platoon was moved along, thrust onto waiting buses, as we twisted and turned about in helpless protest. We vanished into the night, suddenly, becoming the urban myth that later haunted the bays, the whispered story of the all-female platoon that simply up and disappeared one night.

Fort Sill is not Relaxin' Jackson. Fort Sill is Fort Kill and it loves its reputation. An all-male post for decades, it doesn't know what to do with us females. We're shiny and new and very much disliked. They slap paper over the MEN bathroom signs, WOMEN hastily scrawled in black marker, and we ignore the urinals in our bathroom space.

Other units balk at our existence. We are intruders, a sign of the End Times, the feminist-driven social experiment that will bring about the ruin of the US Army, and they will not abide us quietly. Running in the morning, we pass another unit, all male, as all the units seem to be. Their drill sergeant halts mid-cadence, taking in the dirty hair buns peppered throughout the platoon, the telltale sign of a woman beneath all that green. He's silent for a moment, as if we've rendered him speechless. Then he grins, rolls back his shoulders, and calls out a new cadence.

"We're going to rape, kill, pillage, burn!" he calls.

"We're going to rape, kill, pillage, burn," his soldiers shout back.

"Gonna *rrrraaape*, kill, pillage, burn!" he sings, a predatory purr, and they growl back, all teeth, grinning at their drill sergeant's joke, at the balls of it, rolling out the word, prolonging the sound of it into the Oklahoma air.

Another day, another platoon rushes past us, filled with angry eyes, chanting, "Eenie, meenie, minie, moe. Catch a virgin by the toe. If she hollers, let her go. On the other hand, *hell no!*"

Our drill sergeants are better. They don't make us sing about rape, but that's as far as concessions go. This is Fort Sill, after all. Instead, it's just the dick jokes that are prolific. Drill sergeants never pass up a chance for a good homoerotic slur:

"Take that dick out of your mouth, Private! I can't hear you!" a drill sergeant screams into the face of a male soldier.

"Why you looking at me, soldier!" The drill sergeant rounds on a teenage boy, standing so close that his lips must brush the Private's ear. "You're looking like you wanna fight me or fuck me. Either way, I'm on top!"

"Privates, you're more ate up than a dick at a gay bar!"

"Private, if it were raining women, you'd get hit by a faggot!"

"Private! Why are you waiting for cocks to fall out of the sky? Close your goddamn mouth!"

And then there is the degrading of anything feminine or female:

"God*damn*, Privates, you're slow! What, you got sand in your vaginas? Keep moving!"

"Why do you sound like a hysterical woman when you sound off, soldier? If I wanna hear a bitch scream, I'll visit your mother!"

We're all ladies, pussies, bitches.

And "Suck my cock." "Eat my dick." "Taste my Johnson, Private!"—all of which is perfectly unremarkable when screamed male-to-male, but even the best drill sergeant squirms when he inadvertently demands a female recruit get on her knees and take his dick six inches in. His eyes flare wide, his jaw clips shut, and he rounds on a male soldier instead, spouting off the same demand, as if to show he's not serious, he's really not propositioning her. Some drill sergeants have a harder time aligning themselves with the reality of women in their ranks.

Then there is the degrading in general, not gender-specific, but always innovative and unique:

"Soldier, you better get your shit together before I time-travel and kick your mom in the stomach."

"Beat your face till you turn pretty, Private!"

Another drill sergeant chimes in, "We'll all die waiting!"

"Never have I seen so many abortion survivors!" or "Private, I can see the hanger scars on your face."

The perpetual order to "Un*fuck* yourself."

Drill sergeants are made to break you, these monstrosities that never eat, never sleep, never laugh, uniforms flawlessly pressed, pristine, as if the Army birthed them into perfection. They are well trained in how to dismantle our brains and rebuild them as they see fit. *Break, break, break*, they whisper, and we do, in a thousand different ways. The brain snaps under the stress until it simply reacts, all training, no thinking, because that is what a good, effective soldier does. We shave precious seconds off reaction times. Basic training isn't about reforming the body but instead, the mind.

"It's all a mind fuck," we're told by everyone who came before us, and it is. It is and we bond in our shared misery. Embrace the suck. *Embrace the suck!* Until our brains are stripped of the civility of civilian life and we realize it's all fucking hilarious. Because come on, it kind of is.

And the drill sergeants we should hate, who glory in watching us crack and spill open onto the floor, we love. "As long as you live, you'll never forget your drill sergeant's name," promises Drill Sergeant B, a tall, lanky man, graying at the temples. He's salty, old-school salty, rejecting the evolving Army, and hard, from the muscles lining his chest to the severe cut of his eyes and the way his black eyebrows angle down across his forehead. "Fifty years from now, some asshat will ask your drill sergeant's name and you'll know it better than your own." And I do, Drill Sergeant B, named here by the first letter of his name because no other name will do.

In scant moments between formations, the men and women in our platoon secretly practice our marching, adding an extra step into a cadence, a little flair performed in unison, and we show it off for him on the way to the mess hall, dragging our left foot in perfect time, our little surprise for him. He stands with fists at his hip. There is something like a smile on his face, fast and fleeting. He turns to one of the other drill sergeants.

"You see that? That's my platoon," he boasts. We swell at his pride, throwing our shoulders back, voices loud in cadence, eager to perform, ready to bleed for Daddy's approval.

There's a reason they like us so young, with our teenage brains, so malleable, so ready for indoctrination. Humans have a natural aversion to killing, and that just won't do. The recruits are desensitized to violence; we breathe, eat, sleep, shit around the concept until it's ever present. It becomes second nature.

Through the field he was walkin'.
In my sights I was stalkin'.

It's a One Shot Kill from the top o' the hill.
Stalkin' in a Sniper's Wonderland.

In the town there is a lady.
In her arms there is a baby.
You lock and load one round, baby hits the ground.
Stalkin' in a Sniper's Wonderland.

In the meadow we can plant some claymores.
Camouflage and bury 'em real well.
Kill the Commie bastards while they're sleepin'.
And blow their God-less souls straight to hell.

Later on, in the village.
As we burn and we pillage.
It's a One Shot Kill from the top o' the hill.
Stalkin' in a Sniper's Wonderland.

We sing awkwardly at first, stumbling over our new boots, the words spilling out just to appease drill sergeants. I internally writhe a little, staring up at the faces around me as we sing of murdering children. But it doesn't mean anything. It doesn't *mean* anything. And in the beginning it doesn't matter because I'm an awful little soldier. I gasp and gag during the runs. My arms shake during push-ups. At the range, in the prone position with an M16 tucked into my left shoulder, my foot keeps jetting upward.

"What the fuck is this?" Drill Sergeant B kicks my ankle when it swings up into the air.

I grunt at the pain and try to tuck my foot back down. I'm sprawled out on my stomach, squinting to see the green, man-shaped targets. One pops up. I shoot.

"Dostie! Stick that foot in the air one more time and I'll shove my boot so far up your ass, you'll taste Kiwi till the second coming of

Christ." He shoves the toe of his boot hard into my upper thigh, hard enough to nearly flip me over. I gasp in surprise, trying to hide the pain, slamming my foot back to the soil. He hovers there, boot pulled back, ready to deliver more physical guidance. I grit my teeth, concentrating on keeping it on the ground, and miss the target entirely.

Drill Sergeant B stares down the line, at the green man target wavering slightly in the wind, and simply shakes his head. "What the fuck, Private."

I'm no better at grenades. I shiver in the live-bay pit, grenade clasped to my heart with both shaking hands. My knees are weak. Drill Sergeant T, the stupidly sexy drill sergeant with the barrel chest and Disney Prince cleft chin, stands beside me in the cement pit.

"Prepare to throw," he barks. I pull the grenade back near my head, the other arm held out straight for sight guidance. "Pull the pin. Come on, soldier, pull the pin!" My fingers fumble with the tiny ring pin. "Prepare to throw. Throw!" And I hurl that live grenade downrange as hard as I can. It leaves my fingertips, twirls gloriously in the air with a hopeful arc, and then buries itself straight into the ground a few meters away.

"Well, fuck," Drill Sergeant T grumbles, and grabs me, throwing me down, his heavy body pressed over mine as we wait a span of seconds for the deafening explosion that rocks the cement pit. I feel the vibrations in my chest. My ears ring. At least I threw it far enough not to kill us, I think, but he's still annoyed.

"Are you trying to kill me, Private?" Drill Sergeant T screams down into my face. I stare up at him, my gums still pulsating. "I'm not trying to die in a shithole with you," he adds, dragging me to my feet.

I suck. I suck. I suck.

And then I don't. One day I bang out push-ups, up, down, smooth and quick. I move up a group on morning runs. In the evenings, sitting in formation on the hard pavement, my boots shine the best. Drill

Sergeant R strolls up and down the line, bottom jaw jutted out, lower lip pressed out over the top, as if her face is at war with itself, the lower territory slowly invading the north. She pauses as she inspects my boot-shining skills. The black toes gleam like cut obsidian. She grunts in approval.

"Five minutes of phone time," she begrudgingly awards me and I leap to my feet, running to the pay phones to call my mom.

In first aid I shine. It's simple memorization and recitation but I outperform others in my platoon. I can spout off signs, symptoms, and treatments at will, in perfect order, and I can't figure out why some of the others struggle with the information.

In the mess hall line, drill sergeants quiz us on the chain of command as we wait for our food. I never miss a question. Memorize and recite: Enlisted: Private, Private First Class, Specialist, Sergeant, Staff Sergeant, Sergeant First Class, First Sergeant/Master Sergeant, Sergeant Major, Command Sergeant Major, Sergeant Major of the Army. Officer: Second Lieutenant, First Lieutenant, Captain, Major, Lieutenant Colonel, Colonel, Brigadier General, Major General, Lieutenant General, General, General of the Army. I know them all.

"You're one of those smart ones," Drill Sergeant T says one day, pulling me out of line. This is news to me. In my old life I was ballsy, an outlier, but I'm not used to being one of the smartest people in the room. He sits on the edge of a table, one leg half up, elbow braced against his knee. "One of those Military Intel people."

"Now, there's an oxymoron if I ever heard one," Drill Sergeant B chuckles, almost a laugh. He stands to the side, arms crossed over his chest, examining his nails.

"Drill Sergeant, yes, Drill Sergeant." I'm one of a tiny few Military Intelligence soldiers transferred here. Fort Sill is better known for its artillery training than its intelligence.

"What's your MOS?"

"Drill Sergeant, Japanese interrogator, Drill Sergeant." I assume. I'm not promised a specific language at the Military Entrance Processing

Station when I enlist, although my recruiter makes sure DLI is written bold and proud on my contract.

He whistles low, leaning back a little. "You speak that Ching-chong?"

"Drill Sergeant, I speak some Japanese, Drill Sergeant."

"Well, go ahead then." He gestures vaguely at me. "Speak some."

"Drill Sergeant…what, now? Like, what do you want me to say—"

Drill Sergeant B looks up from under his Smokey Bear campaign hat. "What you stuttering about, soldier? You heard him. Say something in Japanese."

So I spout off a few lines, talking about how I hope to become proficient one day, a casual conversation with myself about my love for the language and its complexities. The two drill sergeants stare and I stutter out, mumbling the last sentences.

Drill Sergeant T rocks back slightly, brow high. "You sound like one of those Jap cartoon characters," he says, and his voice is just a shade different—not as deep, not that terrifying rumble in the chest that stops Privates dead in their tracks. Then he remembers himself, crinkling his brow. "Did you just cuss me out in Oriental, soldier?" But he lacks conviction. His heart isn't into it.

"What are you doing standing here, soldier?" Drill Sergeant B saves him. "Get back in line."

But it's said perfunctorily, and I trot back to the mess hall line, grinning because this is the closest thing to honest praise I'll get from them, and I love it.

I love it. I love it. I embrace it all; I embrace the suck. I gobble it all down, the dirt, the anger, the power, *that fucking power*. I am greater than me, I am one of many, one part of a whole, an important toggle in the well-oiled machine that is this glorious Army, the best goddamn military this world has ever seen. I am bigger than *me*, fist up in the air, chanting kill, kill, kill.

Went to the playground, where all the kiddies play, Pull out my
   Uzi, and I begin to spray!

Left, right, left, right, left right, KILL!
Left, right, left, right, *you know I will*!
Go to the mall, where all the ladies shop,
Pull out my machete, and I begin to chop!
Left, right, left, right, left right, *KILL*!
Left, right, left, right, *you know I will*!

It rumbles from the toes, shivers up the spine, sits at the back of the lips and pours out with vigor and zeal. I am fierce, I am fire, kill, kill, kill, head thrown back, screaming with delight to the skies. Kill. Kill. Kill. I am the happy convert.

Mostly.

Because we're sitting in the deck hall, casually testing the journey of a dud bullet from magazine to muzzle by running through all the motions of live fire without the live bullet, and one of the M16s behind me goes off, a live round whizzing past my ear with a quiet little hiss, and embeds itself into the ceiling above.

Drill Sergeant B stands there for a moment, staring at the round nuzzled deep into wood and stone above, a little shocked. "Drop your weapon! Put it down, NOW!" And he rushes us outside, into the parking lot, far from our abandoned rifles.

I keep bringing my hand up to my ear, to where I could have sworn I had felt my hair stir, to where that hiss still burned in my ear canal, and I do the unthinkable. I burst into tears.

Drill Sergeant B turns to me from the front of the platoon. The other drill sergeants linger behind in the hall, examining the smoking weapon, the ammo, clumped together in what might be misconstrued as fear, as if perhaps they realize they almost just killed a Private or two. "Dostie! Why are you crying?"

I clench my fists, try to be hard, to be the better version of me, fat tears rolling down my flushed cheeks, but all I can think about is how my muzzle hadn't been facing up toward the ceiling. They weren't treating the activity that seriously, they didn't keep on us to make sure our muzzles were pointed upward for gun safety, and mine had been lazy, trailing a little down, in the direction of the heads in front of me. "My weapon wasn't pointed up," I sob; I hiccup. "If it went off, I would've shot someone." I could've killed someone. I could've *killed* someone.

The girl next to me rolls her eyes. There are only a handful of us girls here and I'm embarrassing her. "Don't mind her, Drill Sergeant. She's soft like that." I raise my chin, trying to turn off the tears, to not be *soft like that*, but I can't.

"Dostie." Drill Sergeant B shakes his head slightly at me. "We're in the business of killing people." His stare is hard and serious. "You better get yourself right."

Get right. Get ready to kill. I want to hate that part of me that cries at the thought, but I'm not sure I do. I want to hold on to this tiny bit of softness, the softness that has no place here in the world where we sing Christmas carols to the lyrics of murder and plunder. I want to keep that little bit of me. *I won't be like that*, I think. I will never want to kill, I will never burn for it, I'll never shimmer and shine with uncontained violence.

How naive I am.

cry "havoc"

FOG SHROUDS THE HILLS of Monterey, obscuring the Army base from view. I arrive at night, just out from basic training, alone, worn threadbare from memories that still ache with bitter winds, frozen uniforms, and the dark glares of drill sergeants. "The fog is a government experiment," someone once said to me, pointing up at the white, dense cloud cover. "From World War II, so Japan couldn't bomb the Japanese linguists." It's laughable, or plausible. It certainly has an otherworldly effect as you stride up the hill, rising above the clouds, the fog parting and giving way to the open gates of the Defense Language Institute. Despite the swirling mist, you can periodically catch a glimpse of the sharp, craggy coastline of Monterey Bay and Marina, the white foam cascading over black rocks and the baritone bark of sea lions splashing up the hills, echoing across the bright white-brick buildings.

Monterey is paradise. "The best place you'll ever be stationed," they promise, and I can't think of any other post where the sky is perpetually blue, a cool seventy degrees year-round, with running trails weaving between giant redwood trees, over dark wooden boardwalks and past the round, curious eyes of sleek harbor seals, who balance on tiny rocks, silver fins flipped up in the air.

That first night, though, I unfold from a taxi in front of the barracks. I feel a bit lost, white-knuckling the strap of my duffel bag. "Let me help you with that." A soldier materializes from the gloom and reaches out, trying to grab my bag.

"No, that's okay, I have it," I protest, tightening my hold, but he smiles too widely, prying it from my hand. I trail reluctantly behind my bag, feeling off-balance already without its weight. He drops it in front of the charge of quarters desk, the small lobby washed in yellow light. I hug myself with one arm as they find my name on the list, glancing up at me casually, assessing, their opinions quartered off and weighed upon invisible scales.

"Your room is here," the first soldier says, refusing to relinquish hold of my duffel once we reach the room. "We have formation on Monday."

"On Monday?" I sputter, still trying to grapple with the fact that I have an actual room, personal desk and all. "But it's Friday."

He shrugs and drops my bag. "You have to stay on the post and around the barracks, but you're free until then."

"But what do we *do* until then?" My voice rises an octave in panic. It's too much time, too much freedom. It's been over three months since I had this kind of choice, although it feels a lot more like three years, or three decades, and I don't know what to do without someone watching, pointing, ordering. I don't know how to balance and deal with private seconds and minutes and hours.

"Whatever you want."

The prospect crushes me and when he leaves, I stand tentatively at the threshold of the door, craning my neck to stare down the hall with its white, freshly painted walls and bright-blue carpet.

I pull back into my room and firmly close the door. After basic, freedom never quite has the same taste as before.

DLI is much like college with its small classrooms, heavy notebooks, long lectures, and native speaker professors, before you toss in the morning formations, boot shining, enforced PT at 5:30 a.m., and marching drills. We wear uniforms to class; the post is a splash of color with Navy whites, Air Force blues, Marine tan, and Army green. The Coast

Guard is in here somewhere, and possibly an FBI and CIA agent; the school is a conglomerate of government effectiveness.

"So you're going to be learning Persian-Farsi," my advanced individual training drill sergeant announces a few days after I arrive, scanning my papers from his desk.

I stand at parade rest in his office and cock my head slightly in confusion. "Gesundheit, Drill Sergeant?"

He glances up, his hard stare saying he doesn't appreciate the joke.

I try again. "What is . . . Persian—whatever it's called, Drill Sergeant?" Persian. Isn't that the empire Alexander the Great defeated? Why would they want me to learn a dead language?

"Persian-Farsi. It's what they speak in Iran." And where was that again?

"Um, Drill Sergeant, they said at my contract signing that I would probably get Japanese. I mean, I speak Japanese already." It had been one of my main reasons for joining, the illusion of a promise dangled in front of me that very first day I met my recruiter.

"Your paperwork says you didn't score high enough to learn Japanese," my drill sergeant informs me. "Japanese is a Cat IV language. You placed into Cat III." I'm convinced that's only because the tape recorder fell off the desk in the middle of the test, and I wasn't allowed to touch it, so I floundered about for a good few minutes trying to figure out how to get an official back in the room to fix the recorder when I couldn't even get out of my seat. But then again, maybe not.

"Yes, but . . . I already *speak* Japanese. Can I at least get Korean or Chinese?"

"You're not listening to me. You don't have the aptitude to learn a Cat IV language—"

"I can have this conversation with you. In Japanese. Right now."

But he never looks up from the shuffling of papers. "We need Persian-Farsi linguists," he says, and it's definitive.

I leave his office, saving my huff for when I collapse into the black leather couches in the common room. I scrub my face with my hands. "Who has ever even heard of Persian-Farsi," I grumble. I glance at a girl studying, her books cracked open and taking up most of the space of the wood-and-glass coffee table. I read the spine and crinkle my nose in confusion. "Tagalog?" What is it with all these weird languages? "Isn't that the name of a Girl Scout cookie?"

She breaks away from the black scribbles. "That's Tagalongs. This is *Te-ga-lick*. They speak it in the Philippines."

I try to envision a Philippine war. "When will we ever need Tagalog?"

She shrugs and pulls a book onto her lap. "When will we ever need Persian-Farsi?"

The girls live in one barracks, the boys in another. It's the most females I'll ever see in one place in the military. In basic the women had all been stuffed into one bay at night and then broken apart during the day as we mixed with our male-heavy platoons, but here it's more than a bay. It's an entire barracks, three floors filled with women. There is a sense of camaraderie; we sprawl across the common room, legs flung over couch armrests, Army-issued black-socked feet bobbing back and forth as we flip through movies.

"Oh my God, you've never seen *Labyrinth*?" Jones, my new roommate, shrieks at me.

I shrug, sitting in PT shorts and shirt. I don't know how to say that I grew up fundamentalist Christian, that all their secular entertainment was banned, that unless it was a classic musical, we weren't allowed to watch it. People react funny when they hear words like *compound*, *religious leader*, and *the curse of idle hands*.

"We have to watch it, yes, we have to. Right now. You can't go through life and not have seen *Labyrinth*." She yanks the movie out of its sleeve. "It's practically a sin."

I never quite get the appeal of 1980s movies, having somehow missed out on the entire genre. Even after I leave the cult and substantially loosen my Christian beliefs, I never bother to go back to watch all those classics I missed, but I'm included now and that makes it almost worth watching some campy, bad music film.

Suddenly Brown appears, flipping her long pale ponytail over one shoulder. "Marines!"

"Shit, is it time already?" Jones and I scramble over the couches and the girls line up against the tall windows, hands pressed against the glass. Hot breath streaks the windows in clouds.

And here come the Marines. Galloping up the street, every day at five thirty, in rows of three, long lines of muscular thighs, sweat rolling down bare chests and trickling along the grooves of their backs, deep voices ringing out in unison as they sing, running by in tiny green shorts that haven't changed since the 1970s. Their daily route is carefully selected to run by the women's barracks and we wave in appreciation. I'm mindful of the glass that sections us off but I'm not sure which one of us is on display.

This is the closest we're allowed to the Marines; interactions between trainees and Marines are strictly forbidden, even if said Marines are trainees themselves. Marines are the things that go bump in the night. Don't worry about the mountain lion that stalks the Presidio: When a twig goes snap at night, it's the hunched form of a Marine in the gloom that should terrify you. Of course it is all urban legends and myths, until two Marines stab a civilian jogger just to see what it's like, and stuff her body between the rocks, and then it doesn't seem so ridiculous anymore.

I'm not a brilliant linguist—I'm neither great nor horrible, just hovering somewhere around average. My professor often pauses in front of my desk, crinkling her delicate nose, long black hair swept back in a careful bun. "Why do you speak Farsi with a Japanese accent?" she asks with her own thick accent, to the delight of the class. I'm still clinging to my Japanese, as if it were a slowly sinking raft, cramming in reading of

Japanese manga in the halls between classes when I should be studying, because I never quite fall in love with Persian. Josephine Rojas leans over me as I read, recognizing the cover even if she can't read the Japanese, and she huddles down to exchange manga fervor secrets. She's Air Force and pretty, as all Air Force women seem to be, and for a moment I have a connection to that old language passion, but then it's back to class and back to carefully shelving my beloved Japanese and replacing it with *alephs* and *mims* and *sins*.

I can master the Arabic script and reading, but my heart isn't into the rote memorization. Someone will tell me years later, as I am learning my sixth language in Ireland, that I don't actually have a natural aptitude for language, I'm simply stubborn. Stubbornness keeps me in the class because I don't want to admit defeat and "roll" into the class behind us. Or perhaps my tenacity is due to a certain Jonathan Rossiter, an Air Force airman who sits two seats down from me.

I don't know what to do with this crush on a far more experienced and worldly man, the likes of which I never really encountered in my sheltered, Christian past. He isn't the most handsome man on the post but he walks with a type of cocksureness that overshadows all other men; he has an instantaneous laugh that doesn't build but bursts straight from his chest, as if ripped from his body.

"You guys should come out and eat some time," he is saying, blue eyes darting to me, offering a grin that tilts upward and to one side. "What kind of food do you like?" He's asking the group, but he's still looking at me and I'm flushing a faint red.

Marjone, a girl from our class, looks from him to me to him, then rolls her eyes. "For God's sake." She digs a hand into her cargo pocket to produce a pen and paper. "Write down your number."

He does with a small smile.

"Here." She shoves the number into my hand. "Was that so hard?"

I stare at the number, uncertain because I've never been here before—not quite. Jonathan expresses interest that doesn't come with the Christian weight of shame, guilt, or sin. He doesn't see my desire as evil, my lust as something dirty that should be buried away. The openness and honesty of him dazzles me.

Not that I can do anything anyway. I still have a Christian boyfriend who sits on another Army post and we maintain our relationship mostly through phone calls and occasional letters. In truth, though, it's been deteriorating at the seams for weeks, decay born of time or distance, so when he breaks up with me, I'm not overly surprised. The reason jars a little, as he says I tempt him too much, what physical things we've done so far have been too much, too sinful, as if I will knock him off his Christian path. I'm not repentant or guilty. I sit on my barracks bed, cradling the phone in one hand, and try to come up with an emotion. I feel like I should cry, because that's what girls do when they're dumped, but instead there is a potent sense of liberation, like the last tether snapping free from the earth.

They say that the stone statue of an eagle down by Soldier Field will wake and take flight if a virgin ever leaves DLI intact. Suddenly I'm not so sure I want to test the theory.

So I don't. I eventually find myself in Jonathan's small, twin-size bed, my hands braced against his chest, my knees fixed on either side of his hips, very naked.

"Are you sure?" he asks, fingers digging into my hips, holding me in place.

I shiver, gulp down one nervous breath, and nod, because this is okay. I've made concessions in my mind, unable to wait for marriage but surely this is okay. Surely when you're in love, sex is still sacred and hallowed and I'm not dirty if this is how I do it, right? It doesn't matter that he doesn't feel the same. I prefer men whom I have to chase because if I haven't worked for their attention, then I don't really deserve it. He sometimes talks about other women he wants to fuck instead of me, which suits me because if he really loved me, I would've thought him crazy, and then I wouldn't love him anyway. This love feels a little obsessive, a little wildly desperate, but it's love, and that's all that matters.

I feel no guilt afterward, as I nuzzle his neck, breathing in his scent, naked legs tangled around his. "I didn't know it was supposed to feel that good," I say huskily, raising my head to stare into his face. My chest constricts, as if a hand grips my heart and squeezes. I didn't know I could feel this much. I shiver, then place my cheek back against his warm chest and smile. This is okay. This is good.

I make friends through Jonathan, mostly Air Force people, though I'm occasionally faithful to the Army and her members. I have street cred for reading manga in its original language. I've watched Miyazaki's *Mononoke-hime* without subtitles and that's cool. I join a D&D group and laugh because I was always told it was Satan's game, but really it's just a bunch of teens sitting in a circle, eating bad pizza, and pretending to be grand things we're not. I write a (bad) fantasy novel and people read it. I celebrate my first Halloween by dressing up as a vampire in my roommate's everyday attire—leather corset, wine-red lipstick, and fishnet tights. My platoon sergeant stumbles, literally, when he sees me at the rec room's costume party, my skirts slit all the way to the upper thigh, and he stares. "Dostie," he says, his tone more appreciative than reproachful. I arch my brow at him and smile with one side of my newly painted mouth. He releases a heavy breath between clenched teeth, dark gaze rolling from the top of my head to my high-heeled boots. My breasts sit somewhere just below my chin. He notices. "You're trouble," he notes, wagging one finger playfully at me, and I grin. I like that idea. And if you asked me then, I might have said I was raised born-again Christian, but the verb has shifted to past tense.

One morning in September, we have a rules of engagement briefing before class, which means we're in the theater room even before the sun has risen. "It is *way* too early in the morning for this," I grumble to my roommate, Jones, patting my cheeks to try to wake up. I just want to get this over with so I can scarf down breakfast and see Jonathan for a few moments before class, because we're on one of our "off" times and I desperately want to be back "on." Jones is nodding off, her head dangling forward and her eyes half hooded. I kick her foot as a Sergeant stalks up the aisle, searching for sleeping soldiers.

She jerks up, spine straight, eyes forward like a good soldier. Then she yawns and settles back into the hard wooden seats. "What is this about again?"

"ROE." Her yawn is contagious.

We pause as we listen to a spew of directives and I'm shocked to learn that you *can't*, in fact, shoot the downed enemy in the head as you walk past them when you're clearing an area. Life isn't like the movies. Go figure.

"This is so stupid." I lean toward Jones, voice low so that I won't end up doing push-ups in the back of the room. "It's not like anyone's going to go to war with America anyway." My recruiter told me so.

She yawns again, head craned back, and offers me a bored nod in agreement. Standing a few rows behind us, Captain Wasem surveys the room. I nudge Jones to peek, because Captain Wasem is our unit commander and a very sexy one at that. He looks too good to be in the Army, as if he's wasting those sharp cheekbones and warm, russet skin on such menial work. His cell phone suddenly comes alive and he jerks at the sound, as shocked as we are. Slinking to the back of the room, he answers in a hushed voice.

And then a series of chirps fills the theater and officers duck and skulk to join him, phones pressed against ears, hands raised up against mouths.

The speaker continues but Jones and I are distracted, twisting in our seats to see the officers huddle together, pecking like hens, hands gesturing sharply at each other.

"Hey. What is wrong with you?" A Sergeant has spotted us. "Turn around and pay attention," he orders, planting himself behind us, arms crossed over wide chest, a wall between us and the squabbling officers.

More cell phones, more bodies rush down to the aisle to the back.

"What do you think is going on?" Jones whispers, lips barely moving because Wall-Sergeant is still glaring.

"Underage drinker got caught?" Great. That means we might be locked down for the weekend as punishment. I can never understand my peers who so recklessly break the rules. Caught in underage drinking or narcotics use will cost you your security clearance, booting you out of MI and down to the dirty trenches of the Army ranks. The threat of becoming a truck driver is enough to keep me scared straight. And then the projector is sputtering silent, the speaker pauses hesitantly in his presentation, and pretty Captain Wasem is back behind us, cheeks drooping, a sheen of sweat over the brow of his abruptly pallid skin. He glistens sickly in the low light, scanning the crowd, pink tongue jetting out and licking dry lips. "We just received news," he starts, looking a little stunned even as he says it, "that a plane flew into the World Trade Center."

I feel my face scrunch in confusion. "The what?"

A rumble of whispers sweeps across the room but I'm sitting close enough that he glances at me. "The World Trade Center. Those two tall towers in New York City?"

"You mean the Twin Towers?" I've never heard them called anything else, though I know them well, having stood at the top of one, clinging to the cold, chain-link metal fence, dumbstruck by the grand, sprawling landscape of gray New York while I shifted, wind-blasted, in the building's natural sway. "What do you mean, he landed in between them?"

All eyes are on Captain Wasem, and the other officers shift uncomfortably in the background, heads turned away. "No, he hit the tower."

"He hit a building? Like the tallest building in New York?" Jones exclaims. I'm shaking my head.

"How do you hit a freaking tower? It's not like it jumped in the way and yelled, *Surprise!*" someone else says.

But Captain Wasem isn't looking at us now; he's blinking too much. "We're ending early. Get ready for class." Before he turns away, almost as if an afterthought, he adds over his shoulder, "And call your parents."

Call your parents? Jones and I exchange a tense glance. We file quickly out of the theater and into the Monterey morning fog; there is a heaviness in the air that mutes sound. A type of dumb confusion is scrawled across our faces.

I thumb my mom's number on my cell phone, a stab of worry tightening my chest. Connecticut is too close to the city and something isn't right.

"What are they telling you?" my mother rushes once I have her on the phone.

"Nothing really. How did this guy hit a building?" I glance over to where a sea of green fatigues is milling about the doors of the classroom building.

"They're saying something about terrorism." Her voice has the fine edge of panic and again I feel like I'm missing some dramatic piece of the puzzle.

"*Terrorism?*" The word is unfamiliar in my mouth and I spit it out with bewilderment. "I gotta go." I hang up, but that doesn't stop the ugly word from swelling and reverberating in a fine hush.

"A second plane hit the other tower," someone hisses and I whip around, hearing the statement bounce back and forth across the halls.

"That can't be a coincidence." Someone rips the words from my mouth. "That can't be an accident."

Our entire class huddles into one room, some Persian linguists perched on desks, others, like me, squatting on the hard tile. A television on a black metal cart is rolled into the room and the fluorescent light washes us in white, red, and black.

Dr. Dariush, the head of the Persian-language department, demands we watch the news in Persian—"You're still in class, you have to practice, we're not taking a break"—and I squint, scratch, squirm as I try to string together the words but they all sound like buzzing wasp wings.

"Fuck this," Jonathan snaps and he jumps to his feet, switching the television to CNN. Dr. Dariush stands quietly against the wall. He doesn't protest.

The Pentagon is on fire.

"Oh my God," I whisper, grasping Jonathan's hand, intertwining my fingers with his stiff ones, but he's rigid, uncompromising even as I press up against him, and I'm alone.

The towers fall as we watch, a shroud of white blanketing the city until it's unrecognizable. The skyline is distorted.

A plane tumbles and crashes in a Pennsylvania field.

Jonathan casts off my hand and rushes out into the hall to fight the clogged airwaves, trying to get a call in to his Pennsylvania home.

Our Persian professors huddle in the back, hands clasping each other, their lips moving in a pattern of prayer, their dark eyes wide, petrified, and I lean forward, straining to hear their desperate mantra.

"Please, don't let it be Iran. Please, don't let it be Iran. Please, don't let it be Iran."

They get it before we do. We're still gangly kids, still waiting to fill out the wingspan of our uniforms and angrily scrubbing the youthful roundness from our faces.

I swivel, turning back to the television, oily clouds of black filling the screen.

"Oh my God," I whisper as finally it all clicks into place. "We're going to war."

redacted

FALL 2001 ROLLS into winter 2002, onward toward the end of my yearlong training at DLI. War blooms in Afghanistan and just like that my classmates and I become linguistically relevant. Our next duty-station assignments are handed out seemingly at random, as if higher-ups had stood in some room, bent over an elaborate table with dice in hands, guffawing fiercely with each arbitrary cast. We stand in an auditorium after class, milling about as we wait for our orders, names called one by one, reading us our future. The world is an open map and the possibilities are invigorating. Join the Army; see the world. I hope for Fort Gordon, Georgia, but only because Jonathan will be stationed there. It's a young, love-induced desire, but it's also the safe choice because Fort Gordon is a strategic unit and no one deploys to war from there.

My platoon sergeant calls my name and I climb the stairs to the stage at the front of the auditorium. He hands over our orders with very little fanfare. Perhaps he wants to be spared everyone's drama. I flip through the pages, trying to make sense of the military nonsensical jargon, finally noticing the highlighted duty station. Fort Polk, Louisiana.

"Fort Polk?" I crinkle my nose instinctively, even though I've never heard of the place.

My platoon sergeant lifts his head, green eyes bright under the cover of his ruddy hair and complexion. "No luck there, huh," he says with a half laugh that is either apologetic or sardonic.

I stumble numbly off the stage, staring down at the orders, trying to dredge up any memory of Polk. "Does anyone else have Fort Polk?" I ask my peers.

None does. Fort Gordon, Fort Gordon, Fort Gordon around the room, except for me, holding orders to some mysterious post a few states away from everyone else.

"That sucks," says one Specialist. He reclines in his chair, boot crossed over one knee. "That's a tactical unit."

Tactical, those units that focus on the combat aspect of war, the nitty-gritty, sand-in-your-boots, rifle-in-your-hands kind of training. Linguists typically aren't destined for such places. We're better served in strategic units, behind computers, accompanied by the soothing whirl and hum of top-secret machinery.

"Are you sure?" I ask. "Why would they send linguists to a tactical unit?"

He shrugs. "Knew a guy who got sent there. I heard it sucks ass. Good luck," he offers and I walk away, holding my orders limply in front of me, wondering if I lost them, what would happen then? Would I maybe slip through the cracks, show up anywhere I want, make my own orders? Because I know I don't want to go to a tactical unit. In this newly christened "post-9/11" world, I know what *tactical* means. I look around the room, to those designated for Fort Gordon, whose labels now read SAFE, SAFE, SAFE, while mine says PROBABLY NOT.

But before Polk comes Goodfellow Air Force Base, the last six-month leg of my almost two-year training. If DLI is about the language, Goodfellow is about what to do with said language—how to use words, verbs, and syntax for the military. I sit in the polygraph chair before training can start, heart pounding as I'm strapped, fingers and heart, to a machine that reads my every flutter and gasp. Top-secret starts here, with these last few tests, to make sure I'm not a traitor or a liar. And when I pass, when this next level of training starts, I learn there is a sequester of knowledge. I now exist in places carefully monitored and structured for security, enclosed rooms with no windows, no cell phones or internet, these Sensitive Compartmented Information Facilities where anything can be said and everywhere else outside these doors is profane.

"You're one of those spooks," a guy accuses me at a club, and that sounds so terribly intriguing. I shrug, I smile, "I work with computers," I say in my defense, the carefully crafted deflection from what I really do. And I do work with computers, but I also ██████ and ██████ and possibly ██████. It's all so exciting, but also not. I never envisioned myself as a spy, and even if I had, this isn't James Bond. It's a lot of ██████ and ██████ and never ██████. *Spy* is a glamorous title for not-so-glamorous work.

Then there is the silence, the things that can never be said, the nondisclosure oath, the sworn secrecy for fifty years, the perpetual fear of saying too much or letting the wrong thing slip. Never let loose or let go; never ever be out of control. This is my life in redaction, sections blacked out and sliced away. And it's okay. It's not really that big a deal; it's just a job, like everyone else's job. Except that every once in a while, I ██████ something that sinks to the base of my stomach, makes my hands a little cold and clammy, and I want to tell someone, to ruminate over a beer and say, "This is disturbing. This...this really bothers me," except I can't. No one can. If anyone else feels a little off, a little unsettled, I have no way of knowing.

But when I leave Goodfellow Air Force Base for Fort Polk in July 2002, traveling the miles alone in my little green Subaru, because it's not like anyone else got stationed there with me, I still feel a sense of hope, a tingling of excitement as the road expands and unfolds before me. For once, I'm no longer in training, for the first time I'm out there, ready to be utilized, to put my full potential to the test. War dances in the static of my radio and I change the channel, looking for a better station.

Perhaps I should have been a bit more aware. Perhaps I should have noticed the red flags, like when the in-processing unit places me late into an empty room, checking off my name in their database, and then sends me a male roommate, who stumbles in later in the night, dropping his bags heavily by his bed before standing, perplexed, in the tiny bathroom, no doubt staring at scattered jars of makeup and women's deodorant sticks. I wake the next morning, pressing my glasses to my face, and stare back at the young man in the next bed, who leans back against the wooden headrest, chest bare, one hand hooked behind his head.

"You're not a girl!" I stammer.

"You are!" he says back, seemingly just as surprised, but surely he had to have known before that moment. How long had he sat there, staring at the black wash of long hair on my pillow?

I tuck one bare leg under the green blanket, acutely aware of my missing bra, of my PT shorts flung over the back of a chair, of the ticking clock as formation time looms, and of the fact that I'm going to have to flash him one pair of white panties as I climb out of bed. He doesn't seem as uncomfortable as I am. We both laugh, but mine sounds a lot less genuine than his.

Perhaps I should have noticed something was off when I find him again at the end of the workday and he grins at me. "Got myself a pillow," he says, holding it up to show me. "So we won't have to fight over the other one." The room had only one pillow for its two beds.

"Did you tell your Sergeant about this?" I point from him to me.

He shrugs and looks a little deflated, like he doesn't see a problem with having a female roommate. Like he's disappointed I'm going to report it. I'm spoiling the fun.

Perhaps warning bells should have rung when the in-processing Sergeant growls at me when I report the mix-up. "Why didn't you tell me this sooner?" he snaps, blaming me for the mess, tapping my first name with the end of his pen. "You have to wait till the end of the day to bring up this shit?" He's angry at the inconvenience, at the extra paperwork, not the fact that I woke up with a strange man in the bed next to mine.

But I don't see it. I scrub myself clean, ready myself to meet my new unit, shiny and new and hopeful.

welcome

ONE ROAD LEADS into Fort Polk, and another road leads out. They sit side by side, fat lanes divided by a trail of sun-worn grass. The roads are decorated with dull-yellow buildings; the barracks are tall, stacked bricks with black windows.

It's a new unit with all new faces and all I can do is pant against the midsummer Louisiana heat. It presses against the mouth and drowns the lungs, my brown undershirt molding to the small of my back and across my chest. I crinkle my nose; I hate sweating. I'd rather freeze than sweat. I reach under my BDU coat and pinch at the wet shirt, trying to buy some brief relief, but even the breeze is soggy.

"The motor pool is down here," my new acting platoon sergeant, Pelton, is saying. I nod, trying to appear attentive and eager. I can already tell Sergeant Pelton likes to laugh. He wears his smile like a permanent patch, a part of his uniform, and it scatters some of my fears. I'm new here in this terribly dull land of dead grass and monstrous mosquitoes. No familiar faces, no one to sidle up to before formation; I'm standing awkwardly at the edge of the group, wondering how I'm going to crack open this already well-established and tight community.

But two years in the Army have taught me how to play the game, at least in part, and I laugh when Sergeant Pelton laughs. I don't question what I'll be doing in the motor pool, which is a black slab of concrete cluttered with old Humvees from the 1980s, some held tenderly together with military-grade duct tape and 5-50 cord. Two languages under my belt, a top-secret security clearance, and well over a hundred thousand dollars in training and I'm handed a pad on how to keep these old beasts alive. I arch one eyebrow at the maintenance standard operating procedure form. I can decline variant verbs in Farsi, but now I'll be checking for grades of fluid leaks beneath vehicles.

"Don't worry, you'll get used to all this," Sergeant Pelton assures. "Motor Pool Monday! Gotta love it." He grins and I can't tell if he's being flippant or not.

I smile, noticing that the motor pool sucks in all the heat, trapping it between metal Humvee bodies and radiating it off the tar. Sweat trickles down my spine.

Two soldiers escort us around the motor pool, glancing back at me with inquisitive eyes. I shift uncomfortably under their gaze, suddenly feeling on display. One bumps the other with his elbow, and he breathes, in a low voice loud enough for me to hear, "Why is the space between a woman's breast and her hips called a waist?"

The other shrugs, lips upturned uncertainly. They're testing the waters.

"Because you can easily fit another pair of tits in there," the first finishes, gesturing his hands to hold two imaginary breasts and they laugh, glancing backward at me, reading, gauging.

Sergeant Pelton is silent, still wearing that grin, waiting to see if he needs to intervene.

I know this game, the sport every female soldier learns how to play. The better the player, the better the female soldier. I don't narrow my eyes, I can't grit my teeth, although the joke is a poor attempt if they're aiming to offend. Still, I yank up the edges of my mouth, baring my teeth in a smile. I give a little laugh. "Oh, don't worry," I say to ease the wariness in their grins. "You can't offend me." A lie repeated often enough becomes the truth.

Sergeant Pelton is delighted. He half turns and raises a blond brow. "You mean if I pull my dick out right now, slap you across the face, and leave a mushroom mark on your cheek, you won't be offended?"

My jaw works as I struggle for a response. I blink in dumb shock. My acting platoon sergeant. Soon to be my leader. He's not supposed to be a part of these power games. But the precedent has been set, the game already in play. Laugh. *Laugh.* I titter. "No," I say in a pale voice.

They like this, all three men, snickering to each other. I've been tested and the smile plastered on my face says I pass.

Welcome to Fort Polk.

I sit stiffly at the edge of the couch, red cup of some horrid-tasting drink in my hand. I'm newly twenty-one and haven't had much opportunity to acquaint myself with the heavy drinking culture that sustains Army life, so I pretend to sip it and it burns the edges of my lips. I pull at the hem of my jean skirt with my other hand, watching the come and go of others from our platoon. I have never been invited to a platoon sergeant's party before. It simply isn't done in training. But here we all are, at the house of my new platoon sergeant, Sergeant First Class James. He's leaving Fort Polk soon, throwing party after party as he exits, and I accept the invite because I'm stumbling to make a place in the platoon. Everyone has been here longer, elbows locked together in friendship, or, if not that exactly, at least in shared misery. I'm used to starting training in groups of recruits, where we're all glancing around desperately for a new friend or point of contact. But training is over, this is the real Army and I'm alone. I've managed one friend, Andres, the analyst who lives on the same floor as me, but he refuses to engage in anything even remotely work-related unless it's mandatory, so if I'm going to endear myself to anyone else, an after-hours party seems the best way to do it.

When I first walk in I catch a glimpse of the poker game; Sergeant First Class James, First Lieutenant Patron, Staff Sergeant Daniels, Specialist (soon to be Sergeant) Rivera, and Sergeant Forst sit, cards in hand, crammed around a small, circular table. A haze of smoke lingers above them, filling the tiny kitchen. Random bottles of alcohol cram any extra space on the yellow countertops.

Sergeant First Class James leans back in his metal folding chair. He chomps on the end of a cigar, leaning into the stereotype. "Have something to drink," he says to me with a wave when I enter, and someone is quick to throw a series of different-colored liquids into a cup. Its scent is potent, and one gulp burns my esophagus.

"Thanks," I croak. Sergeant Forst glances up from her cards and grins at my ineptitude. She reminds me of a fairy—small in height and with wild blond curls snipped in a careless pixie. Yet there is power in the way she lounges in her chair, and she curls her tongue around the edge of her cigar, swiveling it to the other side of her mouth and clamping it in place with trim, white teeth.

I leave the kitchen for the couch, and Stuart, a Specialist from Supply, plops onto the plaid couch beside me. His knee bumps mine and he pauses, sipping his drink. "So," he says, sinking into the soft cushions and grinning over his cup. "Tell me about yourself, Dostie."

I'm suddenly glad for someone to speak to and I turn toward him, yanking down my skirt again. When his eyes linger at the edge of my shirt, I wonder if I wore something too low-cut. His knee bumps mine again and he leaves it there. I shrug. "Not much to tell. From Connecticut. Joined the Army after high school. Nothing out of the ordinary."

"How'd you get Farsi?" he asks.

I snort. "You got me. I was told I was going to be a Japanese interrogator."

His smile is slow and he shifts slightly so that his leg is resting against mine. "How's that working out for you?"

"Well, considering I have no idea what we do here besides stare at Humvees all day, I'd say it sucks."

He laughs and I press my knees firmly together but his leg follows mine, as if glued. "Yeah, this place sucks ass." He downs the rest of his cup.

I glance around the room and immediately feel like I'm the center of attention. I wonder if I'm imagining the half-turned heads, sideways glances, if they're all really watching my reaction, watching to see how receptive I am. What kind of female will I be? The whore, the bitch, or the lesbian? I'm about to be labeled and I chafe at the rigidity of the situation.

But I'm saved. "All right!" James materializes in the living room, as if summoned and about to make an uncomfortable situation all that much more uncomfortable. "Bored as shit."

"You just hate losing," Lieutenant Patron quips, stuffing what looks like bills into his back pocket, and James ignores him.

"Who wants to hit Pegasus?" James asks the room.

I glance at Stuart for clarification, using the opportunity to shift my body farther away. "Pegasus?"

"Strip club. Halfway decent place. Better than the Pink Lady, at least."

I blink in surprise, and instantly scan the room. I hadn't realized I was one of only two women here. Sergeant Forst emerges from the kitchen in a slow saunter, bringing our number up to three.

Private Woods balks at the suggestion. She's all waves of blond hair and carefully lined eyes of kohl and Tempting Tanzanite Purple. "Uh, no thank you." She makes a show of declining and the men smile at her appreciatively—Woods, with her feminine curves and pale cheeks fused with shimmering powder.

"I'll drive you home," Rivera offers and Woods smiles sweetly, demurely collecting her pocketbook and saying her goodbyes. Rivera opens the door for her.

James looks to me, waiting for me to decline, too. "You don't have to come," he says, and I feel a stab of annoyance. Like I'm being pushed out, purposefully excluded. I suddenly want to fight back. I shrug. "Sure," I say. "It won't be the first time I've been to a strip club," I lie.

I can't tell if the men are annoyed or indifferent to my acceptance but Sergeant Forst smirks as she gathers up her purse, bright-blue eyes a little too knowing. She inclines her head slightly in my direction. I don't know if it's an invitation to come or a warning not to.

Confused, I just smile back. When we leave, I open my own door.

Pegasus smells. It's the first thing I notice in the gloom. It reeks of cigarettes, stale beer, and something sickeningly fruity. Blue lights flash, illuminating a stage where a woman writhes on the floor, legs spread at a painful angle, and all I can do is wonder how much *that* wax job must have hurt. "Here, you sit *right* here, Dostie." James drops his hands on my shoulders and sits me down at a round table. The surface is sticky and the ashtray overflows with a heap of mismatched butts.

A half-naked woman stalks by. Her breasts are high and tight but her stomach sags slightly over her thong, the loose skin bouncing with each step.

The men and Sergeant Forst fill the seats around me, enclosing me in a tight circle of cigar smoke and masculine laughter. The music drums through my bones, a constant bang, bang, bang of senseless noise. Someone has put a drink in my hand, which I don't drink, noting the chipped glass edge.

James yells something, his whiskey-washed breath splashing over my cheek.

"What?" I call back, squinting against the flashing lights. I'm trying really hard not to label that slightly off scent that lingers over the club.

But he's moved on, yelling something at Lieutenant Patron, whose face beams in reaction. They sit back and sip their whiskey and I glance at the stage. It takes a lot of upper-body strength to swing around a pole like that, especially in plastic six-inch heels. I'm impressed.

I don't see where she comes from. She slinks onto the table, all spray-tan legs and taut, slender torso. Instinctively I rear back, space invaded as her ass sways by my face. James holds out cash close to his chest, eyes half hooded, and she shimmies for the bills, perky breasts hovering in front of his face.

I shift uncomfortably, glancing away, only to see Stuart and Patron admiring her assets with open-lipped leers. She makes her rounds of the men and suddenly James is shoving a twenty-dollar bill in my hand.

I stare down at it, then back at him. "For you," he mouths, and gestures gleefully at the stripper. His gaze is off-balance and I suspect he's drunk. The money dangles in my palm—I'm afraid to hand it back.

The girl turns toward me. Fake lashes flutter playfully, and I realize she's younger than I am. I smile apologetically, suddenly feeling like I've become a part of something horrible and oppressive. I slide the money across the sticky table, trying to save her the act of earning it.

A sharp gleam enters her eyes and she holds the bill up over her head, kneeling in front of me and swaying with the beat. She has a heart-shaped beauty mark over her left hip bone. It seems the only safe place to stare at. She leans forward, arching her back to carefully slide the bill down the front of my shirt, tucking the edge into my bra.

"It's okay, you don't have to," I say, softly because she's close enough to hear me.

She turns her face toward me and her grin is lofty and a little hard— she knows something I don't. Wiggling her ass in the air, she leisurely leans down, never breaking eye contact, lips brushing over my collar-bone as she clamps her mouth down on the bill and pulls it free.

All to the thunderous applause of the men. They throw their hands above their heads, clapping, roaring, and I swallow the dry lump in my throat and force a laugh. The stripper tucks the bill into her G-string.

Across the table Forst arches her fine blond eyebrows at me. She salutes me with her cigar, ash cascading down onto the table. Welcome to the fold, she seems to say.

May it shred you to pieces.

jrtc

I'M BARELY AT FORT POLK a month when I learn what JRTC is.

"You got here just in time, Dostie," Sergeant Pelton informs me, leaning against the Humvee I'm PMCSing. "We're going to start Joint Readiness Training Center in two weeks."

"Sergeant?" I toss my checklist board onto the worn seat of my Humvee, next to where Andres is relaxing, debating whether I really want to crawl under the metal beast to check for leaks, like the damn preventive maintenance checks and services list demands I do.

"It's this monthlong war game," Sergeant Pelton elaborates. "Units come from all over the country to train here. It's actually really good training. There's two sides, us and OpFor, the bad guys, and we go to war. Think of it like . . ." He places his palms together as he inclines his head back, thinking of a good comparison. "Like a glorified game of laser tag."

I arch my eyebrows. "That kind of sounds cool."

"That's what I want to hear!" Sergeant Pelton slaps me on the shoulder, grinning widely. I smile with him, because Pelton is infectious. "So go see Sergeant O'Brien when you're done with this vehicle and he'll get you up to speed on what gear we need packed and ready," he says as he starts to walk off, throwing us a friendly wave as he leaves.

"This seems like it could be fun," I say to Andres in the passenger seat, his check board balanced on his knees and fully completed, even though I know he didn't get under a single vehicle.

He turns his face to me and scowls, his dark, thick brows pinned together. "Are you shitting me? Fun? You think this will be fun? This is going to suck dirty, sweaty balls."

"I mean, it could be exciting." I imagine rushing through the woodline, M16 in hand, commando-rolling under laser fire of red and blue, theme music blasting in the background. "Come on, it's laser tag. When has laser tag ever been boring?"

He gives me that hard stare he's so good at, as if he's waiting for me to realize my own stupidity. He then points off into the distance, into the dense green forest that lines the edge of the motor pool. "We're going to be out there. In the fucking wild swamps of Louisiana. With no beds. No bathrooms. No showers."

I forgot about that part, but I'm not averse to a little dirt. I did join the Army, after all. "Baby wipes?"

"For a *month*, Dostie. That's *four* weeks. Time stops in the field. No, scratch that—it goes fucking backward. Four weeks is like two years regular time."

I cringe. Now that I think about it, that is an awfully long time to go without a shower. He leans forward to drive in the last nail. "In *August*."

I groan and sink into the driver's seat next to him as the thought settles in. "Oh my God, there's going to be no AC."

"Dostie, we're not even going to have electricity."

I stare back at him, eyes wide, trying to envision a night without my beloved AC cranked up as cold as the setting will allow. I'm a New Englander. I'm not built for this Southern wet heat. "It's going to be hell," I whisper. "It's literally going to be hell."

Andres snorted. "Hell is spring break compared with what we're about to go through."

He's right, of course. It only takes a few days into JRTC for me to realize this is hell. Even in the evening, the wet Louisiana heat is oppressive. The night is clear, the moon a slim slip of light. The heat is visible in wet, fluttering particles that saturate the air and dance across the beams of the Humvee headlights. One night, I stand by the open Humvee door, rummaging through my rucksack in the dull light. We're parked in a loose circle for protection from OpFor, the Opposing Force, who's been promised a four-day weekend if they manage to kill any of us MI folk. The task shouldn't be terribly difficult—OpFor is well trained in this JRTC war game. Yet miraculously, so far we've evaded.

Not that death would be a release. The training ends when it ends and not a moment sooner, death be damned. I pull at the multiple integrated laser engagement system harness, tossing the glorified laser tag gear down by my feet. The humidity has done its work and my uniform is soaked through. Stepping farther into the dark and using the Humvee as a shield, I peel off my BDU top. It sags to the ground and I shed the next layer, the brown undershirt leaving my skin with a wet hiss. I groan in appreciation of the tiny breeze; even my sports bra is soaked through. I strip down, keeping my clean uniform within reach, but pause for half a moment, trying to remember what it feels like to be dry. I lean against the Humvee, my wet skin leaving imprints on the metal, and sigh, glancing around the black forest, starlight just barely visible between the dense canopy of Spanish moss trees. This was *not* how I had envisioned Military Intelligence life to be. I startle at movement in my peripheral, snatching a brown undershirt from my bag. A silhouette sits perched on top a Humvee hood and I narrow my eyes, straining to see through the gloom. "What the..." It takes a moment for the figure to grow limbs, one leg stretched down the hood, the other bent as he rests one arm on his knee. In his hands and pointed in my direction, I recognize the familiar shape of night-vision goggles pressed against his face.

"Jesus Christ," I hiss, angrily yanking on a sports bra. He casually waves to me and I flip him the bird. I can hear him chuckle, which only annoys me more. I huddle against the Humvee door as I dress. The heavy material instantly sucks up the heat and spits it back out at me.

I contemplate telling someone, maybe Sergeant O'Brien, the track commander of our vehicle, but I bristle at the thought. I'm too new at the unit to be starting trouble. The last thing I need is people thinking I file Equal Opportunity complaints. Besides, our four-man team is leaving for our new positions in the morning and I won't see this guy again. It doesn't matter. It shouldn't matter.

Still, anger simmers as I crawl across the hood of my Humvee, rolling out my poncho liner as a protection against the hard metal. I shove a BDU top under my head as a makeshift pillow and try to ignore the heat, the unforgiving metal, and the silhouette in the corner.

A few days later, I cough up another handful of black ash, stare at the dark smear in my palm, then wipe it against the leg of my BDUs. The sun beats down on our position but the lack of trees creates a wind tunnel of dust and ash, generating a breeze that stings when it crashes against my eyes or down my lungs.

The Devil's Ashtray, Sergeant Burns affectionately named the desolate stretch of land. Louisiana habitually burns acres of forest to prevent wildfires, and a smoldering patch of burnt wood and blackened grass makes for the perfect hiding spot from OpFor. "They'll never expect us to hide in a burn zone," he stated upon arrival.

"Because they'd never expect anyone to be stupid enough to try," Sergeant O'Brien mutters just under his breath. Sergeant Burns is our team leader, and open disapproval isn't allowed.

"Is this even safe?" Sergeant Forst stretches as she gets out of her Humvee, kicking bits of grass that explode into black dust.

"They already burned this area," Sergeant Burns replies with a shrug, as if that should be promise enough of its safety.

"I don't think we're legally supposed to be here." Sergeant Forst plants fists on her hips as she surveys the gray landscape. She's short but sturdy in a way that reminds me of a German tank. Her lack of height never makes her seem petite; instead her thick legs lend her a type of earthy strength and reliability. She has the distinct honor of being the best

Humvee driver in the platoon, and the entire unit knows it. I've seen her rock impossibly stuck beasts from wet, hungry mud pits, all while sitting back with one arm jutted casually out the window. "There have to be laws against this. I mean seriously, those trees over there are still smoking!"

But her protests are ignored and Sergeant Burns's ashtray epiphany ends up paying off. Aside from the burning eyes, cloying smoke, and ash in the lungs, our position has yet to be compromised, leaving us to our OpFor resistance work in relative peace.

I stretch out against the base of a tree stump, trying to pull my fingers through the sweat-and-dirt-clogged mess that was once my hair. With four of us on a rotating schedule, we have four hours of rack time to rest between shifts on the equipment and pulling guard duty. I should be sleeping—the rule is when you can sleep, you sleep—but the sun is too high in the sky and I just can't get used to midday naps. I twist my hair back into a bun and rub my face and arms down with baby wipes. Twenty-three days and counting with no shower. Andres was right. This sucks dirty, sweaty balls.

Sergeant Forst does a halfhearted circle around our position, but we haven't seen another person in days and guard duty has become a half-assed joke. She splashes water from her canteen over the back of her neck and rakes her fingers through the short blond curls. She handles the dirt and exhaustion with experience and ease—as if the uniform is tattooed onto her skin. I'm envious in a wistful kind of way. I don't fault her for it. I want to be her.

"So is this everything you expected it to be," she asks suddenly, a white-toothed grin consuming her face.

"Thought what would be?"

She stands and her wet hair curls at the base of her neck, dribbling water onto her undershirt. She doesn't seem to notice. "This. The Army. The whole thing."

I glance around the Devil's Ashtray. "I didn't think it would be so smoky."

Sergeant Forst laughs and drops down across from me. She watches

me expectantly, like I'm supposed to say more, so I shrug. "I don't know."
I think back to a few days ago when we were hopping from spot to
spot and Sergeant O'Brien was directing one of our Humvees. He stood
in the waist-high green meadow, the grass bending under the thudding
propellers of a Kiowa overhead. M16 rested on his hip, he had reclined
his head to stare up at the low-flying helicopter, Kevlar helmet slung low
over his forehead, obscuring his eyes in shadow but leaving the lower half
of his face stark in the sunlight. It was as if he had stepped directly out
of a film reel. It was a surreal intermixing of expectations and reality.

"It feels like the real Army," I say.

"This *is* the real Army," Sergeant O'Brien yells from the inside of our
equipment box, his voice tiny through the thick metal walls.

"Are you working or listening to our conversation," Sergeant Forst
yells back.

"If you weren't being so fucking loud, I wouldn't have to do both."

She grins, that large, genuine grin that is so easy and infectious.
"Why'd you join the Army, anyway?"

I open my mouth to give the normal response. That I hadn't gotten
into the college I wanted, that I hadn't prepared a safety school, or that
I hadn't had the money for any college regardless. Each of these is true
enough that people nod and move on. It's the simple kind of answer
people expect. The real truth is that I'd never had to leave. Maybe I
could've gotten a scholarship and gone to the local college, or taken
on a lifetime of student loan debt. I could've gotten a degree and a
husband and a small house with a few kids and probably a dog. But the
very possibility of that kind of future strangled the life from me. I saw
the years stretched out before me like a roll of pestilence-ridden sod—
rooted, even, and every blade cut the same as the one beside it. It was
never that I had to go, but that it had been impossible for me to stay.

And somewhere along the way, between basic training and drill
sergeants and grenades, or marching and spit boot shining and brutally
bloody cadences, without noticing it had happened, I realize I'd fallen
in love with the time-old tradition that is my uniform.

But I can't say that to Forst; I can't even begin to articulate it. So I grin and say instead, "My recruiter was really hot."

Forst throws her head back and lets out a full-bellied laugh. "A girl after my own heart."

I laugh with her.

Suddenly Sergeant Burns is flinging open the door of his Humvee from where he had been snoring, ripping free from the vehicle, arms flapping overhead in a comical gait that strikes me as particularly apish.

"What in the world is he doing?" I start to ask but Sergeant Forst has already risen, face immediately serious.

"A Colt! It's a fucking Colt!" He's screaming as he nears us.

"A what?" But I could hear it now—the steady drone of a single-engine aircraft. I twirl around, head thrown back and scanning the sky.

"What's going on?" Sergeant O'Brien sticks his head out from the work box. "What's happening?"

"Get the AT4!" Sergeant Burns is flinging open the box door and grabs a three-foot-long cylinder.

"What the fuck are you going to do with an anti-tank rocket launcher!" Sergeant O'Brien scrambles out of the way as Sergeant Burns twists the tube toward him, nearly knocking over a fair share of sensitive equipment in the process.

Sergeant Burns is already out the door and scuttling up the front of the Humvee hood. He stands, legs braced apart, resting the AT4 on his shoulder, barrel pointed to the sky.

We can all hear it coming, yet when the small plane roars over our ashtray, it's still a shock. Sergeant Burns howls, leading the plane for a moment before he fires, the MILES gear sending a ping from weapon to plane as it tears by.

We stand frozen, breath held, straining, and faintly we think we hear the high-pitched ring of the MILES gear overhead signaling a hit.

"You hit it! Holy fucking shit, you hit it!" Sergeant O'Brien screams, clapping his hands in delighted shock.

Forst thrusts her hands overhead in victory. I roar, and we imagine a fiery explosion, wings snapping off and the plane diving down in a ball of chaos.

Even after it's gone, we stand frozen, Sergeant Burns still perched atop the Humvee, AT4 rested casually on one shoulder. Then Sergeant O'Brien: "He could've called in our position."

An electric shock of adrenaline jolts through us. We explode into motion. "Move, move, move!" Scrambling, we tackle the equipment, ripping down the antennas. Even on our best runs, it usually takes at least fifteen to pack up our gear. But if the pilot called in our position, they could rain down artillery fire in minutes.

We get it done in five. We are a symphony of twist, pull, bag, perfect unity as all four of us squat in the dust and cinders, black smeared along the edges of our uniforms. Sergeant Forst swipes sweat off her brow, leaving lines of war paint across her checks. Her eyes are stark blue in comparison.

"Get in, in, in!" Sergeant O'Brien is screaming and I throw my rucksack into the back of Sergeant Forst's Humvee before I leap into the passenger seat of Sergeant O'Brien's truck, heart racing. The tires tear up the dirt and black soot, the Humvee shooting forward and ripping a trail through the woods.

"Yes! Yes! That is how it's done!" Sergeant O'Brien slams the steering wheel with the palm of his hand. "That is how we get *shit done!*"

A laugh simmers in my stomach then bubbles up, surging outward, and I'm high on adrenaline. Suddenly nothing seems that bad.

Sergeant Forst pulls her Humvee to the side of us, clearing some rocks and catching air. She thrusts one arm out the window to point to us in a show of solidarity and triumph. Next to her, Sergeant Burns clings to the frame for dear life.

I point back, lost in a laugh, the other hand braced against the dashboard as we blaze our own trail between half-dead trees.

And I'm so in love with the Army then. I'm in love all over again.

consumption

DEATH ISN'T SUPPOSED TO STOP the JRTC training, but apparently a mysterious, lethal disease can. I'm pulled from the field when I'm found shivering under a woobie blanket, cocooned beneath the green fabric, teeth chattering despite the hundred-degree weather and dense humidity. A red rash covers my skin, including my palms and the bottoms of my feet. My joints ache; my bones hurt. I can't support my own weight.

"That doesn't look good," Sergeant O'Brien observes, pulling back the edge of the woobie to expose my neck. The rash has crept up from my neck to the side of my jaw and along my cheeks. I'm in full uniform, hands tucked into my armpits, chin to knees, to stay warm. He rests a hand across my forehead. "Jesus Christ, she's burning up."

Sergeant Burns leans over my cot and I crack open my eyes to see him chewing on the edge of his glasses. My eyelids feel hot. "I think we should radio the medics."

"I don't think you can fake that," Sergeant O'Brien agrees. I'm glad for the rash, because at least it's a visible symptom.

They load me up into the Humvee, busing me over to the regiment HQ site, where I'm led to a tent, dragging my boots, kicking up dense clouds of yellow dust. I hurt, from the center of my skull to the smallest toe. I want someone to carry me, but I can't ask for that.

"Well, this is different," says the doctor, an officer, an older woman with a thick, gray stripe of hair that runs the line of her skull. She holds my hand, flipping it over, staring at the red, raised bumps, then back at the soles of my feet. "I've never seen this before," she says with delight, eyes bright, rushing over to her bag to pull out a camera. "It's very odd for the rash to be on your palms and soles of your feet," she clarifies, speaking quickly, thoroughly engrossed in this little medical wonder. She holds the lens close to my body, click, click, click, each done with an appreciative hum. She then flips through a heavy book, tugging at the collar of her uniform in between pages, sweat coating the sides of her face.

"Rocky Mountain spotted fever," she says at last, looking up from the page with a wide grin. "You get it from a dog tick."

I groan, hunched on the makeshift medic's table, trembling from the effort of having to sit up. Not another tick-borne disease. I already had Lyme disease when I was a kid, back in the 1980s, when they didn't know much about the disease, which made for the perfect storm of needles, MRIs, and exploratory surgeries.

"I don't think anyone has ever had Rocky Mountain spotted fever here in Louisiana." She stares down at the book. "You might be the first. You could be in medical books." Her voice holds a level of reverence. I find out later this isn't true, that Rocky Mountain spotted fever has been all over the States, but each doctor murmurs the same thing, wondering how I got it here, caught up in the name of the disease instead of the history of it.

"It has a small fatality rate," the doctor adds, as an afterthought.

"Wait, what?" I jerk my head up, which sends a charge of pain down my spine and settles into my hip bones.

"Minor, minor." She waves it off, although I will later learn it's actually not all that minor. The fever is more lovingly nicknamed "tick typhus" and is the most lethal rickettsial illness in the United States.

And then she leaves, taking her medical book with her, and I'm left on the table, wondering how long I have to wait before I can lie down. I just start to lean toward the table, one elbow planted on the tough green material, when the medics come for me. I'm slightly alarmed when they say they're taking me to a hospital, but the promise of a shower and painkillers is enough to make me move my feet. They load me up in the back of a Humvee and I huddle around myself on the hard wooden bench.

"Dostie! Hey, Dostie!"

I lift my head to see Avery Langley rushing over to the side of the Humvee, lacking his BDU jacket, his brown shirt white with salt stains.

He grins at me, a boy who is more charming than traditionally hand-some, though he has the loveliest pair of green-hazel eyes. He's cheery and laughing, despite the heat, because Avery is always cheery and laughing, a wild ball of chaos, who shrugs off disciplinary action with a chuckle because he takes nothing too seriously. He's young and married to an equally young local stripper, a pretty, quiet girl with long, dark hair and generous curves, who supposedly comes from a strict, Christian family. She is a soft, subservient wife and mother, a good Christian, save for the whole stripper thing.

"Here, take this," he says, and shoves a portable CD player with headphones into my hands.

"Oh," I say, staring down at the gift. "I can't take this from you."

He shrugs, his smile a little tilted. "Take it. You're going to need it more than me."

"Thank you," I mumble, genuinely warmed by the gift. He doesn't know me. I'm new to the unit. He doesn't have to go out of his way to be kind to me, but he does and that little gesture stays with me permanently.

"I hope you like Eminem," he shouts as the Humvee pulls away, shrouding his face in clouds of dust.

I don't, but I'll learn to. I clutch the CD player to my chest, teeth clenched as we bump and jar over holes in the road.

I expect to be taken to an actual hospital, to a tall, bustling building humming with technology and efficiency. But they never take me out of the field, and instead to a field hospital, a small, two-story building that is permanently stuck in the year it was built, with aged linoleum tiles and old metal-framed windows. It's underwhelming. I crawl out of the Humvee, hunched forward, still bipedal so I'm forced to walk, even though my knees scream and grind and my spine bends into a hard C.

They lead me to a lobby, a twisted sort of waiting room with hard, faux-leather blue chairs that creak as the soldiers sitting in them turn in my direction. There's no AC, but large fans are planted around the room, some pulled close to the chairs and those soldiers who sit in them.

"Why, hello there," says one of them. They're all older, significantly older, blatantly upper brass, dressed in a mix of PT gear and hospital paper gowns, clustered around an old television that flickers with light but no sound. There are no women.

"It's going to be a while," says another. "Place is a fucking mess after the helicopter crash." No one offers me a chair.

I lean against the wall. "What crash?"

"They rushed one of the pilots through earlier. Blackhawk came up next to a Kiowa." He gestures with one thick hand, twisting his wrist to then flop the palm up toward the ceiling. "Flipped the Kiowa right over." I imagine the smaller Kiowa going bottom-up, a perfect 180, complete with a cartoonish dust cloud on explosion.

"Killed both pilots."

"Oh," I say, stunned. My mental image is reworked. This seems out of place for the field, for the safety of American soil. This isn't Afghanistan. Pilots shouldn't be dying here. "That's horrible."

The men nod, agree, henpecking the stupidity of all pilots involved. "It's not like they're the first two to die in this exercise," snorts one of the men.

This is gruesome gossip, macabre grumblings from the upper echelons.

"Two got run over by a tank while they were sleeping," says one to me, an aside so that I'm caught up with the group.

"They got run over by a tank?" I ask, aghast. "How do you get run over by a tank? How did they not hear it coming?" I learn later that this is a real problem in the military, that ground guides need to be deployed to walk in front of tread vehicles, to kick awake bodies from the tanks' path. I learn that smart soldiers sleep near the base of trees, or pressed up against the side of wheeled vehicles, anything to protect the body from being crushed in the dark.

And then there was the soldier who fell off the obstacle course before JRTC started, who tumbled from the top of the rope climb and broke his neck. That makes five in a month. I do the math, glance around the old, quiet field hospital, and realize I'm going to die here.

I'm eventually called into a long room with multiple beds. It looks vaguely technical, as if the machines and equipment had been new once, a few decades ago, now clunky but present. The room is awash in garish fluorescent lights, one of the bulbs flickering erratically in the corner.

A middle-aged, stocky Captain greets me. He's an affable doctor, with round, boyish cheeks and a blunt, square hairline. "We'll figure this out," he says warmly as he jabs a needle into the nook of my arm. He fills vial after vial, handing them off, and I grow dizzy. He lets me lie down on the hard green bed as he exits left to do something with all that blood.

I must smell, I realize. I can't remember the last time I showered. I lie on my side, racked with pain, feverish head pressed against the vinyl.

"I can't give you any pain meds," the doctor informs me much later, when he returns. He drops two small Tylenol pills into my hand. "Your liver is bleeding. We can't give you anything harsh."

My eyes grow a little wide. "Is that bad?"

"Well, it's certainly not good," he laughs.

Fear is slinking its way through the pain and filling in the holes of my thoughts. I ask his thoughts about the fatality rate.

"As long as you respond to the antibiotics, you'll be fine," he says. They pump me full of tetracycline. I find none of it reassuring as I down dry pills of Tylenol, my knees, hips, spine unable to even make short distances from hospital bed to bathroom. Though I could now, I choose to not take a shower, not for days even, because I can't stand in the stall, and instead I lie in bed, the film of filth transferring from my skin to the white sheets.

They set me up in my own bay because I'm the only female in the hospital. I have the long room all to myself. There's no AC in this wing because it doesn't make sense to cool an entire area for one occupant. They give me a fan, though, which sits in front of my bed. The windows hang open, white long curtains shifting in the breeze, in the sunlight, which illuminates the entire bay; it's almost romantic, in a quiet, *Love in the Time of Cholera* kind of way.

For the first time in what feels like years, I have no schedule, nowhere to be, left to lie on the bed in solitude. I listen to Avery's *The Eminem Show* album on repeat, "Soldier," "White America," round and round again, reading *The Firm*, a fat book one of the medics gave me to fill the hours.

I'm not allowed to leave the hospital until my unit leaves the field, and the exercise is delayed for days when someone loses a detonation cord. Packs and vehicles are stripped the field over, soldiers left to linger in the heat, and by the time we finally can go home, I can stand without support for short periods of time. The antibiotics do their job and the fever breaks, the rash recedes, the liver stops bleeding. I'm allowed back to my barracks room along with everyone else, where I finally climb into the shower, sit on the bottom of the tub, and wash my hair, the water turning black around my feet as it circles the drain.

The disease does its number, though. My lungs still struggle. I suck on air, mouth hung wide, at the smallest provocation. They put me on profile—no working in temperatures over eighty degrees, which rules out all of late-summer Louisiana. I sit awkwardly in the offices, shifting papers from one pile to another, while my platoon labors in the motor pool and comes to formations with reddened cheeks and sweat-slicked hair. I'm a princess in fatigues. I'm humiliated by my own ineptitude.

My lungs don't improve.

I have an allergic reaction to the tetracycline, my hands bloating red, my fingers unable to bend, my throat growing tight. "Don't take those meds anymore," says the Captain from the field hospital, whom I still visit, this time in a real hospital on the other side of the post. "You're allergic to it now. If you have it again, you could go into anaphylactic shock."

"Oh," I say with a desperate little hiccup for air, and I have to add a red tag to my dog tags so that no one injects me without my knowing.

My lungs still don't improve.

"Maybe it's asthma," says the doctor, and fills my cargo pants pockets with albuterol. I suck on the ends of plastic cartridges, even as I'm finally off profile, finally back to work in the motor pool but gagging on the hot, wet air.

"Maybe it's tuberculosis," says the doctor, when even after months the albuterol does nothing to alleviate the symptoms. He gives me a PPD test, a little bubble placed under the skin of the forearm. The skin turns ruddy and swollen.

"Positive PPD," he muses. "You have tuberculosis." He says it triumphantly, like he's solved a puzzle.

"Like consumption? Like where you hack up blood?" I'm alarmed and loud and nervous.

He waves one large hand at me. "No, no. It's sleeping inside you. It's not active. You just need to have chest X-rays every few years to make sure it doesn't wake up."

I shiver in the chair, thinking of the sleeping creature inside me, shifting and turning and waiting to wake and eat all my organs.

"Take these for nine months." He hands me a large bottle filled with fat orange-and-red pills. "That's for the tuberculosis. And these"—he hands me a smaller bottle with smaller pills—"are vitamin B for your liver." He waggles a blunt finger at the first bottle. "Those things will do a number on your liver. You'll have to take blood tests every month to make sure your liver isn't failing."

"What?" I stare at the bottles sitting in each hand. "That seems really dangerous."

He shrugs. "Better than tuberculosis." Then he adds, in passing, "And no drinking while on these. Ever." He turns to stare hard at me, as if trying to drill the words into my head, like he can see that I'm young and stupid and only half listening. "Your liver can't handle the meds and alcohol. I'm being serious here."

No drinking for nine months? For the entire time it takes for a human to grow in the womb? No drinking in a town that has nothing to do but drink? Where the only non-alcoholic entertainment, the movie theater, bursts into flames every few weeks due to a faulty popcorn machine? It's too high a demand for a twenty-one-year-old, for a girl who has just started to drink, who rarely did it before she turned of legal age, because there was the Christian thing, and then the not-wanting-to-be-demoted-to-truck-driver thing, scared straight right up to twenty-one and now she just wants to do what everyone else is doing, and in excess.

Locke thinks it's ridiculous, too. "Come on," she taunts, straightening a dark tank top against her long frame. She twists in the mirror, examining her silhouette. She slips on one of my coats, then peels it off, back on again, trying to decide if the warmth is worth hiding the lines of her body. "You don't *have* to drink," she reassures, holding the coat open, hands planted on hips, trying for a compromise. "But at least come out."

I slump on my bed. "I don't know. You guys are all going to be drinking and then there's going to be me sitting in the corner like an idiot, sucking down water."

She turns to me with that wild grin she owns so well. "But we'll be daaaancing!" She throws out her arms and spins for effect. She's lissome and tall and powerful. The coat hides nothing. She promises fun and excitement with the curve of her arms overhead, the turn of her hips below.

I groan, lean against the wall, tap the back of my head against the brick, deliberate, deliberate. I'm terrified of being left out, of everyone moving forward without me. I say, "Sure. Why not."

I laugh and dig through my drawers, tossing unwanted articles onto the floor, finally finding a short black skirt and matching mesh top. Locke excitedly dances from one bare foot to the other as I hastily apply makeup, tossing bottles to the side, cluttering up my desk with brushes and tissues. But it's the weekend; I don't have to worry about room inspection until Monday so I leave the room chaotic. I slip on a black leather coat, tall black heels, and totter out the door.

Diaz drives us because Diaz always drives us. He doesn't drink, never drinks, and even though I'm not going to drink, either, why break routine?

The downtown Margarita Bar is one of the few places in town to dance. They have a small, square dance floor, the outside of the square crammed with off-duty soldiers. The Army is the lifeblood of this small town. We clog the clubs and bars. The club is hot, lights flaring to the Reggaeton beat. Locke and I strip off our coats immediately, releasing bare skin, exhibitionists in our own way. I'm aware of the gazes on me, on the way I turn to hang my coat, on my legs as I stride away from the coatroom. I saunter like I like it because I do. I like being the center of attention, feeling wanted from a safe distance. I like it when it's in the periphery, held at arm's length. I am an actor, conscious of my every move, from the turn of the wrist to the sway of hips, but actors don't interact with the audience and I prefer it that way.

Andres stands to the side of me, not my boyfriend but I can lean on his male presence at will, like a beautiful, dark dog keeping the others at bay. He scowls at the crowd. He hates this shit and I brush my hand against his shoulder possessively, reassuringly. Andres has all the broad shoulders and solid frame of a man who can fight, even if I've never seen him do it.

There's a small bar set up near the door, just outside the coatroom, and the bartender behind it waves at me. "Free shots for the ladies," he grins at Locke and me, holding up a small, plastic cup.

"Free? Like as in free?" Locke is already there, collecting the cup and downing its contents in one fluid motion. If she's an actor, too, then she's just as determined to be the star of the show.

The bartender holds out another cup to me, arching his dark brow suggestively. "Free," he reiterates.

I groan to myself. I've barely made it in through the door. I take the cup instinctively, just so he's not sitting there holding it out to me. Locke takes a second.

"I can probably have one, right?" I ask. It smells like cinnamon. Locke has already moved on, slipping through the dense crowd toward the light of the dance floor. Andres and Diaz follow her.

Though I haven't been drinking that long, I've learned a lot about my tolerance that others find impressive in a woman my size. I know how many shots it takes for me to get tipsy. Eight. I know how many it takes for me to be drunk. Twelve. I know my numbers. One can't be that bad, right? I place my lips at the edge of the plastic rim, breathe in the hot cinnamon, hesitating for only a moment more before downing the glass. What's one or two going to do, really? I can handle my alcohol.

And really, what's the worst that can happen from just one night of drinking?

Invasion

entrenching

THE ROAD TO IRAQ is bland. The landscape bleeds into the sky, one interconnected flat plane of yellow that scrolls on and on, endless as the cracked pavement and dirt roads we drive on. The heat is violent, singeing the lungs with each breath. I dangle one foot out of the side of the vehicle—the flimsy canvas doors have been removed, it wasn't like they were bulletproof anyway. I let my foot hang there, the sand road rushing inches beneath the sole, despite the stories of soldiers' feet becoming ensnared on debris and the entire leg being ripped off. I'm too desperate for a breeze. Billows of sand clog the air, settling over uniform, skin, mouth, and eyelashes like dry mist. I cough, spitting up dirt. Holding the wheel with one hand, I take a swig from my bottle, forgetting how hot the water has become. It scorches the inside of my mouth and my throat, settling like a hot stone at the base of my stomach. I angrily toss the bottle back onto the center console.

"No wonder these people are so pissed off," Sergeant Holt complains from the passenger seat, yanking at his flak vest collar. "It's so fucking hot!" Columns of sweat decorate the sides of his face and darken his hair.

I grunt in response. My eyelids are heavy from the lack of sleep, and the constant rumble of the Humvee is a dangerous lullaby. Heat continues to roll off the engine and fills the cab. My nose runs black liquid; my throat is raw from coughing up sand. I don't feel like partaking in small talk. I wiggle in the seat, my undershirt so wet with sweat that it makes a watery hiccup as it plasters against my skin. I'm in desperate need of a latrine and I roll my head back, silently begging for the convoy to stop. Sergeant Holt has the luxury of a bottle and a penis, both of which make for easy in-vehicle bathroom breaks. He tosses his urine out the window and I squeeze my thighs together.

"Another town," Holt comments, though he uses the term liberally. Mud-clay huts, primal in their simplicity, decorate the side of the road up ahead. They're spread far apart, though, so I never understand where the people come from—they materialize from the sand and stand along-side the otherwise empty highway. So many people for so few huts. From a distance I see a small boy galloping across the sand, a plume of dust stretching out behind him. He wears nothing but a dirtied shirt, one that wraps around his knees and brushes his ankles. He runs as fast as his tiny legs will carry him, waving one thin arm overhead. And when he reaches the edge of the road, he stares with dark eyes, a wide grin stretched across his small face. He waves enthusiastically then, eagerly watching as our rumbling convoy rushes by.

Others are not so easy to pass. They flood the road, causing us to slow to a crawl. They rush to the vehicles yet somehow always stop at an unwritten, invisible line. The barrels of our .50-cals swing their way, facing the crowd. Sergeant Holt grips his M16, shifting nervously in his seat. "Don't let them get so close!" he snaps when an Iraqi reaches out and brushes a palm over my knee. As if I can do anything—my M16 sits to my right but I can't wield it and drive. I wish I had been given an M9 handgun like some of the officers, but there aren't enough to go around. I'm lucky I even got ceramic SAPI plates in the back of my ballistic Kevlar flak vest—some have to do without the small arms protective insert.

But these Iraqis are friendly enough. Most smile, more curious than afraid. Many wave, more still ask for water, calling out the word in English. I grab an extra bottle and toss it to a little girl with fluffy black hair and massive eyes. She immediately scoops it up, rewarding me with a brilliant grin. The boy next to her raps his knuckles on her skull, snatching the bottle out of her hands as she raises her little fists over her head, cowering away.

"Give it back!" I yell, gesturing angrily at the boy, but he darts away and it's not like I can follow him.

Sergeant Holt lets out a startled bellow and I snap my head around, adrenaline soaring.

He clutches the side of his face, doubled over, and for a moment I see a flash of red in his hand. "What happened?" I yell. I grab at my M16, ignoring the sharp pain where the hot metal burns my fingers.

Sergeant Holt looks up, angry red welts slashed across his eye and cheek. "That fucker stole my sunglasses!"

I blink in surprise and almost laugh. "Wow, he really got you."

Holt angrily touches the welts with his fingertips, seeing the blood. He curses again, glaring at the crowd. "Go faster," he growls, and I don't blame him. The bodies are pressing too close to the vehicle. We're left vulnerable here. "They'll get out of the way." Which is true enough. They shift to the side when it becomes obvious I'm not going to stop.

There are no walls or guards or territories here. It's the grand wide-open and we're among the first to occupy in late April 2003. We have no armored vehicles; such things weren't readily available to us then. Maybe some of the infantry were gifted the very rare armored Humvees, but the Army certainly wasn't handing them out to Military Intelligence units. We don't matter that much.

There is that nagging, constant fear of attack; a little voice whispers behind my ear that in every dust storm crouches an insurgent with AK-47. But fear stretched too long simply becomes boredom, and the reality of the situation is surreal. It's the instinctual complex duality of a soldier's life—fully acknowledging that any second can be your last, yet never believing you can die—mortality blended with invincibility. I can die. But I won't.

We arrive in Baghdad in the muggy heat of early spring. We are not yet accustomed to the city enough to feel the monotony that fills the hours of war. I wake for the third night in a row, drenched in sweat, heart pounding as another round of AK-47 fire startles me from my sleep. I lie there, wide-eyed, listening to the shots tear through the night. I wait for someone to rush into the room, demand we don our armor and ready our rifles. This is it; this is a firefight. When no one comes, my eyelids grow heavy. I doze, and then another round jerks me awake to suffer the whole cycle again.

I groan in frustration, rolling onto my side. A layer of sweat sits on my skin, making it glisten in the low light. Baghdad, cradled by the Euphrates and Tigris, is far more humid than Kuwait. The air is wet and mosquitoes are everywhere. I won't use a mosquito net—the thin fabric cuts off whatever small breeze might exist. I lather up with military-grade DEET instead, turning my skin white with each application. My lips tingle; I lick them and my tongue goes numb.

I jerk again at the rapid fire of an AK-47, but it is the slow, steady fire of the M16 that spreads cold dread through my stomach. I hear its familiar rhythm and shiver, knowing it means a military guard or patrol is engaging fire. Over the months I will learn to block out the AK-47, but I can't shake the fear of the M16's cadence.

Sleep is impossible. I share a room with four other women from my company, Sergeants Forst and King and Specialists Brooks and Lovett, the last two new Spanish linguist additions from another post. At night we strip down to underwear and sports bras. At dawn Sergeant Daniels or some other Sergeant will quietly pad into the room for a weapons count, but we don't care. I want to be ashamed of the fat that jiggles around my stomach, the widened span of my hips, or the thick thighs that slap together as I move. I don't want Sergeant Daniels to see this embarrassment, but it's too hot for modesty. My cot is drenched; a pool of sweat sloshes from side to side as I turn. In the morning it will become a white stain on the green fibers.

On the third night I break, gritting my teeth against hot tears. I spread my arms out, legs wide, waiting, begging, praying for the slightest breeze. Waiting, begging, praying for the gunfire to stop. For even a moment of sleep. I get none. The burning, clawing frustration gets the best of me. I cry. I hate myself for it, biting my lips to stifle the sound. I feel like less of a soldier. Tomorrow, tomorrow I'll be stronger. Tomorrow I'll be fearless and brave. But tonight I'm exhausted, terrified, and struggling for air in the wet heat. Tonight, I want to go home. Tonight, I cry.

Our unit comes to Iraq and is promptly split up. Some are sent to Camp Marlboro, a cigarette factory once run by one of Saddam's cousins, now reclaimed and renamed by US forces. From our platoon, Locke, Sergeant Baum, female Brennan, and a few others are sent there, while the rest of us are planted in Camp Dragoon, the former headquarters of the Directorate of General Security, and more affectionately known to the locals as Saddam's one-way prison. The DGS was akin to our CIA and, as locals told it, home to hundreds of thousands of files on Iraqi citizens. Upset the regime and your file was pulled, a member of your family murdered. No one seems to mind that the headquarters took heavy US fire during Shock and Awe and is now mostly rubble. Our "rooms" are half-blown-up buildings; our first task is to clean out the broken glass and smash clear the twisted metal of the former window frames. Electricity is the luxury of civilians. Or officers. Our food is MREs and local lake water "cleansed" with heavy doses of bleach. Powdered drink mixes are bartered and haggled over, traded for something as small as reading material or as large as getting out of extra duty. Anything to mask the taste of bleach, which sits at the back of your throat for hours.

I get dysentery. A time-honored tradition; it's not really a war until someone gets dysentery.

"How positively medieval," I grumble, clutching my tight and aching stomach. Dysentery doesn't get me out of work, though maybe it would have had I properly reported it. But I can't risk the medics taking me off duty, especially not for something as pathetic as explosive diarrhea. Imagine what they'd all have to say about that. Instead I just take extra bathroom breaks. I eye the "latrine" warily. It's a wooden shack with a rickety door, put together recently by the engineers. When I pull the thin door open, I'm attacked by the swarm of blackflies that live on the stewing piles of feces and urine inside the half-iron barrels. The smell assaults me. Apparently, I'm not the only one with dysentery.

I could snub my nose at the bathrooms and head over to the bushes, which I've been doing a lot of lately. Just recently, I ran into another female soldier, possibly a cook, and we took turns peeing in the foliage, making small talk with our uniforms around our ankles, one playing the lookout for the other because neither of us wanted to use those wobbly latrines and I'd rather pee with a stranger than with a storm of flies. Public urination is hardly a thing anymore anyway—I've become desensitized, having bared my ass on the sides of roads in Kuwait and Iraq: first trying to be discreet, first covering myself with a woobie, fumbling with the extra material and only getting piss on my boots. Then less so, when there was nowhere to go but a wide-open expanse of sand and silt. Even when I hide behind a Humvee tire, thinking myself finally safe between two vehicles, another unit's convoy blazes by, hoots shouted with each passing of a vehicle, like one continuous holler that grows louder and weaker then louder again as the line of trucks thunders by. Their uproarious attention is undoubtedly scornful. No one wants to see the fat girl peeing. I take it because I have to. I stand, boots firmly planted in the dirt, chin angled up. I'll pretend to be brazen and piss in the open. I'll be a mockery of what they really want to see—not the pretty girl caught in a vulnerable position but the thing that disgusts them. And if I really must care, at least I don't have to let them know.

But too many people have been choosing sparse bushes over the latrines and now new rules have been implemented—getting caught is punishable by an Article 15. So I barely suppress a horrified shudder and slide into the narrow shack, trying to push out the majority of flies. Like a pillar of smoke they swarm upward when I lift the toilet lid.

"Oh, I so don't want you anywhere near my vagina," I tell the flies, but it's inevitable. Even worse, it's become fairly obvious that the toilets were made with only men in mind. The seats sit too far back on the wooden shelf, and if a woman sits to pee, her legs at an awkward angle, the urine pools on her thighs. "You've got to be kidding me," I hiss, and do an acrobatic trick with one leg pressed up against the shack wall. Nice to know the engineers remember us women.

But as with everything in Iraq, we adapt. I learn that crouching over the toilet hole is much more effective than sitting on the seat. Instead of washing with wet wipes, we create a shower, scavenging the blown-up buildings for doors and stacking them side by side against a cement wall, creating four walls. We learn that holding five-gallon jugs overhead is tiresome, so we drag metal bookshelves into the shower room, and haul jugs onto the shelves, where we can tip the nozzle down and create a makeshift shower. We learn that it's easier to have a plastic bin to wash hair, the women sometimes taking turns pouring water over each other's heads, a shared task that becomes somewhat enjoyable as we amass at dusk or twilight to bathe, when the air is cooler. We then use the bins to wash our uniforms, water black with daily sand and sweat. Desperation is the greatest of innovators; every soldier becomes an engineer.

And there is a sort of rhythm we fall into, a repetitive flow of the days. The sun rises and falls with the *azan*, the call to prayer that heralds out over Baghdad with a rich, resonating voice. I learn to anticipate the crackle of the microphone, the silence before that first long, deep note, a haunting invocation that cries out over the city. It's so alien at first, frightening, this startling blare that floods the air, a strange mix of notes that feels foreign. And yet it unfurls itself into a lyrical certainty, a comforting inevitability that marks the day, marching forward, onward despite bomb or mortar, unyielding to war or peace. I curl around my pillow at *fajr*, eat lunch at *dhuhr*, pause for *asr*, watch the sun sink at *maghrib*, and stare out into the darkness at *isha*. The worship marks the moving of hours, the sectioning of days that otherwise blend seamlessly together.

At dusk there's the shit-burning detail, where unlucky soldiers drag out the barrels from beneath the wooden latrines, pour fuel into the waste, and light it ablaze. The shit and piss burn to a blackened tar, stirred with one long metal pole, a scarf over our mouths as we're pelted and splattered with burning feces, turning the front of our uniforms black. Later we'll learn that burn pits can wreck soldiers' hearts and lungs, leading to reduced lung function, asthma, and cardiopulmonary diseases, and the government will evade responsibility, because of course they do.

Tonight I stand back by our company's door with Andres, leaning against the balcony railing and watching the fire pits burn against the backdrop of *maghrib* and the rose-pink sun. Andres is an analyst and works in the tactical operations center (TOC), which he hates because it surrounds him with all upper brass. I only see him in the evenings before or after my twelve-hour shifts, and even then finding privacy is difficult and time is scant. I just barely rest my hip against Andres's side, a discreet caress, because there's no touching in uniform and most of the time this is all we get.

"If you squint, it's almost like a bonfire," I say, my brain clamoring for normalcy. Andres snorts at me. He finds it intolerable when I look for silver linings. The chaplain stands beside him, leaning back against the wall. He's paid a visit to our company, though I'm not sure why.

"Don't worry, we'll be out of here in six months tops," he promises.

"You think so, sir?" I ask, hopeful. We've been given no time frame, just dumped into the sand and told to exist, to work, to not die. There has been no other Army occupation deployment before us, we're the first, and that brings all the uncertainty of knowing nothing.

"I have it on good authority." The chaplain smiles, staring out over the burning shit.

Andres gives him a dark, sideways glare. He doesn't believe him. Andres has a good sense of these things. His jadedness gives him an uncanny insight into the military's interworking because in a few months, this chaplain is gone, relieved by another chaplain, just like Colonel Fox is relieved by another regiment colonel mid-deployment, snatching up their combat patches and moving on, leaving us all here to rot. It's good to be an officer.

In the beginning, it's only MREs. The Skittles are nice and if you're smart enough to snag a vegetarian bag, there's fruit. Supposedly there's a mythical option out there with scrambled eggs and maple apple sausage, but I never see it. The redundancy of the food is disheartening. There are only so many times one can eat meat loaf for breakfast. So when a man who has next to nothing offers us all that he has, we take it ravenously.

He sits cross-legged on the men's bedroom floor. I don't know who he is or why he's here. Perhaps he's an informant. There are plenty of locals willing to help in their own way. Children mostly will run up to Humvees outside the wire and point out where insurgents had planted IEDs the night before. They swing and dance around the vehicles, pulling soldiers into games of soccer, sometimes sitting on the sidewalks and asking for help with their English homework. Some locals will tell you chilling, terrifying stories about the days before. Some, like this man, who may not speak much English at all, will give what he has for reasons I'll never know. His feet are hard and dusty. He is old but bends easily, slanted over an impressive display of food. Silver round tins overflow with ruddy sauces, golden saffron rice, and round chunks of browned meat, all displayed on an ornate red wool woven square rug. He grins, the corners of his eyes crinkle, deep lines embedded in the dark skin. He gestures to the food with a work-worn hand.

"Eat, eat," he says gleefully. His beard is white, bright against the rest of him.

I glance at Sergeant Lee and male King, female King's husband, who are already devouring their shares. I crouch down beside them and the man makes me a small plate of red-curry-like sauce over meat with a side of rice. My mouth waters. I dip the offered flat bread into the sauce and it tastes like Eden.

"His wife makes all this," says Sergeant Lee.

"From scratch?" I yelp over a mouthful, food dribbling out the corners of my lips. "He brings it every week for the soldiers to eat."

The man grins again, gesturing for me to take more, eat more. The brown meat is goat and it is delicious.

"Why?" I ask.

The two soldiers shrug, scooping up the last of their food with fingers.

I say, "Thank you, *shukraan, shukraan*," and the man only gestures for me to take more; his smile seems so genuine, his delight is palpable. I don't get to ask why he's so happy, or why he brings food to soldiers who have entrenched themselves into his country's soil. I can't ask why, when he has so little, he gives so much away. But I say, "*Shukraan, shukraan*," and this seems to satisfy him. I carve his face and his kindness into my brain as my only means of gratitude, because I don't know what else to give him.

The camp finally gets its act together and builds a makeshift mess hall, a hut of green tarp and wobbly tables, powered by fuel and fire. No one thinks to complain about its lackluster appearance because at least we're not eating MREs anymore. But mess hall means kitchen patrol, and that's one hell of a duty.

I arrive before dawn for KP, staring down at my boots, struggling to stay awake.

"Go get water," says one of the cooks, shoving five-gallon jugs into my hands. And so I do, back and forth from the water buffalo, sloshing water over the front of my uniform, because we don't have running water and every ounce has to be hauled into the tent.

"I speak three fucking languages," I grunt to no one, my hands crimped into a permanent claw. No one cares.

I haul another jug up onto a metal shelf in the mess hall. The water is poured into metal bins, heated by open flames. The kitchen is sectioned off from the mess hall by two dirtied nylon flaps, which ensnare the heat, circulating it around the tiny room until my hair is plastered against my skull and sweat drenches my uniform. The cooks mill about, occasionally stirring silver tins of dehydrated food, while those of us tasked to the duty clean the tables, the floors, dumping dirty dishes into the metal bins and scrubbing them clean. There's no way to regulate the water temperature and it's scalding, turning my hands brilliant red and peeling the skin off my knuckles.

"What do we need cooks for," I mutter to the other guy on duty. "They just stand there while we do all the work."

He glances over at the cooks, all huddled around one tin of orange eggs, each taking a turn stirring the watery food. "They certainly have this whole shamming thing figured out," he agrees. Every good soldier knows how to sham—staying in plain sight while doing the least amount of work possible—and the cooks have this down to a science. They shirk the heavier work and shoulder off the labor onto KP, even as they ignore us, as if there is a caste division.

But there are those who don't, who mingle, and McCarthy always stands next to me on the line, coyly watching as I slap food onto trays, grinning a big-toothed grin and saying, "You'll make some man a really great wife someday," and I laugh at the sexist compliment, because he's actually very friendly and sweet, and it's a shame that one day he places the muzzle of his rifle into his mouth and blows his brains out over the back of the mess hall tent.

Soldiers file in three times a day for meals and I clamor for a space on the serving line, because I'd rather smile up at soldiers and dish out food than stand in the blistering heat of the back kitchen.

Sergeant Daniels comes for breakfast, holding out his tray for me to splatter wet, rehydrated eggs onto his plate. He's already covered in a layer of dirt, his uniform pale with salt stains and his face dark with sun and grime. He narrows his eyes at me, holding up the line. "Dostie, how many times have you done this so far?" He means KP, kitchen patrol.

I slosh eggs onto the soldier's plate next to him. "Four or five times now?" I say.

The issue is my language abilities. Up on our work floor, packed away six stories up in a condemned building, we work twelve-hour shifts, seven days a week. But I'm not good enough, I'm not fast enough, I've always been a mediocre Farsi linguist. I struggle to keep up on our ██, leaning over the broken-down desk, clamping ████ to ████, brow pinned, ████ this or that, what little ████, and feeling terribly inadequate.

Sergeant Holt had pulled me aside one evening, standing in the hall-way between floors five and six. He holds my ████, scowling over the ████. It's unsatisfactory. "Dostie, if you can't keep up, there are other ways you can be more useful," he says and I stare down at my boots, nudging away some white debris with my toe. "You could do KP for everyone instead," he offers, maybe because his KP duty is upcoming and no one likes the sixteen-to-nineteen-hour shift. "I'm not saying you have to, but wouldn't you want to help the team out the best way you can?"

I grumble something, because it's not just that I want to be useful, I have to be. War has given me reprieve from the role of the girl who reported—I've won freedom beneath bullets and mortars. Everyone's forgotten either because they have better things to do or because another girl in the unit is raped and they have something new to look at. I won't remind them. I'm not the worst linguist, but I'm certainly not the best, either. I can't draw attention by holding the group back.

"Yeah, sure, I can do extra KP," I mumble, because if I can't perform well enough, at least I know how to work hard.

In line, Sergeant Daniels shakes his head at me, a little angry. "No," is all he says, then strides away, and I think I did something wrong again, my stomach twisting with dread, but instead someone tells me

Sergeant Daniels corners Sergeant Holt in the mess hall, leans in, and reams him out. And when I'm told, I stand dumbfounded because I didn't even know Sergeant Daniels cared. That's the last time I ever have KP.

Outside the wire, there are the convoy details, and it's a very different kind of ride from our journey up to Baghdad. Here there be insurgents. Here we blaze down the streets and begin to calculate:

Lumbering dump trucks filled with Iraqi workers: insurgents with handguns

Crumbled plastic cans on the edge of the road: improvised explosive devices

Glassless windows cut into apartment walls: snipers

Riding the swell of a bridge: explosives under the structural supports

Ducking beneath an overpass: bombs dropping onto the passing convoy

Iraqis on sidewalks: rifles hidden beneath traditional cloth and dresses

This is the way our war is now. Rides are tense. Sergeant Daniels sits to the right of me, one hand on the door, stubble-covered jaw working around a wad of chew. We both see the debris rolled up with cans and loose plastic bags at the same time. My eyes dart to the mirrors, checking my lanes, but there's a stone barrier on my left, a Humvee on my right.

"Dostie, don't run over it," Sergeant Daniels orders, his right arm reaching up to grip the roof. I have nowhere to go. My foot hovers over the brake, my heart pounds, the Humvee on the right blocks my way and I grip the steering wheel, twisting the metal in my hands.

"Dostie, don't run over it!" Sergeant Daniels yells again, one leg rising up, bracing against the dashboard, pushing against it, as if he can shove himself out of the vehicle completely.

It's either crash into the barrier, crash into the Humvee, or risk the IED. I take the risk, every muscle rigid, breath held, body clenched over the wheel as Sergeant Daniels screams, "DOSTIE!," a final attempt at an order, and we both squeeze shut our eyes, our bodies, our fists, our legs, and wait for the blast to rip open the bottom of the Humvee and fill the vehicle with fire.

But it doesn't.

I exhale, a hot, wet sound as the debris passes silently beneath us. Sergeant Daniels turns to me, rage burning across his face, still curled, and for a moment I wonder if he'll reach across the space that separates us and punch me in the jaw. I'd probably deserve it.

"There was the Humvee on the right," I say, but my voice sounds soft and watery.

He turns away, the muscles in his jaw dancing as he clenches his teeth. He says nothing to me for the rest of the ride. He eventually gets a new driver once we change camps.

Inside the wire we live like prisoners behind twenty-foot-high stone walls. Beneath some buildings are literal interrogation centers, complete with a torture chamber in one of the basements. Foreign-language messages are carved into the walls of jail cells. We do our time, staring at the same walls, the same faces, one day scrolling into the next, counting down until we can go home while we coil, and pace, and rage, and itch. Itch to get out, itch to release, to have a target, a new face, a bloodied direction, a visual purpose, gritting our teeth and drowning in a growing fury that makes us say things we shouldn't say and want to do things we shouldn't want to do.

indiscriminate

WE'RE BOTH INVADERS AND NOVELTIES. For as much as any nationalist should hate an occupying force, the Iraqis surrounding our camp seem far more curious than they are angry. American troops sit up in stone towers that sporadically decorate the camp walls and Iraqis are drawn to the strongholds, undeterred by concertina wire and M16s. I think we like the attention. It's good to be the hero, even if our heroism is in our own minds.

Some come to practice their English. "Hello, hello," says a group of young boys. "Me speak with you? Speak English with you?" they ask with such big smiles, sitting down on the dusty sidewalk on the other side of the concertina wire. "I like music. You like music?" or "I go to school. Come to America one day!" Simple sentences but spoken with such intensity, bouncing their stunted language off us in earnest.

Some come to beg for water or an MRE. I throw my MRE lunch down the tower wall to a young kid dressed in dusty trousers and a worn sweatshirt. He halts mid-sentence, snatches the package out of the air, and dives for his bike, pedaling away as fast as he can, as if he now possesses some treasure, as if I might suddenly ask for it back.

"You know that'll probably feed his family for a week," the soldier on guard with me jokes as we watch the kid's dust trail disappear down the corner of the street.

"I doubt it," I snort, because that seems like a stereotype. No one is that poor.

Some come to the tower for the novelty. "I marry her," says one Iraqi man to my guard tower partner, pointing at me.

"Her? Sure, I'll sell her to you."

"What?" I squawk. "You can't sell me!" I elbow him hard in the flak vest.

"Four camels," he calls down to the man. "I'll give her to you for four camels."

The man shakes his head with a grin. "Too much!" He holds up two fingers. "Two. Two sheep!"

My guard partner breaks out into hysterics, face red with laughter.

"I'm worth at least four camels," I grumble, affronted. They both ignore me. "Two sheep and a goat!" the soldier counters.

The Iraqi laughs along with him. "I see what I can do," he says, shaking his head, and walks away with his own little laugh.

Each is equally mocking the other.

Another time, another man is a little more straightforward. "I go to the mosque to pray you be my wife," he says. At least he tells me directly, which is nice.

I smile and wave. "Okay, sure," I say. Two marriage proposals? I'm flattered.

And among all the different types that come to see us soldiers up in our towers are the entrepreneurs. Majid is one such businessman, a young boy of sixteen, scrawny but with a quick tongue and a sharp mind. His brand is trust. Give him twenty dollars for a black-market DVD and he'll return with exact change, waiting to be paid only after he brings back the requested item. He never runs off with the money, he never overpays, he never skims from the top. He earns a reputation among the soldiers; we know him by sight and he works the towers with brilliant efficiency.

Anything that isn't an MRE or DFAC food tastes delicious to us, and Iraqi food has that extra something that melts in the mouth. It's full and heavy and vibrant. Majid knows this. An ATM gets planted in the dusty corner of our tiny PX shop, which means soldiers finally have access to our money, and all possibilities lead to food. Except: We're not allowed to eat anything that hasn't been provided by the Army. In the back of our minds, we understand this. There's no way to regulate food coming from outside the gates. Food is easily poisoned, after all. But Majid has marketed trust and it's never wise to kill off your best clients. Lamb, flatbread, kebab, coffee, tea, even pizza—we can have it all.

I love lamb kebab. I can't get enough of it. Majid brings back the order to the tower and I hang over the stone edge, ready to catch the package when he tosses it upward.

"Come down." Majid gestures to the locked metal door in the wall. "Come get it here."

Frankly, I didn't even know the door opened. My guard buddy shrugs. He doesn't see a problem with it. I glance back toward the camp, making sure no higher-ups are around, and scuttle down the ladder and to the camp wall. The metal door is heavy. It groans as I shove it open, heart pounding, realizing I could be opening the door to enemy attack, to letting insurgents in, to getting shot while standing in that doorway, but it's just Majid on the other side. He slinks through the rows of concertina wire like it's nothing more than a nuisance. He grins, young, with white teeth and dark, gentle eyes.

"You're beautiful," he says, and gestures one hand around his face. "You look like the silver moon at midnight."

I blush red, glance down, because I'm aware that I'm still fat, although I'm not sure anyone can tell under all this gear. "Thank you," I mumble, taking the white, grease-soaked package of lamb kebab.

Majid is a sweet kid. He likes talking with the Americans. He likes American music. He says he needs a CD player to listen to his American music and I happen to see one in the PX one day. I buy it on a whim. Forty dollars isn't much when thousands are loading up in the bank, mostly untouched because what can we spend it on here anyway? I ask our local contract linguist to write a letter out for me in Arabic, a sort of quick little note, and the linguist grins, sitting back in his chair as he scrawls the letters out over a scrap piece of notebook paper. I can sound out the letters, but that's as far as my Farsi will take me with Arabic.

"Wait, doesn't *habibi* mean 'lover'?" I ask, pointing to how the letter is addressed.

"It's for friends," he says, waving away the concern. "Between close friends." He smiles, though he's always smiling, so it's hard to tell if he's pulling my leg or not.

The next day I toss the package down to Majid, who has come to the tower with a few other boys, this side of the wall an open green field where some of the boys play soccer.

Majid tilts his head as he reads the letter. Two boys glance over his shoulder, reading along with him, and suddenly there is a loud bluster, boys rocking back on their heels with laughter, pushing Majid's shoulders. "*Habibi, habibi,*" I hear them mock, and Majid ducks his head, not looking at me. I shift uncomfortably up in the tower, wondering now exactly what the letter says.

He opens the bag slowly, unfolding the paper around the CD player, and the boys flock around him, loud and excited, though he is quiet and still. He looks stunned.

"You said you needed one, right?" I ask, slowly wondering if there is some cultural gap I'm missing. Do I seem like some older woman trying to buy the younger boy? What does *habibi* really mean? He looks up at me with that blank, stunned stare, and it wasn't the reaction I was hoping for. I know other male soldiers have given him gifts, so why do I have to be so different? Why am I always stumbling into ravines and rifts that they all get to stride right over?

He says some kind of thanks, and turns to walk away, but one of the older boys, practically a man and far larger in size, snatches the CD player out of Majid's hands, making to stride in a different direction with the prize.

"Hey," I yell from my gut, my Army voice, deep and masculine and powerful, because tone matters. "Give it back," I order.

The young man pauses, then reaches out, dropping the package back into Majid's hands. I'm surprised, because what does he think I can do from here to stop him? I often forget how I must look, with an M16 slung over one shoulder. He walks away quickly. Majid still appears stunned.

We never mention the CD player incident. Not even some months later, when soldiers have worked hard to fudge his age, to make him older than he really is, to fit the minimum age requirement of eighteen in order to work inside the camp. Then he's in here, doing manual labor moving heavy rocks from one place to the other. It seems like a terrible waste for such a brilliant mind, but he seems happy with the hourly wage.

Moving heavy rocks from one place to the other is a common job for Iraqi locals inside the camp. "Putting money back into the local economy," it's called. The groups of men are guarded by two soldiers, one who strolls behind the group, the other in front, magazines seated into their weapons, hands at the ready. That's called Haji Duty. Not officially, of course, although I'm not sure what the official name for the duty actually is. I've never heard anyone use it. *Haji* is an honorific title given to a Muslim who has made the pilgrimage to Mecca. It's an earned and honorable term, but we use it indiscriminately.

"No, no, not Haji," one Iraqi tries to correct, ducking his head a little with embarrassment at being misclassified, at being given a title he hasn't earned, smiling politely at first, though most stop trying to correct the mistake when the word slides into a racial slur, a derogatory term for all Middle Easterners, be they Muslim or Christian, Arab or not. We take something of honor and tarnish it, muddling it up until the title means nothing at all. Although as far as racial slurs to demonize the enemy go, it's a rather mild adaptation from wars prior.

These groups of Iraqi workers are ubiquitous in the camp. There are the hard laborers, but also those who wash the laundry (mostly women), or who ship in dirty blocks of ice, or those who run the Haji Mart, the store for local items, or the barbershop, who also pluck women's eyebrows with a thin red thread. Eventually they're all over the camp, doing the work we no longer want to do, that we no longer have to do, and the camp shuffles, expands, breeds into a tiny city—or, at the very least, something more than war-torn buildings with black, empty windows and rubble for roads.

During lunch one day I pause at a group of four or five Iraqis crouched over brown MRE bags, towered over by two young American soldiers who snicker loudly, watching the eating men a little too gleefully. I hesitate, trying to put my finger on why the scene feels off, and glance down at the MREs. They all read in bold black letters: PORK CHOW MEIN.

"That's pork!" I say, aghast.

The two soldiers lose it, bursting out laughing.

"Hey, stop!" I say to the Iraqis, waving at their food, alarmed. "That's pork!" And they stare up at me, blank, confused as to why this woman is yelling at them, so I shove my index finger to the tip of my nose, pushing it up in a symbol I've seen Iraqis recognize before, and say, "Pig! Pig!"

An indescribable horror dawns on the group, written clearly on their faces, a slow, slack-jawed realization, food frozen partway to mouths, dropping their boxes as if they're suddenly scalding hot, hands thrown up in the hair in disgust, trying to put as much distance as they can between themselves and the forbidden food.

And the soldiers laugh louder, I suppose because the realization was part of the joke.

"Dude, that's fucked up!" I turn on them.

"It's fucking hilarious, is what it is," says one and his eyes slide toward me, a sideways glare, saying *who the fuck are you* and *why the fuck do you care?*

I could report them, I have the time in service now, the rank, but I lack the follow-through. I'd like to say it is because I don't want to report anyone else, or because I'm threatened by my higher-ups, but really I just don't want to deal with tracking down their command, with the paperwork. I can't be bothered. So I growl a little, threaten a little, then storm off and forget it, which helps no one at all.

Not all such interactions are as grim, though. Some laborers come to where we work, cleaning out the debris from one of the floors. Someone wants to turn the building into offices, and they mean to, sending Iraqi workers in to remove the walls that are now on the floor, until they realize the building sways in the wind, or shudders with each distant mortar attack, or that it's a precarious monument at best, safe for no one and Intel is only there because we need to be invisible. But until then it's nice seeing new faces on the floors. While on break, I lean against a fallen column, watching some of the workers move blocks into wheelbarrows.

One gentleman, a foreman of sorts, joins me. He speaks English, enough to get his point across clearly and with a charming accent. He's middle-aged, in that place in life where wisdom intersects youth, with an amiable face, hair white at his temples, slender, and with a well-kept beard. He asks me about my god. I answer circuitously. Despite a lifetime of history with him, I'm not sure how I'm feeling about God at the moment.

So this man tells me about his god, instead. I won't remember which words he uses, or how he'll phrase his belief, but it's not the words that matter. Rather, against the backdrop of the late-afternoon sky, leaning against a once marble window frame, I listen to a man speak with a conviction I recognize. He speaks of peace, burning from the inside with a spiritual fire that I know, that I've seen, that I've had myself before. I see it in his dark eyes, in the way he leans forward slightly, an eager desperation for me to *hear* him. He's trying to save my soul. I thought only Christians did that. This Muslim man is trying to save my soul because he is so certain he knows the truth, so convinced, so worried for me, except he's not talking about *my* god. He's talking about *his* god.

The axis of my world tilts.

Even after he's gone, that man stays with me. An epiphany, my spiritual question mark. I have no intention of becoming Muslim, but I'm not sure I'm Christian anymore, either. Not after this man so casually rattled the foundation of my world, not with words, but with the power of his own belief.

It's the Iraqi translators that are the real unsung heroes of the nation, though. They serve alongside US troops anywhere a translator is needed, which is everywhere: in the camp, on the streets, into combat—with no rifle, often no armor, and sometimes for as little as five dollars a day. They defy terrorists, insurgents, local militias, and then go home through those same enemies at the end of the day, walking out of the camp at dusk with no protection, only to come back the next morning the same way. Their lives hinge on American success, gambling themselves and their families on the hope that we'll come out victorious. Many apply to relocate to the US. Some make it. Most don't. Many die during the wait for the vetting process. No twenty-one-gun salute here. Thanks for your service, here's your grave, no one will know what you did, except those few of us who saw you once, brave and resilient and defiant. You served your country and mine, and one day we'll repay you by blocking your fellow translators' entrance into our country, because you're still Iraqi, after all.

But not Daveed. Daveed is in his forties, college-educated, idealistic, and kind. He has pale-green eyes, which are vibrant against his tan skin. He grins with crooked teeth and has energy to spare. He has a family in Baghdad, a wife and children, and still he dares. Daveed has no intention of relocating to the United States. He couldn't care less about the five dollars—he comes from money. Daveed loves his country.

He's not interested in leaving. This baffles the soldiers around him. Why wouldn't he want out of this sandbox? Why wouldn't he lunge at the chance to toil away at minimum wage in the good ol' United States of America? But Daveed sees something different in his homeland. He sees optimism in the American forces whom he hopes will help rebuild his country. He sees greatness here and he needs to be a part of it. His patriotism is beautiful.

And then there is Mahmod. Mahmod is in his twenties, a handsome medical student with a dark wash of thick black hair. He wears a brown leather bomber jacket and distressed blue jeans. He uses English slang and sticks close to the men. During a convoy run, the executive officer is injured, bleeding out into his own lap, and suddenly there is Mahmod, tightening his belt around the arm, a makeshift tourniquet that saves the officer's life. He's crowned "Son of the Regiment" and loved. The regiment touts him as the epitome of the Iraqi translator, perhaps better loved than Daveed for his youth, perhaps better appreciated than Daveed because of his dazzling, even-toothed smile. So when he rapes a Staff Sergeant in the translator shack after a game of chess, she knows she can't report it. She's older. She's been in the Army longer. She knows the machine better. He's the Son of the Regiment and she's an American woman. She knows exactly whom they'll believe. So she says nothing, reports nothing, becomes a statistic, and saves her career.

Near the end of our deployment, as we're packing up to leave Baghdad, during the uprising of Sadr, the Siege of Sadr City, the spring infighting of 2004, Mahmod is murdered, cut up into pieces, and his dismembered limbs stuffed into a dumpster just outside the camp gates. Or so it's said. There's no way to know. Those who loved him say no, no, Mahmod got out safely, that he's now living in the US and working in Los Angeles. In Hollywood, to be exact. But I don't care either way.

One day a different Iraqi translator visits my guard tower. He's not a regular at our camp, but he's on loan from the First Armored Division, clearly higher ranking in whatever system they use for national linguists. He is simply making his way around the towers out of curiosity. Tall, with a barrel chest and broad shoulders, he has the bearing of a football player two years out of the game, with a hard beer gut, though maybe that's just the bulletproof vest. He speaks English smoothly, with almost no accent, and there is something very American about him, from his large, stocky build to the ease of his stance, legs spread apart, arms crossed over the swell of his chest. He's handsome in a familiar way. Maybe it's the cocksureness, that edge of arrogance, that's both familiar and appealing.

When he arrives I'm gnawing at the edge of a hard stick of classic pepperoni, sent in from home. "May I?" he asks, pointing to the unfamiliar food.

"Sure," I say, and slice off a chunk with my knife.

He rolls the meat in his palm. "Does it have pork in it?"

I cock my head and try to think what's actually *in* pepperoni. I was born in the Pizza Belt—New Haven, home to the greatest thin-crust pizza in all the world—but I have never stopped to consider what pepperoni actually is. "It's beef," I say, fairly certain, and the other soldier on guard doesn't correct me so that seems about right.

The linguist takes a bite, his dark brow rising in delight. "This is freaking delicious."

"Right?" I grin, breaking off another chunk with my teeth. "Best stuff on earth."

We end up talking about democracy, somehow, although perhaps the conversation is always destined to come around to that when you're occupying another country. He seems excited about the future, and pleased with his own involvement. Then he says something that surprises me. "We don't want to be too Western," he says, chewing on his second slice of pepperoni, as if being *too Western* is a bad thing.

"What do you mean? What's 'too Western'?"

"I mean, we want everyone to have freedom, that's important, but we can't have women walking down the street in short skirts or anything. For example, I mean."

My brow crumples. "But shouldn't they have the freedom to *choose* to wear short skirts or not?"

"No, no." He shakes his head and leans back against the tower wall. "Too much freedom is a bad thing, you see."

"There's no such thing as too much freedom."

"No, but think about it. When given too much choice, man will choose wrong, he will choose poorly. Society must have rules to protect ourselves from our own nature." He points to his chest as he speaks, animated. "From us doing wrong."

"But a woman wearing a short skirt isn't hurting anyone."

"She is hurting herself. She is hurting the men around her. She disrespects herself and those who see her. It is our job, our responsibility, to protect the morality of our society."

My head hurts. "But that's not *freedom*," I stress.

"Freedom is the right to speak against my government. To assemble peacefully and to have fair elections. Freedom is electing our own leaders. But if there are no guidelines, no structure, there is chaos. Society cannot function on chaos. We need sharia to protect ourselves."

"But what if people want to *choose* to wear short skirts, or to be gay?"

He shakes his head, sadly. "Then society will crumble. We will fall."

"America hasn't."

"Has it not?" he counters, raising his eyebrows slightly, as if surprised by my claim.

I tilt my head, pushing up the brim of my Kevlar, stunned. This man fights for democracy, fights alongside American troops, but his democracy doesn't look like mine.

I open my mouth to counter, to clarify what freedom actually is, because I think I've got it all figured out, when one of the soldiers in charge of him pops his head up through the door on the floor.

"We're moving out," he says to the linguist, then pauses. He looks at the packaging in my hand and then points one gloved hand at the linguist. "You know that's pork, right?"

The linguist swallows hard. His face is ashen.

"No, no," I quickly assure him. "It's beef." I scramble with the package, trying to read the tiny script. "Isn't it?"

"Not any pepperoni I've ever had," the soldier replies, and sure enough, there are the words on the package, PORK and BEEF.

"I'm sorry," I say. "I really thought it was just beef." I think of the soldiers who purposefully fed Iraqi workers pork—of their smirks, their elation at a joke fully realized. They reveled in the horror. But that's not me. I didn't mean to do it. "It's okay, you didn't do it on purpose," I say for him and me.

"That doesn't matter. It's still a sin," he says, shaken.

"But you didn't *intend* to," I stress. I didn't intend to cause him to sin, either. It wasn't a prank. I'm not laughing. Surely that means something.

"It is not intent that always matters," he says, glancing up at me with dark eyes. He isn't angry. "Action is more important than intent."

"How does that saying go?" the soldier in the doorway pipes up. "'The road to hell is paved with good intentions'?"

"That's not helpful," I snap. He shrugs.

Intent is important to me. The intent to free this country is important to me. And to me, at this moment in the war, it seems to be working. We intend to do right by these people and certainly there are accomplishments here. I've seen a Christian woman walking with a Sunni and a Shi'ite, their attire ranging from no veil, to headscarf, to full black hijab, and I tell myself this must be some kind of accomplishment, our good intentions fulfilled. But then again, what do I know? I only see the country from the tiny periscope of my guard tower window.

filicide

THE WIND IN IRAQ is painful. It is a hair dryer on high pressed against my skin. I tuck my hands into the cuffs of my uniform sleeves, hiding my face behind a thin scarf. Sweat evaporates into the air like puffs of smoke, leaving white salt stains on my arms. Full battle gear rattles against my rib cage and around my hips, straining on my shoulders. Breathing in is drinking fire.

I shuffle faster, nostalgic for spring with its humid days, when my uniform would be drenched with sweat. Sweat no longer survives out here in the summer sun and my uniform burns. I slip into the shade of our work building with relief, escaping the blazing wind. The temperature plummets and sweat immediately blooms over my upper lip and trickles down my spine. I yank down the scarf, gulping in the shadows. I shove up the lip of my Kevlar, which in turn knocks into the bun at the base of my neck and tumbles forward again. I groan at the stairs. Six flights, 117 stairs, to be exact, in full battle rattle— Kevlar, flak vest (neck collar included) with two SAPI plates, TA-50 harness, six full magazines of ammo (seventh strapped to the butt of the M16), two canteens, and one water CamelBak hydration system makes for over fifty pounds of gear. I'd better be thin and with one fine ass after all this.

Bits of debris tumble down the steps behind me, echoing across the curved stairwell. I pause, half turned, curious. A boy is pressed against the drywall. The marble was all blasted off the walls long ago. He is gangly, his threadbare pants too short, exposing dark ankles lined with layers of dust. Dark hair nearly obscures large, black eyes.

"Hello," he says, out of place in this once glorious palace that is now occupied by khaki, tan, and black metal. "How are you," he says in heavy accent and holds out one slender hand; years of work have rendered his palms twice his age. He climbs toward me, hand extended, teeth bared, and he seems slight and young.

I smile in response, silently shifting my M16 on my shoulder, and extend my own hand. "Hello," I say, then slowly add, "You're not supposed to be here." The building looks perilous with its heavily battle-worn exterior, one side torn open so that nothing but mangled metal frames and shattered stone is exposed to the sun. It's purposefully deceiving. No person in his right mind would work on the top floor of a building that is just begging to give its last breath. That insanity is our cover. It doesn't occur to me that he saw me enter the building and chose to follow. I assume he is a lost worker; he's wandered away from his group and armed guard.

He encases my hand in his, less like the handshake I was expecting and more like a shackle. My hand rises and falls in a quick attempt of civility. "You have to go back to your group," I gently coax.

He steps up another stair, suddenly closer, and I balk at the invasion of my space. I attempt to step back and my boot bangs into the stair behind me, almost knocking me off-balance. "Give me a kiss," he murmurs, trying to draw his face closer to mine.

He crushes my hand; his slightness is a lie. My fingers grind painfully together in his fist.

I am momentarily more shocked than scared. He is all bones, tied together with wind-whipped skin—I can't find where his strength comes from. The pain in my hand intensifies as he attempts to jerk me closer. He's bending my fingers at an awkward angle.

And just like that the old rage is back. Like a red flare I am bright and burning. I breathe out in relief.

I shove. I throw my full weight into it and I have the high ground. He smashes into the wall, gray dust raining down around us. He still twists my hand in his grip, black irises surrounded by white; I bare clenched teeth in response.

His grip slips and I have my hand again. I step back. Repetitive training has relieved me of the need for a fully functional right hand. I shoot left-handed anyway.

I swing the buttstock up from under my left arm; I palm the handguard and continue to swing upward, guiding with my right hand as I thrust the buttstock at his head. I miss his face. And I mean to hit his face.

I'm furious at my own clumsiness. Unsatisfied. Want tastes like blood and suppressed violence feels like pain.

I envision a shattered nose, broken cheekbones, and trails of sticky red blood. I chomp on the vision and want to spit out bones. But he had gotten one arm up and I only smash his shoulder. There is a startled yelp and he stares, one hand gripping his limply hanging arm. Then, like a mouse, he scuttles down the stairs, disappearing around the bend of the stairwell.

I hesitate, listening to him round the last of the stairs and leave the building. I choke on fury; my throat burns with an unexpressed need.

I stare down at my frozen hand, pry open the stiff fingers. My Iraqi silver-and-moonstone ring has buried itself into the flesh, and when I drag it off, the skin is engraved in deep-blue grooves.

My hands shake. I reach the sixth floor just as fury gives way to pride. I walk with a purpose, with the heavy gait of one who can defend herself. This time, at least, I got it right.

The room is brilliant from the Iraqi sun and the glassless windows let in the breeze, made more bearable from the shade. I strip off my gear, still favoring my bent hand. I instantly feel lighter, and I sit cross-legged on top of the old wooden desk. It's only one of two pieces of furniture in the once grand room. It's battered, the delicate wood and gold engravings shattered along most of the trim, but it's sturdy. The torn blue couch is a far less reputable piece of furniture. It somehow appears seedy just sitting there against the wall, spilling stuffing from its ripped cushions,

oozing a suspicious stench that no one can quite name. It doesn't help
that at one point I'd seen a three-inch black scorpion make its escape
under the wooden legs. Now I consider the couch a no-man's-land. Let
the scorpions have it.

I stare at my hand, M16 balanced across my knees. I laugh. Who
makes a pass at a girl with a 5.56 mm magazine-fed, gas-operated,
air-cooled weapon on her shoulder?

Even so, when a roar rumbles through the room my heart jumps. I
lunge to my feet, M16 swinging around, only to see Avery Langley in
the doorway, arms held over his head as he attempts to make himself
monstrous and loud.

"Jesus Christ, Langley!" I yell, pulse still racing. "You just scared the
shit out of me!" I collapse back on the desk in relief. "What the fuck is
wrong with you?"

Avery Langley sweeps into the room with his usual cocksure gait,
lacking Kevlar or flak vest, because he doesn't care much for rules
and regulations. "What up, Dostie," he says, waving, eyes crinkled
in humor.

I gesture grandly at the broken building, its walls stripped of marble,
the gold yanked from the frames and light switches. The crystal chan-
delier somehow survived, reflecting little rainbows across the decimated
hall. "Same old, same old. What are you doing up here?"

But he shrugs, his smile full of secrets. He sits with me on the
desk, body pressed right up next to me and resting his head against my
shoulder, presenting his best puppy-eyed stare. Avery is a shameless flirt,
though he does it more out of good humor and habit rather than actual
want. He's not interested in me. I know that and so does Avery. Andres
still hates him for it, but Andres always has been a little possessive.

"Oh my God, you smell." I shove him with my elbow, trying to bury
my nose into my other shoulder. Some of the men have a competition
going on to see who can go the longest without washing his uniform or
body, and usually those who participate are preceded by a stench that
makes the eyes water. His uniform bears the typical white salt stains,

stiff, unyielding, and smelling all kinds of horrid. "Go away," I tease and he sits up, throwing his cap back. It dangles on the string around his neck.

"What's the matter?" he asks, head half-cocked. "You look fucking pissed."

I shrug. "Nothing. You just startled me, is all. Not a smart thing to do around people with guns, by the way."

He snorts. "I've seen you shoot. The safest place to be is you aiming for me."

"Fuck you, I shoot just fine," I laugh. "I shoot better than you!" Which may or may not be true, I can't remember how well he did at the range.

The door slides open from our small, hidden office and Brooks emerges, all lightly flushed cheeks and brightly lit eyes. "Hey," she says to Avery, a grin crawling across her face.

Avery ushers Brooks out of the hall as I take over the shift, sliding open the thin door that leads into the makeshift Sensitive Compartmented Information Facility. It's a small room, carefully secreted away in one corner of the floor, hidden behind a boring slab of a wooden door and jam-packed with classified equipment. The AC blasts the room with freezing air, and the sharp temperature shift is physically uncomfortable. Female King heaves on her flak vest, smoothing the Velcro down with one hand. Her Kevlar dangles in the other, leaving her blond, slicked-back hair to gleam in the white fluorescent light.

"Who's coming to relieve you?" I ask as I throw my gear onto one of the rickety spare chairs, gleefully stripping off my own flak vest. Cold air slithers beneath my brown undershirt and makes me shiver.

She shrugs. "Sergeant Lee, I think."

That's good. I work well with him. King can't leave until he arrives, though, so she leans against the wall, soaking up the last of the AC.

"Would you believe some Iraqi kid just tried to kiss me in the hall?" I toss the question out to her casually, snorting with a short laugh.

"What?" King freezes, green eyes suddenly intense. "Are you being serious right now?"

I hold up my hand, the mark from the ring still engraved in my skin. "Yeah, look. He fucking crushed my hand." I extend the fingers until they're five widely spread points. Everything seems to be working just fine.

She stares, aghast. "Dostie, you have to report that."

I pause by my equipment, tilting my head, trying to read her face. She actually means it. "I'm not reporting that," I snap, far more sharply than I intend to.

"What did you—what even happened?" She leaves her gear at her feet, pale brow angling down over dark eyes.

I shrug, but a feeling of unease is starting to crawl across my shoulders. "It was nothing. He grabbed my hand and tried to kiss me. I threw him into the wall and buttstroked him. I hit his shoulder."

Something in my story alarms her, but I can't quite pinpoint what it is. "You seriously have to tell someone about this."

"No." My voice rises in annoyance. We stare at each other in mutual perplexity. I can't grasp why she's so upset, she can't understand why I'm not. The confusion saturates the small space. "They're not going to do anything about it." I point out the obvious. "They're not going to care. They don't give a shit about that kind of stuff."

She doesn't believe me that no one will listen. I find the trust in her expression offensive. I can't be that girl again. Once reported, shame on them. Twice reported, shame on me. An anxiety seizes me, clutches my throat, and my lips peel back. "Don't say anything."

"You have to tell someone—"

"No, I don't, and I'm not. It's not a big deal." It wasn't at all. That she doesn't grasp that infuriates me. I will *not* be the girl who reports twice.

I am heavy with rage, muscles rigid with the weight of it. I regret opening my mouth. I despise this incessant need to speak, to be heard.

When I turn my back to her, she leaves to wait for Sergeant Lee outside. I fiddle uselessly with ███ and ███ on the ███. I ███ in frustration, pulling on my ███ and thrusting my feet onto the desk. I distract myself with the empty ▮▮▮ of ▮▮▮, fingers perched on keys as I lose myself to the familiar ▮▮▮. Hours slip by. Plywood covers the windows, cracks clotted with layers of green tape, sealing out the sun. I do not exist in here. Occasionally, I hear Sergeant Lee at the desk outside, guarding our boring little door, kicking loose bits of marble across the floor.

The door shudders as it opens and I thrust the book I wasn't really reading under the table, letting it slide down my leg. I cover it with one boot, casually glancing up. Sergeant Daniels pulls the door closed behind him. He is too big for the space. He stares at me for a moment, and a cold sweat rolls down my body. I look down at my work, as if a ▮▮▮ is going to abruptly appear and I will see his chest fill with pride and approval.

Except I have nothing.

I shift in the chair and the silence digs into me. I grind teeth into my tongue to keep from opening my mouth. I taste metal.

He sits, legs spread in a flawless pose of casual ease. "I heard an Iraqi grabbed you while you were coming to work."

Oh *fuck*. I want to strangle King. That she means well doesn't lessen my anger. "It wasn't a big deal. I took care of it."

Sergeant Daniels's jaw tightens. He leans back in the chair, rifle balanced across his knees. The Airborne Rangers patch is stark on his arm and my eyes trace the lines of the screaming eagle. He's angry because I said something to King. No. He's angry because I *didn't* report it to him. No. He's angry it happened at all. That he has to deal with it—no, that he has to deal with me. I can't place the reason for the way he glares over my shoulder, the way his shoulders have risen in tension. Emotion stings my eyes and makes me hunch forward, pulling inward, away.

He turns toward me and even in the dull light I can see his hazel eyes widen. "You look like I'm going to hit you," he remarks.

I wish he would. Hit me and believe me. Beat me and be convinced. If only a little pain would make them all just believe me a little more, what a willing trade I'd make.

I have no response and he gives the reasons for why I should've come to him, why I should've reported some kid making a poorly attempted pass, why I should've told them about how I efficiently handled the issue. I can't recall his words, just the worry that writhes in my stomach, letting me know I'm branded again, marked, I can see it there across my face, perhaps I should write it on my Kevlar: PROBLEM CHILD—YOU'RE THE REASON WOMEN SHOULDN'T BE HERE.

And when he leaves I don't cry because this isn't something I should cry about.

I assume this will be all. It is all so *insignificant*, so petty, they baffle me with their sudden interest and worry.

Three days pass and then First Sergeant Bell is standing by my room. Not directly in, but in front, as if guarding the small door. He smiles when he sees me, which I don't remember him ever doing much of when we were back at Fort Polk so I watch him suspiciously from my cot. His big grin causes the skin beneath his chin to jiggle and his eyes to disappear beneath the heavy weight of his white brow. His uniform hangs uncomfortably on his frame, the cuffs too short, exposing thick white wrists with pale-blue lines.

"I wanted to be the one to tell you we're taking care of the issue," he beams, as if I should be impressed. He gestures me out of the room.

"What issue, First Sergeant?" There are too many to list; I rank them in my mind, our lists disproportionally imbalanced.

"We just need you to point out the Iraqi who grabbed you and it'll be all taken care of."

My arms cross over my chest, an empty hug. "I told Sergeant Daniels that it wasn't anything major." Why are they making such a big deal out of this? My exasperation triples.

He claps me on the back, twice, chest puffed up. "This is important. You just have to point him out."

I want to roll my eyes and tell him there's no way I can find one guy among the nearly hundred Iraqi contract workers. I nod accordingly, pacify, pacify, yes-Sergeant, yes-Sergeant, can I go back to my cot yet?

"So come with me." He waves one comically oversize hand.

"What, now?" I blink dumbly. "First Sergeant," I add hastily.

"Yes, come on." It's an order.

The wind burns again. He leads me behind the company building, my head bowed against the heat, scorching sand tearing the inside of my throat. I see Sergeant Daniels first; he doesn't smile but acknowledges me. I balk at the Sergeant Major; the rank on his collar blinds his features and I shy to the side. Captain Wells stands to the other side, looking bored. He doesn't glance at me.

That beautiful rage snaps to attention and burns in my chest, threatening to spill over, and I wonder, really wonder, if he ever fears me, that I might actually do it, a slip of the finger on a little piece of metal, carefully timed, carefully aimed.

But he knows I don't have the balls.

The Sergeant Major, Sergeant Daniels, First Sergeant Bell, Captain Wells: They wait on me, duties paused, appointments held, heads turned to watch me, and I wonder if they believe me. I hate that they're there, staring at the newly resurrected "victim" label where my face should be. The Sergeant Major? Really? I remember trying to get an appointment with him back in America, scheduling a meeting, only to find it changed, shifted at the last moment and First Sergeant Bell filling in for a Sergeant Major who didn't have the time or the inclination to listen to a girl's tears.

And then I see them. They're lined up in some perverted version of a military formation, standing in rank and file, every head swiveling at my approach. They stare with eyes like holes in wind-torn faces.

I feel my jaw slide open, my knees lock, cold chills battle the heat. They wait, watching, somehow defeated already. I want to run away.

"So who was it?" Sergeant Bell asks, so calm despite the trails of sweat that slide down his cheeks.

A wild kind of horror grips me as I stand at the front of the formation of nationals, suddenly unsure I can even pick out the kid. I glance up at Sergeant Bell, lean a little closer, whispering a little softer, "What if I can't pick him out?" It was dark in the hall and there isn't much that's distinctive between the younger ones, all about the same frame, similar clothing, and I hate myself for not knowing the difference between one pair of eyes and another.

"It doesn't really matter," Sergeant Bell responds. He is wholly unworried. "It's more to make an example anyway. In their culture, the father protects the daughter. But they look at the Army women and see no father and think you have no one protecting you. So we have to let them know the Army is your father."

I consider patricide.

He waves one hand toward the group. "So just pick who you think it is and don't worry about it. It'll be a good example." I'm suddenly transported back to that room, before Iraq but after rape, when Sergeant Bell had turned to stare at my mother and asked, "Does she really want to ruin this guy's life?" The juxtaposition breaks me.

"What will happen to him?" I ask as I scan the crowd for anything distinguishing, anything I can remember.

He shrugs. "Nothing really. He'll get fired and have to leave the camp. But it's really to make sure this kind of thing doesn't happen again. They need to understand that we won't allow it."

Lies. Lies made further disturbing when they all nod, heads on swivels, yes, don't you know, we'll protect you. See, we're protecting you!

One boy glances at me frantically, up then down to his feet, up again, down, mixed with terror and shame, a wild, flittering stare, and he reeks the most of guilt. He can't be over eighteen.

I can't tell if it's his face or his apparent guilt that convinces me. "I think that's him," I say, trying to convey my uncertainty, but they couldn't care less. They are here to make a point. Let's not let facts get in the way.

Two soldiers flank him, and the boy's eyes widen, his gaze stays glued to the ground, but he doesn't protest, he doesn't speak. He walks between the much taller soldiers, compliant, defeated between their shadows, and no one looks at me now. I am contagious. The formation of Iraqis stares at the ground; the soldiers up front have better things to look at.

They dismiss me. I don't run but I walk quickly. My feet find the familiar path to my work building. The shade gives only a small relief this time and I climb the stairs numbly, until the fourth floor where I turn and climb over broken walls, cement blocks with iron rods bursting through the surface. I stumble over blasted marble, dust settling around me like a white shroud. I find a room and burrow in the rubble, spine shoved against failing drywall. I dig my feet into the floor, heels pressing down so that I am one with the wall, arms wrapped protectively around my M16.

I cry where no one can hear me, cheek pressed against the warm metal, fighting for air between body-racking sobs, tears dropping into the dust. I bawl like a child, like a girl, until the shadows lengthen and I have nothing left to give. I'm nicely empty, and quiet, and dead, and then I can go back to work.

respite

JUNE 2003 ISN'T KIND to us. Two soldiers from the regiment are kidnapped and promptly murdered, their remains found thirty-two hours later. Then there's an attack on our camp's back wall. Rumor has it that insurgents were actually aiming an RPG at a tank but missed, blowing up one of the guard towers instead. Two soldiers are killed, eight wounded. We make CNN. There's McCarthy's suicide, which takes everyone by surprise but doesn't make CNN, but the suicides never do. Rumor also has it that First Sergeant Bell was there with McCarthy, trying to talk him out of it, but, true to character, said the wrong thing and McCarthy pulled the trigger right there in front of the command. That part probably isn't true, just wishful gossip of soldiers who long for the ultimate *fuck you* aimed at an ineffectual command. There's also EOD, the Explosive Ordnance Disposal, who keep forgetting to tell the little MI unit they're about to make a controlled detonation of an IED, so that we're left scrambling for gear and instructions as our buildings sway with the roar of the unexpected blast.

It all becomes normal. There's a lot of space between these chaotic markers, and there's a kind of desperate joy in downtime as soldiers bind together to survive the boredom. There's the popular and traditional means: card games, chess, wrestling, movies on portable DVD players with groups of soldiers bunched around tiny screens. Everyone reads anything. Anne Rice's erotica series the Sleeping Beauty Trilogy sweeps through the unit, much to the amusement of the women who read it first. There's the dancing and, if you're unlucky, the singing. Then also the less traditional, like scorpion fights, running from rats, running after rats, pranks that involve throwing camel spiders at shrieking troops. The innovative, like darts with toilet plungers, donning MOPP gear and running amok. We sit in circles and smoke apple or mint tobacco from the hookah. When the time comes, we'll dress up for Halloween from random supplies found in care packages. We'll dress up for Christmas with reindeer headbands and tinsel. We hate it here but we find ways to make it home.

I spend much of my time reading, both on shift and off. When I can, I sit beside Andres on his cot, back rested against his, and devour one book after another. Eventually male McDonald will buy a TV from the locals, along with bootleg American movies, and we'll watch bad copies of whatever we can find.

Female King, female Brennan, Brooks, and Lovett make Friday date nights, where they'll climb up to our work floor, take off their uniforms, and dress up in jeans, smoking the hookah and pretending to be civilians again. I'm invited but I never go. There's something circular about the women and their bond. I can't break in. I never know if their invitation is genuine or out of pity.

If I'm not with Andres, I'm with Starre. I enjoy strolling across the camp with her, especially in the evenings, when the temperature drops to ninety and it feels cool, conceptualizing views on the universe and God's place within it. She's Christian and I'm possibly not. The farther from home I get, the larger my questions become.

Before we left Fort Polk, Sergeant Pelton issued her an M249 light machine gun, because he laughed at the idea of such a small woman carrying such a big gun. When it's slung over her shoulder, the buttstock nearly brushes her ankles as she walks. The joke's on him, though; she carries it with both confidence and ease. Starre is just that kind of soldier, meaning she's the very best kind. Back at Fort Polk, she'd drop concrete blocks into her rucksack on marches. On run days, she'd lead the pack, and the men would say she's so fast only because she's short, because they can't handle that this tiny woman has outrun them all. But she's eventually sent to the cigarette factory and I feel her absence instantly. During supply runs from one camp to the other, we pass fat envelopes filled with long letters to each other. We collaborate over a shared fantasy story, where she writes one section and I the other. She draws out a plot full of intrigue and adventure, while I add a romance between the personifications of war and death, because my writing always is a little too on the nose.

At Camp Dragoon, we get one phone call home a week on a large satellite phone. This usually entails a four-hour wait in line for a timed five-minute call. My mom misses my call once and then never again. She straps her cell phone to her body and always has the volume set on high. My father is harder to reach. There is no cell phone service in his part of Maine.

Eventually an internet café will be set up, a small room with old desktops maintained by Iraqi workers. We pay for internet access in fifteen-minute intervals, which is just enough time to send a few emails home and browse Amazon, which is mostly just books at this time. There's a careful algorithm to maintain between ordering books, when books will arrive, and how much is read in between. I grow a small library in my room. Even random soldiers I don't know come in and ask to borrow this or that. My dad sends the newly released *Harry Potter and the Order of the Phoenix*, which also makes its rounds, but I make sure to get it back, because he's written inside the cover, and I keep every little card and letter he sends in a box under my cot. I would keep my mother's letters, but then I would have no room for anything else.

We make a life at war. We don't think to ask for more but instead make do with what we have. We find hilarity and comfort between the rumbles of mortars and the rounds of AK-47s, because that's what soldiers have always done. We're no one new, just the next iteration of the same old story.

the way we're trained

BEFORE IRAQ THERE WAS KUWAIT, a holding ground for troops ready to head into war. We sit here for weeks, temporarily inhabiting long tents built upon plywood floors with no electricity, tucked between red sand dunes, our tent city stretching behind walls and walls of stacked metal connex boxes. We're waiting to be sent to Iraq, stuck at this holding base that is, quite literally, in the middle of a desert.

Kuwait has a way of depositing itself in odd places—gritty sand up the nose, pressed against the back of the neck, dark lines embedded between the legs or under the arms. It inhabits from the inside out, sandstorms crawling down our throats and back up again in inky spit or long tendrils of black snot.

We're left mostly to our own devices. We're woken up at 0530 every morning in order to do nothing. Occasionally, there are the random training sessions, like sitting hours in full Mission Oriented Protective Posture (MOPP) as we test our chemical and biological gear, wearing thick green overgarments, black rubber gloves and boots, and trying to read books through the round lenses of our gas masks as we wait for the session to end. There's also the frisk training, how to pat down locals, which is particularly invasive as well as useful, especially for us women, because eventually there will be times in Iraq that they'll need females to frisk local women workers as they come in through the gates, which could have been humiliating for all parties involved had some of the Iraqi women not made a charming game out of it, trying to hide non-contraband in odd places to test if we'll find it, not done in malice but to make us better.

Most of our time, however, is spent enduring the long trek from our tents to the DFAC hall. The deep sand hampers any movement. Sometimes along the way, Andres and I will slip between the connex boxes, fitting our bodies between the metal walls, hiding from everyone else because if we want to touch, this is the only way to do it. I find these short sessions chilling, staring up at the tall containers, wondering if one will slip and crush us, and then how long it will take for them to find our bodies.

The only eventful thing to happen in Kuwait is the tent fire. Somewhere down the line, a tent catches ablaze. No one considered this possibility when the tents were placed, because they're too close, and in the dry weather the fire leaps from one tent to the next with ease. We stand in our tent doorway, watching the growing flames in general amazement, clicking photos with our disposable cameras because this is the most action we've seen in weeks.

Then there's Lieutenant Patron racing the fire down the line at a dead sprint, kicking up a cloud of sand behind him. "Get out, get the fuck out," he's screaming, waving one arm over his head to get our attention. We all snap to, realizing the fire is rapidly coming our way, jumping from tent to tent and swiftly devouring everything inside. NCOs start barking, "Grab your gear, grab your gear," and shoving us out the back door. There isn't enough time to get everything so I pick the mandatories but swing back for my rucksack, which has my hygiene bag and a few personal items. All the gear is heavy and I lean forward, practically to my knees, trying to fight the shifting sand as we move a safe distance from our tent. Avery and a few other soldiers dash back into our tent, scrambling to grab the grenades and what ammo they can find, but it's not our tent that matters.

"Oh fuck," says Sergeant Daniels, mostly to himself. He turns around and bellows, "Move! Move! Move!" gesturing for us to go farther back.

"The ammo tent," says someone else, and sure enough the flames are licking around the edges of the tent. Everyone forgot about the ammo. We hasten farther back, slipping in our rush. Sergeant Baum, the young star sergeant of the platoon, leans down and plucks a tumbling soldier up by her rucksack and flings her back up to her feet.

"Get down!" one of the higher-ups orders, and we bury ourselves into the sand, in the prone position, like we're going to fight the fire with bullets.

The ammo tent goes up in a blaze, sounding like popcorn in a micro-wave. Heart pounding, I get my first real taste of adrenaline. I shift farther down into the hot sand and watch as the flames reach out and surround the fuel tanker that sits behind the ammo tent.

"It's going to blow," I whisper over and over, hands clamped over my ears, wondering if we're far back enough for this. But it doesn't. The fire dies out over the sand and, surprisingly, the fuel tanker is no worse for the wear.

The fire stops one tent from ours. The firefighters make it just in time to save our stuff. We trudge back into our tent and wonder what will happen to everyone else who lost their everything. "Lucky them," someone hypothesizes. "They'll probably get to go home now." But they don't. They roll out with the rest of us, with significantly less gear, and wait for replacements in Iraq. Sucks to be them.

Beyond that, the days are dull. Get up, find nothing to do, go to sleep. Rinse repeat. The living conditions don't make our stay any kinder. The engineers have electricity (that's what started the fire, or so we hear), but not the Military Intelligence units. So instead the heavy flaps of the tents, meant to keep out the burning sand, simply lock in the heat. There's nowhere to escape the insufferable temperatures. Sergeant Lee pours water into a ramen noodle cup and sticks it outside the tent wall, a rock holding the paper top in place, and in fifteen minutes it is cooked.

The camp hadn't anticipated women, so while there are some men's shower vans, we women have nowhere to bathe. So we hold up our woobies for each other in the tent bay, creating a makeshift curtain as we use wet wipes to scrub the dark sand off our skin. They leave a pungent, floral-scented layer of grime under the uniform.

One tent holds an entire company, a hundred or so of us crammed side by side, the women scattered among the men. I often toss and turn on the plywood floor, my bed made up of a woobie blanket and a deflated rucksack for a pillow.

I'm propped up against my duffel bag, trying to read a book in the gloom, when someone from Supply flips open the tent door, splashing the dark bay with stark sunlight. I blink my eyes angrily at the intrusion, but his hand is wet around the slick canteen he's holding and I lift my nose like an animal, water-starved. "Where did you get that?" I ask.

He jerks one thumb over his shoulder. "There's a water buffalo out there."

Female King's head snaps up. "There's a water buffalo?"

"Wait, when did we get a water buffalo?" Starre looks up from her book.

Locke swivels in her seat, several beds down. "Water buffalo?"

"Is it cold?" I start to ask but the guy has slunk away, and I don't really care if it's cold anyway. We have access to bottled water, but a water buffalo means disposable water that can be used for more than drinking.

King is already rummaging through her pack, collecting her hygiene bag. Locke, Brooks, and Starre are following suit. I dig out my travel-size bottles of shampoo and conditioner and hurry after them.

The water buffalo is only a few tents down, a very short walk even if the shifting sand sucks at our boots and the temperature screams at 120 degrees. We huddle around the four-hundred-gallon green-and-black portable tank like zebras at a watering hole. The water pours from a spout, creating a dark puddle in the sand, and King leans down, dunking her head under the flow. We take turns submerging our heads, releasing hair from tight buns so that the sweaty, sticky tendrils gather around our shoulders until we can hang our heads upside down under the spout.

The water is warm from the sun, almost hot, and my hair is so long that I have to hold the tips to keep the mass from dragging in the mud. I don't care. Flipping up my head so that water dribbles down my temples and neck, I gather my hair and scrub with shampoo, breathing in the fresh scent with a sense of wonder. My fingers dig into my scalp, as if I can remove the top layer of flesh, and I point my face to the sky, savoring the stunted lather.

But then I happen to glance to the side, outside our small huddle. A row of male soldiers has taken up residence outside their tent, nylon chairs planted into the sand, reclining back to watch the show. They're from some other unit, one without females. Hands laced behind their heads, they are grinning, watching.

Locke pauses, her fingers sunk into the suds on her scalp. "They do realize we're just washing our hair, right?"

King's wet hair hangs around her face and soaks the shoulders of her brown undershirt. "Fuck them."

I shy away to the side, acutely aware of the fat around my stomach, the extra bit that hangs over the top of my uniform belt and is so obvious under the stretch of my undershirt. I try to hide behind Locke to block their line of vision. Suddenly the act of washing hair seems very private, and I nervously wring the moisture from my curls. I feel on display, shockingly exposed for some reason. I think that if I were thin, perhaps the scope of their gaze wouldn't bother me. I assume that Locke and King, with their svelte forms, must not really mind, but Locke's brow is pinned together, back purposefully turned away from them, and King already has her sleek blond hair wrapped up into a bun.

A few of the men in the row clap as we walk away, and the skin at the back of my neck tightens. It's not even a quick getaway, my feet sliding in the uneven sand so that we skid and stumble in a slow retreat. We were just washing our hair. The ordinariness of the act somehow infuriates me more.

But in a camp comprising so little entertainment, even the mundane becomes exotic, so it's not long before some unnamed officer from one of the other units complains to Captain Wells that his women are distracting, that they shouldn't be walking around in their government-issued brown undershirts, that surely he must see how the fatty tissue on our chests, visible beneath our T-shirts, is highly inappropriate. Of course Captain Wells immediately informs us females that should we venture outside the tent, we now must don our DCU tops, buttoned fully up the front, even if we're just going to the latrine and back.

"This is so unfair," I protest as the men come and go in their brown shirts.

"They're fucking breasts," Locke snarls, roughly grabbing her tight, small breasts in both hands and shaking them up and down. "It's not like we can fucking take them off."

"That's not the point," King adds. "It's a T-shirt. A fucking T-shirt! How can someone be distracted by a T-shirt? It's like they've never seen a woman before."

"We haven't been here that long that they can't handle a T-shirt," I agree. And we haven't, maybe two weeks max. The other units couldn't have been here that much longer. Had we all lost sense of ourselves already? "And on top of that, maybe *I'm* distracted by *them* in their brown shirts. Have they ever considered that?" But of course they haven't.

Then Chief Warrant Officer Steele arrives, cornering Captain Wells in the middle of a bay, her sinewy arms exposed under the rolled-up sleeves of her undershirt. Her gray hair is brushed back from her sharp face and clasped in a bun, which somehow makes her features more pronounced. She does not wear her DCU top. She stands inches from Captain Wells, chin raised. She's smaller, but not really, only in physical size. She lays into him. I can hear the general rise and fall of her intonations and there is no wavering, nothing quick or slow, just an even stream that she will not allow to be interrupted.

Although Steele is in Captain Wells's unit, she is not under his command, and is protected by her title of chief warrant officer. Captain Wells is struck dumb by her even-keeled aggression, his chin tucked.

His furrowed brow makes him look like a primate trying to understand human language.

"If I have to wear a DCU top, then you have to wear a DCU top," she finishes loudly as she is walking out, turning to point one long, skinny finger at him. I want to stand and applaud.

After that, the men have to wear their DCU tops.

And then pretty soon no one does, because command realizes rather quickly how cumbersome it is to strap on a long-sleeved blouse in the desert heat just to use the bathroom.

Not that any of this is unexpected. We are the same but separate, we females in our government-issued uniforms. Narrowing the gap of separation is our ultimate goal. If to be soldier is to be male, and to be male is to objectify, then I started to learn the rules of this game long before I ever ended up on a sandy strip in Kuwait.

Some weeks into my time at Fort Polk and shortly before the rape, a few of us from the company pay another visit to the Pegasus Lounge, the finest strip club Leesville has to offer. The long room is shrouded in a haze of cigarette smoke. The purple and blue lights cut through the dense cloud, the stuffy air visible in swirling circles. I lean back in my chair, manspreading my legs and tapping the empty plastic cup against my knee. The Jack Daniel's makes me light; a warmth is spreading across my stomach and cheeks. I signal for another shot, because I don't like the taste of alcohol, and I prefer to shove it quickly down my throat rather than savor its bitter taste.

"Yeah, I'd fuck that," one of the Supply guys murmurs, and I glance up at the stripper on the stage.

The stripper is a small woman, but perhaps the word *woman* is being used a little too liberally. She is almost childlike in appearance: tiny waist, petite bare shoulders, her thong barely visible around her narrow hips. She twists artfully around a gleaming pole, eyes half closed against the harsh spotlight, as if she is dancing alone in her room to Chevelle's "The Red," oblivious to the leering crowd as she flips upside down on the pole, clasping it with her taut thighs. She crucifies herself, inverted, arms stretched wide as pale hair hangs down and brushes the stage, all in time to the screaming, raging swell of the music. Her breasts are small but tight with rose-pink nipples.

"She has great tits," I say. The words are clunky in my mouth, as if they don't exactly fit, but the men around me grunt in agreement, some tapping their hands to the beat on the plywood table.

Leesville, Louisiana, the small city that grows on the corners of Fort Polk, isn't exactly known for its class, and the fact that the Pegasus Lounge can't even be bothered to cover all its rickety tables with thin, plastic tablecloths says a lot about the surrounding clubs. Route 171 is littered with neon lights of triple X's, tattoo parlors, strip clubs, drive-in liquor stores, more strip clubs.

Court wrinkles her small nose at the stage. "I can do that."

"Yeah, okay," I say over the glare of the music, because no way can I hang upside down simply by the power of my own thighs. That takes a certain kind of cultivated talent.

She jerks her head in my direction, her hazel eyes appearing black in the shifting light. "You don't think I can?" And she is off her chair, sauntering around the table in my direction.

"Are you going on stage?" Avery Langley says a little too hopefully. Court is still hanging on to her femininity, inside her uniform and out, brushing golden hair off her shoulder, her tight V-neck T-shirt sculpted perfectly around the heavy weight of full breasts. Suddenly she is straddled over my lap, gyrating her hips against my chest, tossing hair across her flushed face, holding her cup of water and lime slice out to one side (because Christians don't drink alcohol).

"What is happening right now?" I glance around the table and sit back, arms spread in a gesture of surrender. She dances with a sensuality accomplished through youth and inexperience, the edge of her shirt occasionally rising, exposing the soft, vulnerable slope of her navel.

The men turn, they watch, because Court has that kind of unabashed femaleness that will eventually, in the streets of Baghdad, through no fault of her own, make men ask me to pull convoy guard instead of her, because that kind of feminine fragility needs to be protected.

A soldier from another unit turns his chair toward us, smirking. "I knew you MI girls were all freaks," he says. I ignore him, because I'll never see him again and I don't have to prove anything to him.

Farsi linguist Jackal slaps my shoulder as he cheers me with his beer bottle. "I'll trade places with you."

I smirk back. "I get all the bitches."

Court snarls slightly at the title and I tilt my head up, ignoring the sudden stab of discomfort, and grab her ass, yanking her closer to me because it's what they would do if they could, but they can't, and I can. "Bring it on," I jeer to a crowd of laughter. Court and I are both playing parts. But I don't understand hers and I don't think she understands mine, either.

The late-afternoon Baghdad sun beats against the back of my neck as I walk across the flat rooftop of our six-story work building. Waist-high clay-brick walls surround the roof, which provides a sense of privacy and security. I flip open my Gerber and slice the serrated blade through the empty plastic water bottle I had been carrying. I cut off the top and toss the upper half. With no working plumbing or electricity in the building, we all find it's too much of an effort to walk down six flights of stairs to a latrine when a bottle can easily answer the call of nature. I drop my bottoms and squat over the bottle, yawning as I gaze at the smoky skyline. Finished, I pull up my DCU bottoms and toss the urine over the wall, pausing briefly to hear if anyone unfortunate has been walking below. Silence. I happily hum and stash the bottle behind a broken piece of concrete for later use.

As I reach the door leading back downstairs, low laughter catches my attention. Only our platoon has access here so I move toward the voices, stepping over downed columns of concrete and mangled rods of metal.

"Dostie!" Brooks's petite face lights up when she sees me, and she waves me over. "Come here for a sec." She's sitting on the edge of the wall, Lovett leaning against the brick beside her.

"What's going on?" I hike my M16 higher on my shoulder and lean on the other side of Brooks. I don't have the balls to sit on the wall. One tough gust of wind and there you go, the quick way down six flights of stairs.

Lovett shrugs, rolling her eyes behind her black-framed combat glasses. "She won't tell me." She gestures to Brooks.

Brooks's grin deepens, her young face marked by lines of dark sand mixed with sweat. "It'll be worth it—ah, and here we go." She points to the building standing parallel with ours. One floor below us, through the glassless windows framed by jagged metal frames, two male soldiers drop their hygiene bags onto the floor. They don't think to look up and across the way so we're invisible to them as they toss their dusty DCU tops to the side.

"Ooh, shower time?" Lovett murmurs appreciatively as one of the males strips off his dank brown T-shirt, revealing a sleek, toned torso underneath.

"Shower time," Brooks says.

One of the males leans forward, pouring his canteen over his newly shorn head, the water splashing across his shoulders and trickling down his spine. They are oblivious. The other starts to undress himself, working off the uniform trousers that hang low on his hips.

We're enjoying the show, but this isn't about voyeurism. Revenge doesn't work if they don't know we're here. "That's right, baby!" Lovett cups her hands around her mouth to project her voice. "Take it off!"

Both of them start, heads jerking up in surprise, one turning around to see if the voice is coming from behind him.

"Come on, we don't have all day! Take it off!" Brooks calls and follows with a sharp whistle.

The male to the left finally looks up, seeing three females waving from our post. He immediately ducks backward, jumping out of the line of sight.

"Aw, don't run away," I call after him.

"Pussy!" Brooks yells loudly, so that the insult bounces back and forth between the stone walls of the buildings.

It's the second male who catches my attention. He stares up at us, mouth slightly agape, and he's rooted in place, caught on display, unexpectedly exposed.

"That's right, bitch," I mutter, very low, just under my breath. He can't hear me but I can.

He slowly lifts his brown shirt to cover his chest, the limp material barely blocking anything. There is something terribly vulnerable in that tiny gesture. I realize he's very young. He suddenly snaps awake and jumps backward, out of sight.

"No, come back!" one of the girls yells.

I turn around, my back to the now-empty windows. My heart is pounding. I press a fist against my stomach.

"Boo, that was too fast," Brooks pouts.

Lovett is leaning against the wall, trying to still see them. "They have to come back for their bags eventually."

My mouth is dry. "They can't take a fucking joke," I try, but the words don't fit right.

Brooks hops off the wall with a heavy sigh. "Back to work, I guess."

I wonder if anyone else finds it so stifling in here, or if it's just me who can't play the male right.

uninspired

I CATCH A GLIMPSE of Avery Langley out of the corner of my eye. He strides out of the command operations center with that bowlegged swagger of his. He doesn't see me; he glides down the dark hall, his back to me. At the last moment, just as I'm about to call out, he playfully leaps into the air, stretching one large, sun-bronzed hand for the low-hanging ceiling, his fingers slapping the already crumbling plaster. He slips around the corner and I smile to myself. At least someone is happy.

In my room, I drop my M16 by the base of my cot and peel off my uniform, which drops to the dusty floor with a wet plop. I choke on the air, slathering on military-grade DEET. My skin tingles. I spread out on the green cot, pools of sweat already forming around my body.

The recent arrival of electricity has allowed us the luxury of a fan, and the plastic ticks loudly as its head swivels. I roll my eyes back, exhaustion heavy on my shoulders and the arches of my feet. I ignore the periodic AK-47.

I'm woken by a curt yell. It's the middle of the night. Sergeant Daniels stands at the mouth of our room, seeming vaguely red in the dim light. "Put on your gear." Then he is gone into the blackened hall.

I fling my feet over the edge of the cot, tugging on my DCU bottoms, fingertips brushing the muzzle of my M16 for reassurance. I heave on my flak vest as I strain to hear the sound of M16 gunfire. There is unusual movement outside our room, heavy fall of boots on warworn carpets, but otherwise the night is distinctly quiet—no customary splatter of gunshots or the familiar boom and rumble of mortars.

Through the dim light I see Brooks shuffle into her gear, her slight body disappearing beneath the bulk. "What do you think's going on?" I ask, but she simply glances back with a stark, wide-eyed stare. King is missing; her cot is empty and I quickly rack my brain to place her—guard duty or night shift, I can't remember, but the importance lies in the distinction.

I stumble out of the room, shifting my vest into place. One of the engineers stands in the wavering electric light, jerking at our approach with a disjointed stare. "You're supposed to go to Sergeant Daniels's room," he mumbles, and there is something in the way he shifts his bulk and averts his eyes that ignites my dread.

"Where's King?" I ask Brooks but she simply shrugs in response, her Kevlar falling forward on her forehead and consuming her.

Sergeant Daniels's room is shared by what is left of the other men in our platoon; it's ablaze with lights despite the late hour. I'm immediately assaulted by cold air as I step through the door. A coughing, sputtering AC unit sits at the far end of the long room, and for a moment I'm distracted by the relief.

The guys are placed around the room in senseless order, flak vests and M16s laid at their feet. Male Sergeant Brennan's towering height is broken in half, his elbows on his knees, face lost in the cusp of his hands. They are still; the silence is physical.

I quickly scan the room of green cots and metal-framed bunk beds pushed up against the cracked walls. King perches on the edge of a wooden fold-up chair that has seen better days.

I let go of the breath I didn't know I was holding. She looks up at us and her face is white.

"You guys can sit down," Sergeant Brennan says, composing himself, straightening up and running a hand over his shorn blond hair.

I pull up a piece of floor, stripping off my flak vest and glancing around. "What happened?"

Eyes dart across the room, waiting for someone else to speak. It's Sergeant Lee who finally says, his voice heavy and grating against the bright lights, "Langley's been shot." No preamble. No warning.

I simply blink. "Is he okay?"

"He was shot in the head."

"He was shot in the head," I dumbly repeat. I find myself looking around the room again, waiting for someone to tell me it's a joke. "But didn't he have his Kevlar on?" If you have your Kevlar on, you can't be shot in the head. That's the delusional belief that keeps me going. "Why didn't he have his Kevlar on?"

But my questions are drowned out by a crescendo, a thin, wavering wail. Brooks still stands by the entrance, face crumbling under the weight of her cry. Her grief is instantaneous and her tiny hands clamp over her mouth.

The room is too bright, the sound of fabric brushing against fabric deafening. I blink again. "Are you sure?" I ask, and no one answers because it wasn't a real question.

Instinctively I reach out for Brooks, pulling her into a loose embrace, and she leans her thin body against mine; I never noticed how breakable her frame is.

Sergeant Daniels materializes out of the hall and grabs a chair, his exterior slightly cracked along one edge. He looks older. The rank on his lapels is dragging down the skin at the corners of his eyes and around his mouth. He rubs his face with one hand, then the other. I watch him faithfully, breath bated. But instead he says something terrible, something impossible, something uninspired, about the stupidest way a soldier can die, about "self-inflicted," and Brooks freezes, her breath stuck in her throat as she processes the sentence. Then the wild sobs take over once again. She is rocking back and forth in the circle of my arms.

"Dostie, bring her to the aid station," Sergeant Daniels orders.

I'm still trying to figure out why everything is so bright. I tell my legs to move and they do. I tell my arms to carry Brooks and they do. Dully,

I lead her out of the room; I don't glance back. King comes with us, leading or following, I'm not sure.

The aid station is similarly bright and I blink several times, staring back at the faces of the medics. They've been warned or perhaps they are always this grim, perpetually laden with visions of legless torsos or bloodied trunks.

"I don't understand how this can happen." Brooks is sobbing, her arms around my neck. I'm grateful to have a task. I pat her back.

I should be crying. Everyone else is crying. I probe my inner emotions, trying to stir something up, but there's nothing there to grasp. The harder I try, the more it slips between my fingers. I stare. At the thin curtain that is supposed to be a wall, through the threads that make up the curtain, through the stone walls behind, now cracked from US air strikes and periodic mortars.

"How could he do this . . ." Her sentences have no ends; she trails from one thought to the next, then glances at me for affirmation. "Dostie?" she asks, though I can't figure out why. I'm right here. "Dostie!" She strings out my name, the inflection rising in alarm at the end. I move my head so that her face fills my vision and I can see through her skull, past the mushy material of her brain and the fibers of her wheat-colored hair. "There's something wrong with her," she cries to the medics, and I could've told her that a long time ago.

There is a doctor there, a woman; she grips my arm with an iron squeeze. I can't see her features but I know that beneath her eyelids are white, spherical orbs attached to wiggling vines of red. "Can you hear me?" she asks.

I can hear you but I have no mouth. I should nod but I can't find the energy. I could motion to her but my arms are too heavy. So I stand. I stare. More hands. More medics. I hear a string of familiar terms—blood pressure, skin texture, respiration. I'm on a table, seeing through the ceiling, hearing Brooks's probing questions begging for reassurance.

I hear the term *catatonic* and it strikes me as an odd word. Cat, cat, it should be a good word—anything with a cat in it is good. I hear the doctor's voice at my ear, whispering threats of needles. Am I supposed to care about needles? "We'll do this if you don't . . . and that if you don't, we will, we will." I hear the drone and I can feel the weight of my body all the way down to my fingertips. My nails are concrete slabs.

I've been here before, in my world of white, and I wiggle down, comforted by the vast nothingness. I'll peek out in a few minutes but right now I take solace in the blankness.

I can hear the panic now, catatonic—catatonic—not responding— and I probably should respond, just a little.

I turn my head and say, "I'm fine."

Except I don't. My lips are sealed; my neck is iron. Through the haze I feel a dull prick of surprise. I fall back on old tricks, little ways to get out of this white place. Yet when I tell my hand to move, to twitch, I'm met with nothing. I envision the member, slender with blunt nails and mud packed beneath the bed. Move your finger. Move. Your fucking. Finger.

It remains dead against the paper bedding. Panic roars through my skull, screaming that I'm trapped within a prison of bones and flesh and I snatch on to the emotion, wrapping myself around it. I ride its waves back to existence. I move my finger.

My finger, my hand; I sit up. The doctor jumps back, startled, and I swivel my head to finally see her. She has blue eyes—that kind of vivid blue you don't really expect to see looking back at you. She's older, with lines around her mouth and thin, white lips pressed firmly together.

Brooks is near the bed, white with shock. "Oh thank God," she breathes, but she doesn't rush me, she doesn't hug me. I think maybe I scare her.

Sergeant Daniels stands just to the side of the entrance, looking awkward against the medical instruments and sterile environment. Too large against the doorframe. I must have called him away from far more important duties.

I swing my feet over the edge of the makeshift bed, staring down at the pattern of my uniform on my knees. When I look up, he's gone.

There is paperwork, of course. I am seated in a wobbly chair with one missing wheel. The officer sits on the other side of a laughably small desk—no doubt dragged from one of the blown-up buildings. It lacks authority.

What the desk lacks, however, the officer makes up for. Her papers are spread over the torn wood, black pen perched in long, steady fingers. I shift uncomfortably on my chair, which rocks loudly to the side. Brooks has been taken away; I have no idea where King went. The other medics cast quick, fleeting glances at me and I twist my fingers into awkward angles in my lap.

"I've...had this happen before," I say, and the doctor scribbles something far too long to be a repeat of my phrase. "I was...it's how I deal with things." I chew the inside of my cheek. "Before we came here, I was..." The declaration is caught behind my teeth. "...raped." I spit the word and it writhes on the floor in the dirt. "This is just something that happens sometimes," I quickly add, trying to brush it off, trying to scream for help.

The officer's blond head bobs and her hand flies across the page. "Your vital signs remained consistent from when you were standing to when you were lying down..." Medical term, medical term, I don't understand what she's saying but I get the gist. You're fine.

"I'm fine," I affirm.

Again that dismissive bob of the blond head.

Avery Langley's memorial service is mandatory. Work is postponed. Soldiers assemble in the theater, a small auditorium with a still-functioning stage and oddly slanted floor. Andres fumes in the seat beside me, arms crossed over his stocky chest and brow furrowed. "This is such bullshit," he complains. It's not a full ceremony but someone has managed to scrape together music, and I listen with head bowed. Tears blur my vision.

Andres grumbles another complaint and I shoot him with an angry glare. First Sergeant Bell climbs onto the stage, lingering to the side in his gangly height. He begins the Last Roll Call, plowing through the names with little care until he gets to *L*. "PFC Langley," he calls into the darkened room.

Silence responds.

"Private First Class Langley," he calls out again.

The dark room is stifling, the heat presses at my throat.

"Private First Class Avery C. Langley," a third and final time. I despise the silence.

"Let it be known that PFC Langley has been removed from the unit roster. His name will not be called again."

A strike through a name, a complete removal of existence, done with nothing more than an eraser. I contemplate the letter *D* and the precariousness of the space between *C* and *E*.

"We shouldn't even be here," Andres leans into me to whisper.

"He *died*," I snap back. "Can't you have a little respect for that?"

Andres rears back, handsome face darkening. "I'm so sick of having to talk nice about someone just because they're dead. Did everyone forget that all he ever did was cheat on his wife?"

"You don't know that," I say, but Andres is already shaking his head at me.

"He had a kid. He did this to his own kid." For all his cynicism, Andres wants nothing more than to be a father. He glares up at the stage for a moment, his hands planted firmly on his knees, knuckles white as he tightens his grip. "He was a fucking coward," he adds, softly but still bitter. "He was an asshole in life and he's an asshole in death."

I step out of my seat, desperate to put space between his anger and my uncertainty. Suicide leaves everyone off-kilter. The ceremony is over and some drift up to the stage. I follow, hesitant before the display of helmet, rifle, and boots. His Kevlar, complete with name tag, sits on top an inverted M16, dog tags dangling from the pistol grip. I reach out and gently brush the softness of the well-worn boots. Not the ones he'd been wearing that night. He had been sitting. There would be brain matter and blood all over them.

I pull my hand away. Avery had been killed in an entirely different kind of war—one with few similarities save for the bullet.

I turn away from the memorial, one arm hugging my middle. I glance up and happen to cross gazes with Specialist Price. We know each other in passing, once friendly smiles and pleasant exchanges now tarnished by the reason we avoid each other. She steps into the aisle to meet me and we hesitate there, smiles strained and trembling as we attempt to find words of comfort. We stumble into a hug, made further clumsy by our unacknowledged commonality.

Rumor has it that Price recently reported that she was gang-raped, by either a small group of Iraqis or US soldiers—the details remained muddied. Her claims are met with derision; she is either a depraved slut or a flagrant liar, the vehemence of her status wholly dependent on the one reciting the rumor and the participating party that is named.

Perhaps I partially believe the rumors, because it's easier. Perhaps she believes the rumors about me. There is never a joining in shared experience or sisterhood between us, just averted gazes and hollow phrases of nothingness. Maybe we are afraid to get too close to each other, as if our two negatives would tear a hole in the unit. Maybe we worry about the possible rumors that could come from the two raped girls huddling close together: conspiring our next rapes, collaborating our new stories. Or maybe we are both embarrassed by our own guilt—that for no matter how short of a time, we bought into their pervasive rhetoric about rape and didn't believe the other until it was too late.

I can cry now, a small spattering of tears, though I never reach Brooks level of devastation and I feel something empty in that. I hadn't been able to, at first. I recall being in that room the night it happened, moved out of the aid station to another room where there is a chaplain, though I don't recognize him. He is young with a shock of black hair. His earnestness rings false.

Grief counseling. He looks tired and I realize it's nearly three in the morning. I want to sleep but I haven't cried yet. It seems like the proper thing to do.

I'm placed in a corner, and I spread out on the floor, arms flung out to claim my space. Then it comes—the tightening of my throat, the burning of my eyes.

Relief: I'm still human.

Just as the tears slide down my temples, sinking into the loose strands of my hair, I accidently sidestep. The ceiling blurs and the tears dry on my cheeks.

"Hey, stay with me." The chaplain snaps his fingers in front of my nose, a loud, obnoxious sound, and I jolt back.

I waver back and forth between my safe white place and this precarious reality. I see, flashing like an endless loop before my eyes, the very last time I ever see Avery. He's leaping into the air, fingertips straining, stretching for the low-hanging ceiling.

ace of hearts and clubs

EXACTLY TWENTY DAYS AFTER Avery's death, Sergeant Daniels storms in our room, kicking my cot with one boot. "Get up!" He's in full battle rattle, M16 slung over his shoulder. "Get up and get your gear on!" he barks, kicking Brooks's cot. Then he's gone, devoured back up by the gloom of the hall.

The four women around me are leaping up, moving automatically into their uniforms in the dark. I think of the past month and wonder who else has died. No one wakes you up in the middle of the night for good news.

There's no time to reflect now, though. I fumble with my woobie, throwing the poncho liner on the floor. I hear it then, the cry of AK-47 fire, the occasional slower rumble of a .50-cal. I've learned to sleep through the AK-47 but the .50-cal startles me. No one shoots the .50-cal unless they mean business. My hands shake as I tug on my uniform, my gear rested carefully by my cot. I slam closed my flak vest, shrugging on the familiar weight of my TA-50 gear.

Then we're racing out of the black silence of the company building, into the warm night air. The entire city is ablaze. The sky is cut apart under the barrage of tracer bullets, like thin red fibers, crisscrossing in a quilt of fire and metal. *Star Wars*, I think to myself. I tense for falling bullets, my skin tight with anticipation of a hit, running with head ducked, watching my feet, *moving, keep moving*, a sprinting target under the burning sky.

We hurry inside the enveloping blackness of our work building and I feel an instantaneous rush of relief. There's no time to pause. My fellow platoon members flitter by like shadows and I heave my flak vest higher, trying to buy a breath of air, eyes widened for a scratch of light. No flashlights allowed—the quickest way to get shot in the head is to put a light on your helmet.

But this is well-known terrain. Sergeant Daniels has drilled this route into our skulls, so that tonight we can move quickly, we know each step and stone, and there is a brilliance in that efficiency. Sergeant Daniels, ever the Ranger, has set up the six-story building into a complex maze, a crisscrossing of floors with blocked exits and dead ends, a course we know well even in the dark, easily defendable, filled with nooks and crannies to take out invaders. We dash across the floors, up flights of stairs, past our work floor, out onto the roof, back out under that fiery sky, to the world roaring with gunfire.

"Here, here." Daniels directs us each to our own dark nook and I hunker down in position, M16 braced, and glance over the roof wall. I can see below, out across the expanse of the city, to the streets lit up, car horns blaring just under the sound of all those AK-47s. Tonight I am the sniper, the shooter in the dark, and I press against the stone structure, eyes focused on the camp walls, ready should shadowy forms flitter up and over.

The firing goes on and on, tearing the night apart, shrills and screams of heavier fire, of more dangerous things, and the terrifying *thunk, thunk, thunk* of a .50-cal. Sergeant Daniels strides across the roof, stalking like a lion, fearless of the bullets overhead. Unwavering, he is the vision of a warrior, epitome of everything I should be, but am not. He commands, we follow, and I draw strength from his calm. I stare up at him, this steadfast man, and realize this is how you get soldiers to love you—lead with fire and fervor, burn everything before you, not because you're interested in victory but simply to get your troops home. This is how you get soldiers to die for you.

Adrenaline burns like a drug, sweet at the back of my throat, and suddenly I'm alive, *so alive,* like the world is burning in high definition, aware of every part of me, every aspect of life narrowed down into this chilling moment, this glorious moment, beautiful and horrifying and wondrous. Suddenly I am giddy, almost laughing, burning up with a rage to live, an itch to destroy, and this is how the soldier becomes who he is.

Sergeant Daniels abruptly gets new information filtered in to him from his radio and the tension in his wide shoulders eases. "They're celebrating," he calls out in a slightly baffled voice.

"Celebrating? Celebrating what?" someone asks.

"Uday and Qusay have been killed."

Saddam Hussein's two sons: the Ace of Hearts and Clubs. I know their faces well from our military-issued personality identification playing cards. Each card contains the name and photo of one of the fifty-two most-wanted members of Saddam's government. I also know the stories. Iraq celebrates for a reason. Uday can no longer "discover" women on the street to rape and murder. Qusay can no longer order the execution of thousands. It's a good win.

We blink in surprise, glance at each other, startled by the suddenness of the news. It's our first real victory, the most demonstrative sign that we are winning, and we need this.

There is a sharp laugh, a bark of delight, I see my fellow soldiers' faces break into grins. "Fuck yeah," someone hollers. We unfurl, unroll our tense bodies, uncurl legs, straighten crooked fingers. Then we roar, rifles overhead. Adrenaline thundering through my veins. This moment I'll remember, so clear and vibrant, effervescent and intense. This feeling I'll chase forever.

"All right, calm down," Daniels yells over our cheers. He knows better than we do that just one gun turned the wrong way can morph celebration into a full-force attack. He knows the swinging of an RPG in the midst of rejoice can demolish our walls. He leads us down one floor to our work site, where we are to guard our top-secret materials and equipment.

"Get away from the windows," he orders, and I pull farther back into the hall, legs sprawled out in front of me. I continue to stare out the window, though, watching the tracers flash by, casting red flares of light against all the broken shards of glass on the floor.

And so we wait. Giddy, awed, yet anticipating. Because even when it's good, you always, always wait for it to go bad.

what isn't mine

UDAY AND QUSAY ARE KILLED. Saddam eludes capture. Life in Iraq rolls on. I'm trying to keep a relationship alive in this shithole camp, and I'm failing. Andres doesn't seem to notice.

Sex between soldiers is strictly forbidden in Iraq. It doesn't surprise anyone. Had we been ordered not to breathe we would have nodded and said "sure, sure," then taken to the task of breathing when no one was looking. The difficulty isn't in the order but in not getting caught while breaking it.

It might not surprise anyone, but it does make life difficult, especially if sex is the only way you know how to keep a bond from dying. Most soldiers explore dark corners among broken-down walls and nest between concrete and shattered drywall. Andres and I have been there, done that, but a couple of weeks ago I got startled by a very large rat in a very dark room and so I demanded we find less infested places. The most convenient place is the outside shower (the only shower), the makeshift room we had created when we arrived, walls built not with drywall but with broken wooden doors. At the request of the women, the cracks were eventually sealed with duct tape and bits of rags. It offers a small piece of solitude, if you can catch the room in between shower times, which are typically early morning or late night, before or after the crux of the heat, when the five-gallon jug of water doesn't instantly turn to sweat the moment it hits the body.

My uniform top is unbuttoned and my brown undershirt raised so that the air can cool the sweat at the base of my spine. Andres slips a hand farther up my shirt, thwarted by the sports bra, but there isn't time to take any of it off. He playfully nibbles my neck, trying to make it romantic, he's always trying to make it romantic, but my palms are pressed against one of the doors, uniform pants wrapped around my ankles, boots still tied, and there's nothing sweet about this. My head lolls forward, eyes open; I try to find the pleasure in the jarring thrust, the slap of skin on skin bouncing across the door-walls, but this feels like rutting to me.

I resent the rules that reduce me to bending over in a dark, dank room somewhere in Baghdad, with dirty water splashing around my feet, in order to get some human relief—but even this doesn't make me question them. American law is foreign to us, we belong to the Uniform Code of Military Justice now and the UCMJ isn't all that keen on individual freedoms. Sign on the dotted line and suddenly nothing is mine. *You're government property now*, and none of it is sacred.

Our bodies aren't ours. When Andres complains, "We're all fucking Commies," I can't actually argue and at the time it didn't really matter. We had simply moved from one parental institution to another, so that years later, when my enlistment is up and my rights are finally placed back into my hands, I won't quite know what to do with them anyway.

Andres murmurs something against my cheek, my hair escaping from its bun and tickling my ear. I want to snap, *Just finish already*, but it's not his fault he started dating me when it was just a few weeks too late and there was already something hard and dead growing in my chest. More than this emotionless sex, I want to instead grab his arm, to press my palm against his bare forearm, as if I can draw comfort from that touch, but even I know that's weird.

Andres hears it before I do, his hand snaking out and clamping his sweaty palm over my mouth even though I haven't made a sound.

There it is again, the hard *rap, rap, tap* against one of the wooden doors. My eyes widen and my breath freezes behind Andres's palm. I turn, Andres falling out of me. "Someone's in here," I stutter and Andres is jerking up his pants, fastening his belt.

Again the knocking and my hands shake as I fumble for my pants, my fingers tangling in the buttons.

"Who's in there?"

Fuck, fuckidy fuck, I know that voice. Involuntarily my teeth clench together. Captain Wells. Jesus Christ, couldn't it have been anyone but him?

"I'll be right out," I respond as Andres is doing wild little circles, frantically looking for a way out, but thanks to us women the doors are securely taped and there's no other exit.

Captain Wells is knocking at the door again, as if I've kept him waiting for hours, and my heart is hammering. I quickly sling my M16 over my shoulder as I look up, as if Andres could scale the sleek doors and escape over the walls.

"Open this door now."

Fuck you. "I'm changing."

Andres gestures at the door, for me to open it and he'll slip out the side, he even whispers it, as if his voice can't carry through wood. It's as good a plan as any, and I grasp the one loose door that serves as an opening into the shower. I lift it, tilting it outward to block Captain Wells's view, and Andres darts outs and around the corner. In another world, it would've been the perfect getaway.

Captain Wells steps toward the corner, short, stubby neck craning, making his prominent forehead all the move noticeable as he snaps, "Who was that?"

"Who was who?"

Captain Wells follows the dark shadow that was Andres, calling after him as Andres darts into the company building. With his other prey lost, Captain Wells turns back to me, his dark eyes glittering in the low light. He enjoys this. "Who was just with you?"

I'm rooted in place because I've never really been in serious trouble, unless you count the time I served detention in elementary school because I was chewing gum, and it was all Lilly Morrison's fault because she was the one who gave me the gum in the first place. "No one?" I say hopefully, conflicted, not wanting to give up Andres yet not prepared for the full scorn of my superior officer. I know I'm going to cave in because I don't know how not to. It'll take years before I learn I can stare into the eyes of a man and not give a shit about his authority or opinion, but not now. I'm not there yet.

I nervously kick dust around my boots as he waits, unmoving. I squirm, relent, and whisper, "Andres," though I don't really have to. Andres hasn't gone far, waiting at the mouth of the company building, maybe because he knows I'll be so easily broken.

In my peripheral I see Captain Wells smirk; it makes his moon-pale face even uglier. "Both of you." He points at Andres, who is now visible again. "Let's go talk to Sergeant Daniels," he says, and my stomach drops.

Captain Wells likes that I'm having sex. He gets a chance to punish me, but it also proves his point. Girls like me shouldn't be having sex. Girls like me shouldn't be *able* to have sex. It must all be lies if I can do it so easily. I can see the accusation in the assured rise of his shoulders. *This proves everything*, he seems to say in the lengths of his stride.

I want to tell him that it's the exact opposite. I was a stupid girl before, when I had thought sex was all so sacred and special. It's for love, I had thought. It was something to be cradled, drawn close to the chest, then passed with the utmost care from my hands to the ones I've painstakingly chosen. Idiot that I was then.

Now I know what is mine can never be taken, and if it's taken, it was never mine. We're all just meat sacks tied together with skin and tendons, grotesque when you actually think about it, your flesh no more yours than a pair of jeans or a particularly fancy pen. I didn't understand anything back then. Such blindness was just a defense mechanism, I've come to learn. Ways to create roads and pathways so that I would feel safe, saying, "Well, *I* wouldn't have done..." or "*She* shouldn't have done..." thinking that would protect me, as if I had some measure of control, because if I ever stopped to contemplate, I'd realize that all those carefully constructed roads of *wouldn'ts* and *shouldn'ts* create nothing more than a slender, glittering web that can be easily swiped away by a careless hand. Control and possession are nothing more than beautifully decorated delusions. I realize this now.

But Captain Wells wouldn't understand that, and I can't find the words to say it anyway. Instead he brings me before Sergeant Daniels, who sighs, rubbing the bridge of his nose with his forefinger and thumb. *What am I going to do with you*, he doesn't say, but I feel it in the way his dark eyes wearily stare back at me. I want to respond that at least I'm putting this meat sack and tendons to good use. What does it matter if I lend it out and give a bit of pleasure here and there? But then there's that hard, dead thing in my chest, and I wonder how much my realizations have cost me, so I look away, breaking his silent gaze, and say nothing.

I absently rub the space beneath my left collarbone, as if I can warm it, thinking that perhaps the thing has grown, remembering when I first noticed it here.

It was on a weekend of R&R that I first noticed it, when I was given a short leave into the Green Zone, where they told us to *relax*, as if that were possible after they had taken away our rifles. They let us aimlessly wander through one of Saddam's old officer retreats, complete with movie theater and blue, Olympic-size pool. I had been on R&R once before, when I was randomly almost blown up by a stray mortar, but this time there were no Delta forces situated across the river to volley mortars with insurgents, so the nights were uneventful.

Andres was sent with me on this weekend getaway. I think Sergeant Daniels purposefully arranged it because he knew we were fucking. Dating, actually, but everyone calls it fucking. Sergeant Daniels hated rules that made no sense; he trusted his soldiers were smart enough not to get pregnant. He got to help out one of his soldiers while holding a middle finger up in the air at the command. Two birds, one bullet.

Andres and I sat in the theater and watched Robert Redford's *The Last Castle*. They always played military movies, like we'd forget we were in the army if they showed anything softer. I liked the movie but Andres didn't. Anything that revolved around soldiers rallying behind a single man was bullshit to him.

"None of that would happen in real life," he complained as we left the theater. We were in PT gear and the rules were flexible here, so no one complained when we held hands.

"This coming from the man who thinks *Scarface* is the pinnacle of filmmaking."

"I can't date you if you don't like *Scarface*."

"Well, then," I joked with a shrug, and he gripped my hand tighter because we both knew I had all the power here. He always said he loved me first and I repeated it because it was nice to be loved.

The other soldier zeroed in on me as we exited. He ignored the hand-holding. He ignored Andres entirely. He played the kicked puppy well, resting his hand on my forearm, trailing just to the side of me, as if the very act of touching me somehow soothed him. He had a stare that was off. He wasn't actually staring at anything but instead through it, to the other side of it, as if he could see the inner workings of things that the rest of us were blind to. I know that stare. I hate that stare.

He cornered us at the edge of the theater, spoke about nothing, perpetually holding my arm until Andes stormed off, expecting me to follow, and I wanted to, but my every attempt was blocked with injured protest.

"Please stay with me," he begged, staring at my cheekbone, tugging at my forearm, and so I awkwardly followed him to his room, not sure how to untangle myself from this situation, or how to ignore his mournful coos and plaintive manipulation, and that's probably why he chose me— because I didn't know how to tell him to fuck off.

"Don't worry," he reassured me, "I'm safe."

No one's safe, I started to say, but I could see already that he was broken; there was no power in the slope of his shoulders, and his head hung forward, as if it were dragging down the rest of his body. "It's okay, it doesn't work anyways." He gestured to the space between his legs. "It hasn't for weeks. Just stay with me, please?"

"Just for a minute," I said, afraid to just turn on my heel and leave because he reminded me of a baby bird I had once found on the gravel outside my bedroom window, back before the Army. The bird was gone the last time I checked on it. Maybe it flew away, but a cat probably ate it.

I sat on the bed in his room because there was nowhere else to sit, sinking into the soft comforter that they would never give us outside the Green Zone, and he immediately crawled across the space between us, hunkering down before me and placing his head against my lap. Shocked, I raised my hands, uncertain where to put them, but he didn't notice. His knees curled upward, as if he wanted to hug them, a half-fetal position with his head pressed against my womb.

I glanced back toward the door and worried what Andres would think. I worried about rumors and insinuations. But I also worried about the baby bird that was going to get eaten by the cat.

"I'm a medic," he said, his mouth brushing against my knee, one hand curled beneath his chin. "I've been on R&R four times now. They keep sending me here. They think it'll help."

I didn't have to ask what the rest and relaxation was supposed to help with—it was written all over his face. "They should send you home." I finally placed a hand down, letting it rest on the side of his head, fingers sinking into the soft brown hair.

"They won't. They'll never send me home." His voice was so very thin. "I go back tomorrow."

I waited for the catch, the hook, for him to say he was going to die so why not? Just this once? Give a dying man a good memory. I hardened myself against it but it never came. Instead he nestled down and began to talk.

"I was there for the UN bombing—"

(So was I, when the explosion shuddered through Baghdad, so loud and instantaneous that it had stolen my breath, my legs giving out so that I crumpled to the ground, hands clamped over ears, and the newly installed glass windows shivered, rippled, miraculously held while rattling in their metal frames. Then I scrambled to my feet, dashing around the corner to my room where I shouldered on my gear, the heavy press of my Kevlar vest smacking against my ribs, then back, running around the corner to stand by the open door, staring slack-jawed at the growing column of smoke, a pathetic imitation of Nagasaki's mushroom, yet pluming, curling, swelling around itself in inky black lines, already filling the air with the stench of burning rubber and metal, and First Sergeant Bell was screaming, demanding all combat-lifesaver-trained soldiers meet at the aid station, where I reluctantly turned, heading to the station, knowing how to stop a sucking chest wound from a bullet and place a tourniquet on a demolished limb but *knowing* and *doing* are two totally different things and I knew I didn't want to do that, but then there was Sergeant Daniels, grabbing my elbow, saying, "No, she's mine," so that he could collect his platoon, ferreting us away to the top of our work building, because Rome could burn and Sergeant Daniels would play the fiddle but only with his platoon tucked safely behind him.)

"—and me and these other medics, we had to run into one of the buildings because there were people in there, you know? Or at least we thought there had to be. So I end up alone in the basement, I don't know where the fuck my sergeant went, and there's water up to my thighs, like this cold, fucking nasty water, I don't even know where it's coming from. All I'm thinking is there's going to be a spark somewhere and I'm going to be electrocuted to death, just poof, go up like smoke and no one's going to find me because this water is *black*.

"So I pass by this room, I'm calling out for anyone who needs help, and I swear to God I almost kept walking. I stopped for a second and I looked at the guy, and I was like, nope. Just keep moving. No one would even know. I didn't have to go in there, you know? I mean, I really just stood there and honestly thought about turning around because *Jesus fucking Christ.* And he was making the most horrible noise, too, like he was screaming at the back of his throat. Or coughing but it was wet and just fucking...

"I don't know, maybe he saw me, but I couldn't leave him. He was so fucking dead, he just didn't know it yet. This metal frame had him pinned down and I couldn't tell if the rods actually went through his body but the water was rising and here I am thinking I *should* be worried about him drowning but fuck if he's not burned over every inch of his body. It's like his uniform is melted onto his skin and his skin is just melting in general. It's all stringy, kind of like plastic? You know, like when you were a kid and would try to melt one of your toys? The way the plastic becomes that thick, pink goo?

"I don't know where the fire came from. I don't even know where the *water* came from but he had obviously been there a while and I'm like, shit, how are you still even alive? So I pull out the gauze from my bag. When you have a bad burn patient, you always have to put dry bandages on it. No ointment or water or shit, it has to be dry. And here I am, pulling out the bandages from my bag and I *drop them* into the fucking water. I stand there, staring at these bandages, and now I don't know what to do and he's *looking* at me, like I'm here to save him and he's so fucking excited, maybe, or maybe he just wanted me to do something about the pain, and I literally can't *do* anything because I just dropped the fucking bandages.

"Then he begins to choke. And I'm thinking he maybe swallowed something in the water so I go to open his mouth so that I can check his airway. When I put my hand on his jaw, you know, to open it, it just...came off in my hand. Like the entire bottom half of his face is just sitting there, in my hand. And he's still fucking alive. He's still choking and I don't know what to do because his jaw is missing, I still have it in my hand because what am I supposed to do with it? Throw it away? He was literally choking on his own skin that was breaking apart in his throat and he's still *staring* at me."

He fell silent for a moment and I realized they really should send him home. Or maybe they shouldn't. He was dead anyway. His body just hadn't realized it yet.

"I can't sleep," he added.

"Just close your eyes for a little," I said, lightly running my hand over his head, petting him, sickened. But I couldn't just leave him there.

But he didn't close his eyes. He stared, and finally said, "What if I can never feel again?" His voice was ragged, and it planted the seed between my second and third ribs even as I squirmed uncomfortably away from the thought.

But the seedling didn't really sprout until a day later, when another soldier caught me sitting alone in a room. Andres had gone to get food and this guy plopped down across from me into a wingback chair, the beaten down royal-blue cushions the last remnant of opulence, covered in dust and clashing with the sandy desert uniform. He didn't share the medic's gaze; his eyes were blue and direct, they bore through my skull, daring me to look away, the end of an unlit cigarette butt clenched in his mouth.

"It's the easiest thing in the world to kill a man," he boasted after a quick introductory exchange, as if he had been waiting to say it. As if my reputation had preceded me, whispers exchanged between soldiers: "Her, that one. Yeah, get her, she'll talk to you *all* night long," as if I were Mother Soldier, here only to be unburdened upon.

"All you do is line up your sights"—he held up an imaginary rifle, one cheek pressed against an invisible buttstock—"and pull the trigger." He was all tobacco-stained teeth and half-closed eyes as he lounged in the chair. "Easiest thing in the world."

His grin flagged slightly at the corners, though, pulled down in lines that for an instant made him look very, very old. "I'm afraid to go home, though."

"That's crazy," I responded. "Everyone wants to go home. What could you possibly be afraid of?"

"I'm afraid to see my wife and kids again." He stared over my shoulder so that I wouldn't see something very old consume the corners of his eyes. "I don't think I can ever love again."

I don't think I can ever love again. I felt the statement hit me like a slap. It had never occurred to me before then that that could happen, that we could lose our love, but now it was like he had rung a cast-iron bell between my ears. It was all I could hear.

These are the things that are supposed to be ours, I wanted to say, though I'd have to shout to hear my own voice over the noise in my head. The ability to love can't transfer ownership, I almost said, but instead I leaned forward and gently patted his hand. "It'll be fine," I lied, to him and to myself. "Everything will go back to normal when we go home."

He gathered himself, watching my face; I don't know what he saw there. Then he snorted, his grin returning full tilt. "Fuck yeah, I'll be all right," he also lied with gusto.

And there that hard, dead thing sat. There it grows, a little thing in my chest that I rub, just below the collarbone, as Captain Wells discusses punishments with a terribly disappointed-looking Sergeant Daniels.

The sentence suits the crime—Andres and I are no longer allowed to openly consort. He is grounded to his side of the company and I must stick to the other, and we must be very careful never to let our paths overlap.

Andres huffs, puffs, kicking the wall as Captain Wells strides away, growling, "He can't even prove anything was happening! He didn't see shit. It's his word against ours." I almost ask him why he even bothers. Captain Wells doesn't need proof; his word is god.

"But you can pass notes to each other, if you want," Sergeant Daniels leans down to murmur in my ear; this is his peace offering, spoken softly so that Captain Wells can't hear as he walks away.

"I get it," I say to Sergeant Daniels.

But I don't. I don't get any of it, not then. Years will accumulate while I try to dissect the tinnitus of cast-iron bells, obsessing over my dis-interest, my aloofness, memorizing the words for love (عشق, 愛, amour, amore) though the sounds will roll around in my mouth, incomplete, like some Sanskrit root lost without its suffix, entangling myself in bedsheets and limbs, somehow hoping I'll eventually find the etymon of the word. Until I'll realize feeling nothing is *something*, and I'll think this is what it must mean to be adult. "Yes, let's call it maturity," I'll coo to lovers, dressing up the growing chasm between them and me as emotional wisdom, knowing it's all just meat, it's all cold and hard, and if you don't know that, you're the fucking fool, not me.

And when you all look at me with that patronizing sneer, smearing me with your superior pity, saying, "I'm so glad you came home safe," with one side of your mouth while dropping the words like "hopeless" or "traumatized" from the other, I'll sneer right back, saying, "You, stupid, blind people that you are, how does delusion taste? At least I know what isn't mine."

rage against the machine

IRAQ IS THE PERFECT place for rage. War cultivates it, nurtures it with careful hands, like a fine pruned flower. I don't realize how far the roots go, or what will send it blooming.

On duty one day, nearly a year into deployment, I pace the dark hallway of our work building. Sergeant Daniels has turned the entire floor into a skiff, a Sensitive Compartmented Information Facility, meaning the floor needs to be guarded at all times, protecting our equipment and sensitive information. I kick at small bits of debris, watching the white stones tumble down the long hall. I'm bored. I'd read a book if I had one, but I long ago went through not only my own stash but also everything in the company's library. I hop onto the desk, crossing my legs and balancing my M16 over my knees, just for something to do. The sun shifts, cutting through holes in the walls, flooding sections of the hall with broken shafts of light.

So when I see a shadow dart into one of the rooms at the far end of the hall, I think it *must* be my imagination. I freeze, clenching the rifle with one hand, breath held. I blink, rub my eyes, and lean forward, straining to hear, staring hard at the corner where I thought I had seen it. Did I hear footsteps? The stirring of debris?

I swallow hard, my throat suddenly dry. "Hello?" I call down the hall, very unofficial, very startled. I shake my head at the civilian-sounding attempt. I jump off the desk and pull the soldier on for size. "Halt! Who goes there?" Now I sound firm, professional.

No response.

I glance back at the doorway I'm guarding. Sergeant Lee and our Arabic linguist are inside the blocked-off office, working on our equipment. I can call out to them, pull one of them out here to back me, but if there's nothing here but rocks and wind, will word get out that I'm afraid of shadows?

Pulling my rifle to my shoulder, I take a few steps down the hall, breath caught in my throat. I must be imagining things. My heart is aflutter; I can't tell if I'm terrified or excited. It tastes the same.

I move close to the wall to make myself a smaller target and to better assess the space. Training has set my body to auto-control. *Stay next to the wall but not close enough to brush it. Don't give your position away.*

A doorway into a room.

Had it been a room in any other building, I could've walked right past, heading straight to where the figure had darted. But in here, the walls are different, the stone and drywall destroyed. Nearly every room has holes wide enough to be doors and anyone could walk from the first room to the last simply by hopping through rubble.

A wave of adrenaline rushes through me. Now I can see better, hear better. It's a pinpoint existence—the world in Technicolor. I don't have much training in military operations in urban terrain, but I know the basics, enough to make me dangerous. I meticulously walk a semicircle around the corner of the doorframe, scanning half the room from corner to corner. I quicken my pace as I pass the "fatal funnel," where I am the most exposed. I swing to the other wall, making the last terrifying turn to make sure no one is right there, pressed against the wall in my blind spot.

No one.

Relief is short-lived. I'm not sure how serious to be, if this is part of my imagination and I'm a fool clearing rooms in which no one exists. I feel like I might be chasing shadows. But then I hear something. I *know* I hear something. Or at least, I know I *think* I hear something, and I move to the next room. I realize my rifle is still on SAFE and I thumb the little knob, reluctant to move the switch. A hundred scenarios race through my mind telling me not to switch from SAFE to SEMI. A soldier playing a very stupid joke? Sergeant Daniels testing me? Rifle tucked into my shoulder pocket, I recall the urban legend of the Iraqi woman who was said to have approached one of the gates, who supposedly didn't stop when they screamed "Halt" and "*Qiff! Qiff!*," who kept on moving until they shot her down in the street, the rifle fire cutting her in two, and the bundle that was in her hands, which spilled out onto the pavement, wasn't explosives at all but instead cookies for the soldiers.

I can't shoot someone by accident. That I will not do.

I hesitate by the next doorframe, presented with a new dilemma. If I continue down the hall, the person can dart through the walls, pass the room I cleared, and come up behind me. But if I go through the holes in the wall, they can do the same trick using the hall. This is a two-man job. But I don't go back for help. Someone is here, *maybe*, and turning back would give them free access to the hall and rooms. I grit my teeth, furious I left the radio on the desk.

I take the hall. It's faster. I repeat the process, clearing half the next room, darting across the doorway, clearing the other side. The room is dark and empty.

I turn from the doorway, glancing once over my shoulder to make sure no one is lurking behind me, and a man steps out from the next room, directly into my path.

I halt instantly, but he's so close I can see the dark hairs on his face, the fine dust on his dishdasha. I swing my M16 up, half gasping, but he's too close. I register this even as I point the muzzle at his face, realizing all he has to do is bring up one hand and slap it away, wrestle it out of my grasp, turn it on me, pull the trigger, and unload the clip. I have a sudden epiphany, a moment of clarity as I realize he's bigger than me.

I jump backward, boots sliding on the rubble, screaming, "Get back! Back the fuck up!" It doesn't sound like my voice; it's deep, hard. Masculine. "I said back the fuck up!"

But he's rooted in place, staring at the end of my rifle.

My brain freezes up, too. I back up, putting more space between him and me so that he can't reach out and touch the muzzle. But I don't know what to do. He's not listening to me as I scream and for one terrorizing second I realize I might have to do it, really, actually do it, but my rifle is still on SAFE. I take in a short breath, but it's not to steady the rifle.

And then an American soldier trudges out from the room behind him, glancing from my rifle to the Iraqi with a dull, almost bored expression. "Hey," he grumbles in greeting. "He's with me."

Hey? *Hey?* With all the adrenaline pumping through my system, for a second I can't process what he's saying. The relief is abrupt enough to make my knees weak. But in place of all that emotion, rage fills the void.

"Yeah, we were just up here looking for—"

"What the *fuck* is wrong with you!" I scream, dropping my weapon, and suddenly I'm very close to his face. I invade his space. His head pulls back in surprise but I can't stop. Rage vibrates through me and pours out of my mouth. "Didn't you hear me asking who was there? Are you too dumb to read? You can't see all the TOP SECRET, DO NOT ENTER signs everywhere?"

He blinks dumbly at me, a short kid from the First Cavalry unit that just rolled in. "I just thought—"

"I could've shot him because you're a fucking idiot!" I want to hit him for being so stupid. I want to smash the butt of my rifle into his oversize nose, again and again, simply for putting me in that position. I'm suddenly enraged at his inexperience, his newness to the war and Iraq, his youth. "Get off my floor! Get the fuck off my floor!" I order him and he stumbles back, quick to turn back the way he came. He doesn't run, and I almost wish he would. "And don't you *dare* come up here again," I call after the both of them.

I can't stop shaking. My hands tremble, my knees are wobbly. I feel it in my teeth; they ache, my gums throbbing. I can't breathe; I'm being suffocated by my own anger. It squeezes my chest tight and I'm not having a panic attack, I'm having a rage attack.

The door to the work office swings open. "What's going on?"

It's our Arabic linguist. I wave him away. "Nothing. I got it." But I'm hyped up all day, stalking the halls, tense, trembling, brimming with rage.

And I don't really know why.

But with every day it grows.

monster in a box

FEMALE KING AND I are on guard duty the day the Red Cross is blown up. It's a day shift, and even though it's now autumn, my undershirt is saturated and my boots are filled with sweat. My gear weighs on my shoulders. I lean against the wall, resting the edge of my flak vest on the concrete ledge of the window cutout, relieving some of the pressure in my muscles—but my neck is already tight. We aren't allowed to sit, and by the second hour my knees are sore. I lift one foot at a time, trying to shake away the pain in my ankles and at the arches.

King mirrors this dance and though she's even more weighted down with her M203 grenade launcher and ammo, she bears it without complaint. The bright sun washes over her profile as she watches the streets. "I don't get why anyone would feel ashamed for being raped," she is saying. She might have shrugged her shoulders but it's hard to see under the gear. "It's not like it's her fault."

We are talking about it in a roundabout way, saying neither *I* nor *you*. I will learn later that she didn't actually know. She came to Fort Polk after my assault, and I'm inserting subtext that was never there.

It's not that easy, I'm about to say when King perks up, straightening her posture. "Hey, look." She points below. I pull my gear off the lip of the window and lean forward to see the street.

At the base of the tower, standing several feet from the glinting rolls of concertina wire, a woman stands. She's young and pretty, her face tilted up toward us. King waves and the woman smiles, tentatively, her cheeks round, flushed from the heat. By her side and tightly gripping her hand, a small girl buries her face against the black folds of the woman's chador. The woman leans down and whispers something to the girl, who peeks out. Her face is dominated by large, dark eyes. The woman points at us and I can hear the lyrical rise and fall of her voice. The girl purses her lips, as if in disbelief.

I grin and tug at the chin strap of my Kevlar. I've done this before, mostly only on request, when mothers hold up young girls to better see the "woman soldier," or young boys and even men come to the towers and gesture for me to remove my Kevlar. I tug at my bun, releasing a long tail of black hair. It's dirty with sweat and sand, sticking together in greasy strands, but the effect is the same. The little girl's eyes widen, her mouth puckering into an O. The woman, perhaps her mother, grins, now crouched next to the girl. King turns her head so that her own blond tuft of hair is visible in the light. Eyes still wide, the girl waves, first a flash of one small fist, then more vibrantly, a grin brightening her face.

We wave down to them, a wordless exchange of greetings, and I'll never get tired of seeing this.

I tug my hair back into its strict bun and quickly replace my Kevlar. The woman gives one last wave and has to tug at the hand of the little girl, who keeps throwing glances over her shoulder as her mother pulls her along.

"I wonder if she's ever seen a female soldier," I muse as the two disappear down the road. "I saw a woman driving the other day. Like driving her own car. I started cheering."

King gives a short laugh. "Probably scared her half to death."

"When I was like fifteen or something, I went to Haiti on this missionary trip and I remember being on the street and seeing all these US soldiers drive by in tanks and Humvees. Now that I think about it, I don't even know why they were there." I pause for a moment to consider that. "In any event, we waved like crazy and I remember them all waving back and smiling." It's a fond memory, seeing those soldiers perched half exposed in their tanks, somehow bigger than life, almost mythical, part man, part metal beast. "They were really friendly."

King glances at me with a wry grin, blond brow raised. "Yeah. We are."

I turn to her, face blank in sudden realization. I bark out a loud, single syllable laugh. I'm no longer the civilian girl on the street. When had those tables turned? "I guess we are!"

She is good-naturedly rolling her eyes when the explosion rocks our tower.

The sound knocks the air from my lungs. Sudden. Deafening. The tower sways; my ears ring. The floor tilts and I wonder for a moment if the stones will hold—if it will all tumble to the side, dragging us down the twenty-five feet and burying us below, brick by brick. My teeth vibrate with the residual noise. I reach out, fingers brushing against the stone, then wrapping around metal. Once again my training kicks in, my body operating on reflex—a puppet I don't need to control. I'm already at the ledge, hip pressed firmly against wall, M16 buttstock planted firmly into the pocket of my shoulder. I don't remember moving.

"What the fuck was that?" King yells. She has jumped into position, too. The radio squawks. The air tastes of metal and blood. I gulp down endorphins. We scan the skyline.

A column of smoke twists like a black, uncoiling snake but the actual explosion site is blocked by rows of sandstone houses.

"Shit, shit, shit," I mutter through clenched teeth, trying to better fit my rifle into my shoulder. My cheek can't reach the right spot on the buttstock, I can't align my sights because the SAPI plates block the pocket, throwing off my hold. I had never touched a SAPI plate until my boots hit foreign soil. It's an issue I noticed my first day on guard duty when I realized I had never shot my rifle from the standing position—only in a foxhole, training that was better suited for World War II than Iraq. Now my bun is caught between the collar of my vest and the lip of my Kevlar, forcing the front of the helmet to slide forward to block my vision. I yank at my hair tie, fingers ripping out hair by the roots, until I can slap the Kevlar up.

I see a white Toyota pickup truck barreling down the road, nose pointed at the tower. It weaves wildly through the tight-knit traffic.

"Fuck." A single, soft expletive. My sloppy hold tightens.

Silence. There is no yelling between King and me. This is no fast-paced movie scene. We stand in terse silence, our muzzles swung toward the vehicle as it draws to a halt just outside of the concertina wire. A man in a red-and-blue-plaid shirt jumps out from the back of the white Toyota.

I flatten my cheek to my M16, as if pressure alone will improve my aim. The vehicle is too close to the tower. Perfect location for a suicide bomber.

I know I should be shouting some kind of order but I can't remember what, so I simply stare. My thumb pad rests against the metal safety switch. I hesitate.

Back then, when I was more human than monster, I didn't know if I could do it.

Another man swings open the passenger-side door, half outside of the vehicle, hand planted on the doorframe. He yells something I can't understand.

The safety selector indents my fingertip, still pointed at SAFE.

The man stops outside the wire, dark hands cupped around his mouth as he shouts up at me. I attempt to focus on center mass but my gaze keeps drifting up toward his eyes. "What is he saying?" King asks. She covers her side of the tower, leaving the yelling man my sole responsibility.

I pull my cheek just slightly from my rifle. I don't know what I'm doing. "What?" I yell down at the Iraqi.

He waves both hands over his head now, urgently, body tense, fingers stretched wide and upward. "They bombed the Red Cross!" he yells in heavily accented English. "The Red Cross is on fire!" the man reiterates, then he spins and turns back to the car. The passenger is still shouting something in Arabic, his tone hard and fast.

"Wait, should we let him leave? I don't think we're supposed to let him leave!" My own voice rises and I pull off the wall, glancing from King to the retreating car. The uncertainty burns like an ache in the back of my throat.

King stands there, rifle hanging in her hands. The truck is already gone.

I stare at her as the adrenaline trickles off. My knees are weak. The realization that we are safe is euphoric. I have to lean against the wall for support.

King's lips stretch slightly, the quick rise and fall of her shoulders the only indication of an outward emotion. "The fuck?"

But I'm swollen with pride. Pride and exhilaration and relief as my skin buzzes and hums. I glance down at the rifle I still hold firm and grin. My body had moved with confidence. My M16 had found its way into my hands; I hadn't cowered or hid. I had stood in position, in the window, in the eye of danger, and it hadn't occurred to me to do anything otherwise.

And yet my safety switch had never found its way from SAFE to SEMI.

I never quite considered myself a conscientious objector, but when I enlisted, the idea of war was an intangible one.

"I don't think I could ever kill anyone," I confessed once, back in Fort Polk as we prepared for deployment. I was passing a cigarette back and forth with Andres as we sat in the motor pool on a muggy spring evening. I was mostly just twirling the smoke in my mouth before spitting it back out, because it felt like a situation in which I should smoke. As if *not* smoking would somehow be wrong.

Andres took back the cigarette, his back pressed against the tire of a deuce and a half, one of the trucks in the motor pool bay waiting for inspection. It was dark enough that I couldn't see his face but I knew his profile by heart.

"I can," he said, the white smoke shifting in the fluorescent light from the inspection bay. We should be inside, but I didn't know if Kevin Hale might be in there—this was where I saw him last—so I preferred this, hiding underneath the huge truck, out of sight and, theoretically, out of mind. "What are you going to do, wait for them to shoot you?" he asked.

I shrugged. "Who says I deserve to live any more than someone else? I mean, what makes me better than them? They're just another soldier but on the other side." I was overthinking it. Or perhaps everyone else was thinking too little.

"That's just dumb," someone said. I craned my neck around the side of the massive tire and watched the two soldiers from Supply sauntering up. They folded themselves down onto the pavement that was still smoldering from the hot April sun.

They grinned. "I can't wait to get there and blow me up some sand niggers," one laughed, gesturing with an imagined rifle at his shoulder. He closed one eye and squeezed the air trigger, savoring his fantasy kill.

I looked down at the concrete and flicked a small stone out from the treads of one of my boots.

"I heard," started the other soldier, clearly savoring an anecdote that was possibly true, but just as plausibly not, "from one of my guys already there that they were shooting off the .50-cal at this guy, and they missed. But the velocity of the bullet was so strong, it ripped off his leg. Bam. Just like that. Guy just stood there for a second, totally confused. Then, plop. Fell over."

"That's fucking awesome!" the other roared. I imagined a man staring down at his bloody stump, baffled.

I'm not like you, I thought, still flicking pieces of asphalt away from my feet, hating the joy these men found in the violence. *I'll never be like you*, I swore.

I meant to mean it, too, but promises made in peace are rarely kept in war.

The moment when I discover I can kill comes and goes without much fanfare. It isn't during a perceived attack, like the Red Cross bombing. One day, on guard, I notice a man pausing at the side of the road in oddly spaced intervals. His shoulders are rounded, hunched forward as if protecting something close to his chest. He doesn't glance up at our tower, but his shuffling rubs me the wrong way. As he closes in on the tower, I work my rifle into my shoulder, past the ill-fitting SAPI plates. With no need for second thoughts, I thumb the safety selector switch to SEMI, forefinger held straight but ready at the side of the trigger. I even out my breaths, finding comfort in my steady, slightly elevated heartbeat. I empty my brain, as if I'm simply pouring out a cup, until there is nothing but a white buzz and a body on autopilot. I am ready.

But the man moves on, cradling his arms, continuing his odd gait down the road. Once he has retreated a safe distance, I thumb the rifle back to SAFE. I turn back to the busy intersection, looking for the next point of interest.

Still, having the *ability* to kill is different from *wanting* it. That begins with a flicker of indignation. One afternoon I stand on guard, body aching with the passing hours, until: *fizzzz, pop*. I blink at the strange sound. *Fizzzzz, pop*. Crumbling rocks hit the pavement.

"We're being shot at," I gasp in disbelief, ducking behind a beat-up pillar for cover. The other soldier on duty seems surprised not at the gunfire but at my amazement. Although I've been in Iraq for several weeks, I'm not used to being shot at yet. Before I can process it, our attacker is gone.

But some months later, careening through the clogged streets of Baghdad in the back of a Humvee, I stare up at the yellow stone buildings with their black, gaping holes where windows used to be and think, *What a perfect place for a sniper*. Before the thought leaves my head, I hear it. *Fizzzzz, pop*. I know that sound now. *Fizzzz, pop!*

"Goddamn it all!" I snarl, instantly shouldering my rifle. The air is filled with the coppery scent of blood but it turns out only to be a newly disemboweled goat hanging by its ankles, its intestines splashed over the mud and rock below. We drive past safely, and I never see the shooter.

"Fucker," I hiss through clenched teeth. *You can see me but I can't see you.* The rage in that thought eats at me. This feeling is familiar to me now—of being left open, raw, with a target meticulously painted across my body. That kind of helplessness breeds hate. I grind my teeth as the Humvee jostles down the road, picking up speed to avoid a firefight. *Try me! Test me, let me show you what I can do.*

Fuckers. They're no longer human to me. The inability to ever see the enemy, to find a single face, makes *them* a conglomerate—if any one of them shoots at me then they all have and I'm not going to be their little bitch. I realize my thumb is at the safety toggle already, itching to switch to SEMI.

A few weeks later, I feel the *want* more clearly. I stand in the guard tower, eyes narrowed to slits as I peer across the street. I swear there's a sniper in the building over there.

I had noticed the sun glinting off his scope, flashing between the shifting branches of the single tree that separates us. Our entire guard shack is open, with windows on all sides, so even as I try to hide my body behind the brick-and-concrete column, there I am, exposed in the wide-open, white-knuckling my M16 and staring at the spot with the flashing dot of light.

The vulnerability. It makes me want to kill someone.

I don't say anything to the other guard. The kid stands in the corner, oblivious, almost cowering against the wall, though it's not Baghdad he's afraid of. It's me.

When he had arrived to guard duty, he climbed up the ladder into the eight-by-six-foot box, poked his head up through the floor door, spotted me, and froze. He had been expecting another male, possibly even someone from his own unit, and instead he got some random MI girl. I had imagined most of the combat unit males would relish the idea of being sealed in a tower with a woman, but more often than not, as soon as they were separated from the pack, these boys grew meek and quiet, the prospect of speaking exclusively to a female for eight hours being too much to bear.

Still, I smiled at him. "Hi. I'm Ryan." He shuffled the rest of the way up the ladder, eyes wide, and mumbled something that might have been a greeting. I pushed on. "You know, like the guy's name," I added, because while standing in full battle rattle, my long, dark hair tucked into the back of my Kevlar or my breasts flattened against my flak vest, you might never know. He ducked his head, gave a brief introduction, then retired to his corner, staring out the window and down onto the Baghdad street.

Eight hours is a long time to stand in pregnant silence.

He is young. Perhaps two years younger than me but time isn't measured in years. He's fresh into Iraq, part of the First Cavalry Division who recently rode into Baghdad looking for a fight. He sparkles with newness. I feel ancient in comparison. A year of Iraq has bowed my spine and made an old woman of me. Now I stare at him across from me, noting the chasm between us, and how he never glances at the shard of light dancing across the street.

I wonder if he'll ever be like me. If one day on guard he'll suddenly realize he's no longer quite human—as if something cold and indifferent has crawled up into the space of his skull and taken residence there. I wonder if he'll care. I'm not sure I do.

Inside the walls of Camp Dragoon, guard duty is the most dangerous task—perhaps because it isn't exactly *inside* the walls but instead *on top* of them. Before duty, we have to line up for a safety briefing, which mostly consists of *drink water* and *this is how to operate the radio*. The radio is a single unit and our only contact for reinforcement. As we stand in formation, the non-commissioned officer in charge strides up and down the ranks, tapping on our backs. His knuckles rap hard against my back SAPI plate, checking to make sure the ceramic is in place. Recently a few soldiers had the brilliant idea of pulling out their back SAPI plates to reduce the weight of their equipment. At the time, it seemed ingenious, until a soldier got shot in the back and died with a bullet in his spine. Now the NCOIC routinely checks our gear, along with the reminder, *Don't die for stupid reasons.*

I stare out at the building across the street, aware that my spot of vulnerability is physically small—the flak vest protects my center mass and the Kevlar shields the top of my head. But my face, my face is open and wide. The bullet would probably enter through the left eye, popping the orb, blazing a trail of hot metal through to the back of my skull, and splattering bits of bone and brain against the guard tower wall. If this were a movie, the kid would get sprayed with globs of bone, flesh, and teeth, because exit wounds are just that nasty, the perfect prop for this boy's war trauma as the opening credits roll. But this isn't a movie and he's not standing close enough to me for that. I probably wouldn't even feel it. Maybe. Quick and done. Any minute now.

My neck muscles tighten with anticipation. "Fuck you," I whisper under my breath, a silent message to my killer. I glare at that spot of light. I wish he'd step to the right or left. Just a little. Just enough for me to see a face. To see dark eyes, perhaps with a brow slick with perspiration. He'd be about my age. No, a bit older. Maybe he'll look a little bit like the soldier who raped me. I've gotten better at my aim. Maybe good enough for one shot. His head would snap back, that sort of quick, ugly jerk like a cord had been attached to the back of his head and yanked hard. I'd see the pink mist then—that cloud of blood that hovers behind the body when the back of the skull is blown out. His body would linger there for a moment, not realizing it was dead or how what had once been there is now missing. I imagine things I don't know, having been told enough times by soldiers who actually saw, and I think the images real enough only because I'm lucky enough not to know any better.

I replay the scenario. My chest burns and my fingers dance against my rifle with pent-up energy. I rapidly tap my boots against the floor. Alive. Like I hear a really good song that makes me want to dance. *I want you*, I mouth to my sniper.

A bark below startles me and I turn my head just in time to see a small, reddish-brown stray dog dart out into traffic. I wonder what's on the other side of the road that he'd risk the danger of rushing cars. He makes it halfway when an older Mercedes clips his hindquarters. The back legs collapse and his body spins with a forceful yelp. Round and round he twirls on the pavement before sliding into the opposite embankment, where he slumps against the concrete barrier.

The boy and I both silently watch the listless dog, waiting to see if he'll move. He doesn't.

Once I'm sure he's dead, I turn my attention back to the shifting light across the street and spend the next six hours waiting to be shot in the face.

the way we break

I DON'T DIE THAT DAY, and neither does the sniper who never existed. I take comfort in my rage, that toughness that says I'm no one's bitch. And for a little while, life rolls on. Iraq is much the same, day after day, peppered with shocks of mortars, IEDs, and gunfire, but mostly the same. I tell myself I have put Fort Polk behind me. Everyone else has moved on, it seems, or at the very least no one talks about it anymore. I'm not over it but I'm not under it, either, just ignoring, sectioning away bits of rage for later, and it's all going well until Sergeant Daniels finds me one day and accidentally rips the whole thing wide open again.

I sit on the sixth floor of our building, by my equipment, a book carefully perched on my lap. My body is turned just so, poised to shove the book away at a moment's notice. I'm the first desk, positioned in front of the stairs, aware that it's not insurgents I'm on the alert for but higher-ups. I hear the stairs creak and strain, a telltale sign, and silently slide the book out of my hands. I kick it under the desk, placing one hand on my M16 and resting the other on the desk. See, I'm a good soldier, just sitting here, staring at the wall. I fight the urge to flippantly twiddle my thumbs. I glance at the radio, ready to key the mike the second the brass head down the hall, giving a heads-up to the two soldiers in our SCIF.

Sergeant Daniels strides into the room, giving me a brief nod in greeting. No matter how many times he shaves, there still is a light shadow over his jaw. It makes him look rugged but also defiant. I expect him to move on, down the hall to the platoon members he actually likes. I remember when we first came to Iraq, I used to try to impress him, to get him to notice me, like the time I drew some pictures at Brooks's request, shades and lines copied from magazines of bare chests and slimly curved waists, because those are the only magazines to be had and the only models to work off. Brooks liked to plaster some of the pictures on her wall, because artwork seems somehow better than magazine cutouts ("*more cultured*"), and the walls are otherwise depressingly bare. Sergeant Daniels stepped into the room, half turned toward the artwork, and my chest swelled. "I drew those," I said loudly, pointing, and in the clunky pause before he eventually said "Okay," I realized I sounded like a child, like a girl tugging at her daddy's coat, and I wrapped an arm around myself, lips pressed together hard in humiliation.

But there is no way I can impress him because I'm still fat. Less than a month ago, I had shuffled through a PT test while Sergeant Daniels watched from the company concrete stairs. His face was professionally blank. "If you feel you can't do this," he said slowly, his attempt at being kind, "we can separate you." It's not a threat; it's an offering.

"You mean send me home?" I asked, cheeks flushed red from the exercise, sweat molding my gray PT shirt to the folds of my body. I peeled it away, trying to hide the unnecessary curves.

"You can separate from the Army," he said, not harshly but it still hurt.

I stared up at him and I'd never felt more useless. "Can we wait until we go back home?" I asked, not sure I'm willing to leave the military, but so very certain that leaving now would make me a coward. I've already seen how this plays out: Sergeant Forst seriously injured her back early in the deployment. She couldn't bear the weight of her gear; she was in constant pain. They sent her home, after accusing her of malingering, some whispering about what a shitbag soldier she was, forgetting that she had spent years before being the best they ever had. And then, after a few weeks, they forgot about her entirely, as if she had never existed. If I left, everyone would have their fill of gossip and then forget, but I wouldn't.

"I can't just leave everyone here," I said. Let me finish with honor; give me this last shred of dignity. Sergeant Daniels said nothing.

I hate being the fat soldier with the round face who cries. I nervously toe the book farther to the side and better out of sight. Instead of walking past, though, he pauses by my desk, regarding me with dark eyes, as if just noticing me there. Then he pulls up a tattered cushion chair, left over from the building's fancier days. He looks odd in it, tan and brown and perched on plush blue.

"How are you doing, Dostie?" he asks.

I don't expect this, feeling surprised and flushed. I'm looking for too many fathers and always finding none. "Doing well," I lie.

He leans forward so that his elbows are planted on his knees. "Look, Dostie, it's no secret that you have an issue with Captain Wells."

"Doesn't everyone?" It comes out a little sharper than I intend and I quail, afraid I'll scare him away. He levels an unflinching stare at me. I have to look down at my hands. "I can't stand him," I finally admit, to break the stiff silence.

"Care to share why?"

I twist my hands, a nervous habit, and bite my lip to keep from snapping, *Isn't it obvious?* I squirm, wanting him to tell me I'm not wrong, that I'm not the bad soldier everyone makes me out to be, but haven't I already learned this lesson? Rape just isn't one of those things anyone wants you to talk about. And yet in the end, that obsessive desire to hear someone say, even once, "It's not your fault," wins out. It always does. The compulsive need to be heard keeps me talking, even when everyone else wishes I'd just shut up.

"When...that thing happened before we left, Captain Wells totally sided with him," I say to the desk. Frustration burns at the corner of my eyes, and I realize with horror that I'm going to cry. I dig my nails into the heel of my palm. The sharp pain clears the fog in my head. "He's supposed to be my commander. He's supposed to protect me." I spit the words, sounding bitter and childish, instantly wishing I could take them back.

Sergeant Daniels drags that ridiculous, heavy chair closer. "You know," he begins, speaking softly, something I've never heard him do, and I lift my head, startled. "That's why I wanted you in my platoon. When I heard what happened, I had you moved over to me so that Lieutenant Patron and I could fix all this."

Liar. I remember how he hadn't wanted me in the beginning, his startled expression when he saw me nestled there in his ranks, quickly ousting me with an impatient gesture, how I had stumbled between the two platoons, ostracized to the back of the company. Lieutenant Patron, our platoon leader, has never said a word to me about the rape. I didn't even know he knew. I'm acutely aware of all this, but I don't remind Sergeant Daniels. I don't ask him why he's waited months to even broach the subject, why all this time has gone by and he never once tried to fix anything. I never think to even ask, *Why now?*

I'm starved for acknowledgment, devouring scraps like a dog.

Whatever his reasons, Sergeant Daniels is astonishingly faithful to his word. I don't know how he manages it; Captain Wells had always seemed so resolute, heels dug in, refusing to meet with me even when I threatened the command with the IG. I wonder what Sergeant Daniels must have said, how he wrangled Captain Wells into a meeting. Had he threatened? Demanded? Or perhaps he simply asked, because he was Sergeant Daniels, after all, and there was power in that. However he did it, a few hours later I find myself in a room with the Captain, suddenly, with very little preparation.

Captain Wells is combative the second I step into his room. He sits in a green nylon chair; his room is fixed with a plush Iraqi rug and a black air conditioner in the window. Sergeant Daniels and Lieutenant Patron flank me, offering silent support. I'm shocked by their presence, like a drowning victim surprised to suddenly find a life ring next to them. Captain Wells glares as I walk into the room, the low brow of his forehead hanging over his eyes. For a moment I entertain the image of his brain matter splattered across the drywall behind him, dribbling down in pretty crimson lines. I imagine the dumb look of shock in his slack features, the way his body would slump to one side.

The thought cheers me considerably.

But then he opens his mouth. He starts with some useless formalities as I sit down on the trunk across from him. First Sergeant Bell stands off and to the side of him, his boots off, his feet covered in thick, white, non-government-issued socks. The room is divided, the command on that side, rank and file on ours.

"There's no evidence that anything happened," Captain Wells is saying to Sergeant Daniels, not to me, as if convincing Sergeant Daniels will finally put an end to this.

"Just because there's no evidence doesn't mean it didn't happen," I snap, my mouth loosened by months of silent rage.

"Don't get self-righteous with me," Wells growls, spearing a chubby finger at me. "Don't *you* get all self-righteous with *me*."

"You're my commander, you were supposed to be there for me," I counter, my voice rising a little too high—a little too feminine.

"I was his commander, too. You want me to side with you just because?"

"You sided with *him* just because!" I nearly choke on my own words. "Sir."

He glowers. "I just went off what was in the report—"

"You were on his side long before the report even came out." Now that I'm here, now that I have him here, I'm not letting him go. "And even if you didn't believe...if you don't get what happened, it said in the report that he *said* he was going to go to 'that Dostie-chick's room because she's so wasted.' He said it. *That's* in the report! He *knew* I was drunk and purposefully...and in some states, like in California for example, it's...it is *rape*...if you do that to someone you know is too drunk."

"This isn't California, Dostie." He sneers. "And he had a few drinks, too. Does that mean *you* raped *him*? Should I get CID? Maybe we need to report you, too?"

That knocks the gale right out of my sails. For a moment I sit there, stunned, robbed of my rage. "But..." I start feebly. "He did it *on purpose*. I went to my room. I closed my door..."

"It's what you said in the report that's important." He leans back in his chair, crossing his arms over his chest. "*You* tied my hands when you said it wasn't rape."

"That's not what I said," I whisper, a soft desperation that goes unheard.

"I can't prosecute a rape if you say you're not sure." He drives the nail home then, a little too smug, one side of his mouth curled up nastily. "So I don't know why you're so mad at *me*."

The realization destroys me. I slump forward and stare at the floor. I finally get it then—why the whole case was closed, why everyone turned me away, disinterested. It was my own fault, my own words, and I shouldn't have let them push me around, I shouldn't have withered so easily, trying to do what they wanted. I should've stayed strong. I have no one to blame but myself. This is what happens to the weak. Tears roll down my cheeks, off my chin, onto my hands, and I have no idea what's being said anymore. I can't hear past the white haze in my skull.

I'm done. I feel myself break. I don't have the energy or the desire to sit here, to hold my head up, to breathe. I had been tying myself together with makeshift wires and 5-50 cord, thinking it would all come around in the end, that somehow it would be made right, because that's what's supposed to happen when you've told the truth, when your cause is just, and I was stupid and young and naive. I see it then and let go, spilling onto the floor, undone.

In Captain Wells's room, that relatively eventless evening in Iraq, I learn there is no justice.

I drag my feet out of the room. I don't remember being dismissed, or how the conversation ended, or even hear Sergeant Daniels and Lieutenant Patron follow me outside. I huddle against a cement wall, curled between the staircase and the wall, trying not to be seen. I sob like a child, arms wrapped around my knees, pressing my back into the wall, breathless.

"I'm so stupid. I'm so stupid," I gasp out again and again between sobs, trying to bury my face into my knees. "It's all my fault."

I can no longer escape the truth that I had always been afraid of. It wasn't Captain Wells who fucked me over; it was *me*. It was me saying the wrong thing, not believing in myself that night in that interrogation room, and I can't face it. I wish I could take back the last few minutes, to dig the conversation out of my brain with a utility knife. I wanted to unhear it all.

"It's not your fault," Daniels tries to comfort me, crouched by the stairs. Lieutenant Patron sits on the pavement beside him but I can't see their faces. I want to slip into the wall, be swallowed up by stone. I want to disappear.

"You're not stupid," one of them offers, too, but really, what can they say? They didn't sign up for this. No one trains them on how to deal with a deranged rape victim. And I am deranged, trying to push myself through the wall, hands tangled in my hair, pulling at the roots, as if I can physically rip the memories out of my skull. I don't know when they leave or how long they waited there; I'm just relieved when they go. There is no privacy in a camp in Iraq and I just want the right to break in silence, with no one trying to coax me out with pretty and useless lies.

It takes me several minutes to realize someone else is there with me. I look up to see a Lieutenant sitting beside me. He's a medic; I see the symbol on his lapel. I might know him vaguely, but we don't greet each other. He simply smiles. He doesn't ask what's wrong. He doesn't try to comfort me. He sits in silent support. He doesn't judge my tears, just calmly waits, until I become calm along with him. When I finally reach silence, empty, tears dried in streaks on my cheeks, he leaves just as he came, in silence, with a soft smile.

It was probably such a small action for him. He probably never thought of it again, while I remember it always. Rumor had it that some weeks later his truck hit an IED. They said his skin burned off completely. I wish I could remember his name. I wish I knew if he lived.

reconstruction

SOME WEEKS AFTER my meeting with Captain Wells, male King carves ANDRES LOVES THE FATTIES into the stone on one of the guard towers. It's meant as a joke. People laugh. I never see the actual statement, but I hear about it, between their chuckles and tobacco-stained teeth. I stand in my tiny bathroom, a shared room newly fixed up and working, and stare into the silver haze of an old, shabby mirror. I stand naked, towel hanging in one hand, and see heavy breasts, round with fat, hanging downward, mouth sloped downward, the extra roll of fat around my waist sliding downward, as if my body is in a state of depression, spiraling down. The Iraqi sun has blasted my face and hands a deep bronze, but beneath the uniform is nothing but the white, fleshy rolls that have been building since the rape. I grab my stomach, fingers sinking into the softness there. ANDRES LOVES THE FATTIES.

I dress quickly, dragging on a dusty uniform over wet skin, turned away from the mirror, as if to shield myself from it. This is who I've become. I've lost it all—the strong, wiry legs, the thighs thick with muscle, the slender curve to my waist, the arms hard and unyielding, and with it the girl who had held her head high, her gaze straight. I pause while dressing, hands hanging limply by my sides.

"No." I turn back to the mirror, to its dusky reflection. "No." I say it firmly, the single syllable loud in the tiny room. And then I undress. I toss the uniform to the side and pull on my PT shorts and shirt. I lace up sneakers, toss my personal effects onto my cot, and run out the door.

I huff and choke on air, heaving around all that fat, my body swaying with each step. And I run. Sweat pours down my spine, plasters to my head, and still I run.

I run at night through the compound, watching the bats scatter over the walls, avoiding stray dogs that wander through the broken buildings. In the mornings after night shift, I commandeer the small, makeshift gym and do crunches, sit-ups, and push-ups. I eye my food and obsess, flicking out carbs, eating only meat and vegetables. I separate, divide, calculate anything that goes into my mouth. No concessions are made; no cheats allowed. I pop Hydroxycut like candy, carrying around an oversize bottle in one of my cargo pockets, regardless of the heat and the threat of dehydration. And I run.

High on rage, I whittle myself down, my final attempt at a *fuck you*. I don't swallow the end of a muzzle like Avery Langley did, like I have sometimes wanted to do. Instead I decide that I can slice off half of myself, the part that thinks too much, that cares too much, the part that replays Captain Wells's words over and over again, and I shove it down under a trapdoor, stomp one boot down, and lock it shut. I will *not* be broken.

I delight with the ability to no longer care. I stitch together my parts, hastily, haphazardly, and I'm beautifully and fiercely remade. I'm in love with this new me, because I don't give a fuck about you, and that's glorious.

A few weeks into my transformation, one of the medic captains grabs my arm in the hall, swinging me around to face her. Her blond brow is pinched together. "Dostie, you've lost an awful lot of weight," she says. She's concerned. No one else is.

I grin in response. "Forty pounds so far."

She hesitates, her hand still clamped on my arm. "Are you doing it the healthy way?"

"Sure."

Sure.

I run all the way to relevancy, which I never intended, but here I am, no longer the fat "shitbag soldier," and people take notice. Specifically the men. Sergeant Daniels makes his way down the long, dark hall of our work building. I expect him to walk on by with his usual nod, a vague gesture of recognition, but instead he pauses by the edge of my desk, looking down at me. He stands there for a moment, as if weighing something I can't see, then grabs that same old battle-worn chair he'd sat in months earlier when he took me to see Captain Wells. Now he turns it, straddles it backward, crossing his arms over the back of the chair and resting his chin on his forearms. It's a charming, boyish gesture.

I surprise myself by not flushing.

"You're looking good," he says, light and airy, making it sound more like a compliment on my hard work than a sleazy pickup line. "Make sure you're drinking plenty of water with those," he adds, pointing to the bottle of Hydroxycut that sits on the desk.

"I've been drinking a ton," I promise and meet his gaze, a little startled by the casual attention. I allow myself to wonder if he's hitting on me. Then I realize that although my waist may be small now, he likes women with large, heavy breasts that can't be contained by the brown undershirt or the buttoned-up DCU top. He picked a few girls out of the platoon like that, or so the gossip says, girls he held close to him for a brief moment, who got special treatment, and I'm not up to par. For all my weight loss I've been awarded small breasts that get lost in the uniform top, and for some reason I'm relieved.

Sergeant Daniels trades a few tips about dieting and exercising. He has a loud laugh and an ease with himself that I still envy. And yet something is different here. The dynamics are suddenly askew. I'm not sure if it's because he respects me now or because I don't care if he does. I'd like for him to like me; I respect him and there's still a sense of basking in the sun when he's nearby. Yet I match him in tone, no longer burying my gaze into the ground. There's sharpness to my confidence. Like me or don't, that's on you, not me. I'm done giving a fuck.

Toward the end of our first year in Iraq, Captain Wells transfers out. He goes home or to another unit, somewhere else, and I don't care as long as he's not here. It happens suddenly. I never ask where he went; no one does. No one cares. We like Captain Noble, our new company commander, who is young and slender and a bit nerdy. There's a general consensus that he's a little weird but he's not Captain Wells so that makes him tolerable. He doesn't know my past. It's like being awarded a clean slate, and I smile at him. Maybe a little too much.

He approaches me as we're packing up to leave Baghdad. Our year deployment is closing and the unit is pulled together, some returning from other camps. We're all finally in the same place again. We're moved about the company building as equipment and gear are prepped for our journey home. "So I hear there's a picture out there of you girls," he says. I know exactly what he's talking about. King, Brennan, and I posed for a photo in uniform pants and bras, rifles in hands, sunglasses to hide our faces, and meant to send it to *Maxim*, although we never did. Brennan suggested the photo shoot because she's always been comfortable with her sexual potency. This was just good, clean fun to her. King probably did it because her strong sense of self was unwavering, so this was neither empowering nor demeaning, simply neutral. I'd jumped at the chance because I'm thin enough to do this now, and being considered sexy is a new label I gladly take over any of my old ones.

I try to hand Captain Noble the digital camera but he leans over my shoulder, his thigh and hip brushing against mine, waiting for me to bring up the photo myself. He doesn't move. Neither do I. I'm done looking for father figures in powerful men. I'd rather crush them instead.

"That's fucking hot," he says with a laugh when I show it to him. "I heard about this and I was like 'I have to see it!'"

I smirk. "It was just for fun."

"It *looks* like a lot of fun," he says slowly, turning the phrase over in his mouth with a grin. He's not much taller than me. He's married and has a pink dolphin tattoo on one arm. I'm not sure what to do with him but his flirting doesn't fluster me. Later, he shows me around his private space, the stacks of bottled water, an extra, empty room. "Come over anytime," he says softly. First Sergeant Bell is in the other room. "We play cards late at night, you should come by and play sometime."

"Can I take a bottle?" I point to one of the large plastic bottles of water. Fresh water, water not from the buffalo, that won't taste like swamp and bleach. Gold.

"Sure, sure." He waves at the bottles and I take two. "Come by anytime," he repeats.

That night female King finds me and reports, "Captain Noble wants you to come by. To play cards." It's late. The sun has set and I'm sitting out on the pavement, headphones in my ears. I can barely make out her figure in the electric-lantern light.

"Okay, thanks." I sit there on the warm concrete, watching her leave, and consider what I think is a proposition. It's not an order, yet there's something weighty in the request. If I go, I'll be agreeing to something simply by showing up.

I hesitate. I think about the boxes of bottled water and other perks. I consider the position of a Captain; it's good to be king and even better to befriend him.

I crack open the second bottle of free water, take a slug, then head back to my room. There's power in being asked, and even more power in saying no.

I'm no longer the insect squirming under the microscope lens. I smirk at this male gaze, lips curled enticingly. You can't fuck me over anymore because I'm waiting for it, bristled with thorns, just daring you to try.

getting out of baghdad

IN APRIL 2004 we're told we're going home. We've done our time, our year in the desert, and now we'll head back to the safety of our US bases. Books have been packed, foam mattresses passed on, metal shelves, extension cords, and battered fans sold to the newcomers. I stand one last time in front of the AC unit in our window. Spring has come around again, hobbling along as the temperature already begins its steep climb toward summer. Flattened cardboard boxes are taped across the glass to block out the searing sunlight. I lift my arms, letting the cold blast of air shiver up my spine.

"God, I'll miss you," I say to the AC unit.

"In two weeks we'll be home and in actual AC," King promises as she collapses her cot into a bundle of sweat-stained canvas and bent metal legs.

"Yeah, after two weeks of hell," I remind her. But after a year of Iraq, what's two more weeks? I sling my M16 over my shoulder, give the AC one last mournful glance, and grab my own cot. We step outside and are slapped by the heat. I toss my cot and my last duffel bag into the back of our Humvee.

"I'm going to see if there's anything good at the PX," I call to King, darting toward the store. Of course the tiny shop will have nothing but *Maxim* magazines, male deodorant, and the odd CD, but I need to peek in one last time. Maybe they'll have some powdered drink mix. Or a book.

Just outside the PX I pause for a moment, one boot halted in midair as I realize I'll never walk this stone path again. I glance at the sandstone buildings, the sprawling prison walls and the muggy skyline of Iraq, and I'm saddened, overcome with nostalgia for this place I never loved. It squeezes my chest. This has become a type of home— more so than my barracks back at Fort Polk. And there's no coming back to this. Not ever. I twist about, soaking in the dirt-laden road, the crumbling walls. *I want to remember you*, I think, because no one else will.

I'm sad to leave, though I can't understand why.

I return to my Humvee a little heavier, and I fill my lungs with Baghdad air. There is excited chatter in the convoy line, some soldiers sitting on top of their Humvee hoods as we wait for the orders to roll out. I hop onto my hood, the hot metal searing my back as I sprawl out and stare up at the cloudless sky.

"Last letters?" Sergeant Daniels calls out as he walks the line, a bundle of crumpled envelopes stuffed under one arm.

I shove one hand into my cargo pocket and pull out the letter, dropping it into Sergeant Daniels's waiting hand. A different kind of sweat breaks out across my upper lip as the paper leaves my fingers. These are my last words, should I die on our convoy ride into Kuwait.

"Everyone should write a letter to their family and send it home," First Sergeant Bell had strongly suggested two days prior. "Just in case you die." He doesn't sugarcoat it, but it might have been nice if he had.

The convoy will stretch from Baghdad to Kuwait, miles upon miles of sprawling, barren space with no walls, no concertina wire, nothing but our guns and our severely depleted ammo supply to cover our backs. No one whispers about how dangerous it is, but we all knew as we were handed lined paper, pens, and a single blank envelope.

I keep my letter uplifting, scratching words of pride and bravado, that I'm all right dying for this (for *what?*) and it's all surreal anyway, because who writes a last letter? I write it for my mother, not for myself.

But watching Sergeant Daniels stride away with that small envelope, I wonder if I said enough.

One hour, two hours, three hours, more, the sun shifts in the sky, the metal swells with contained heat, and we down canteens of water only to sweat it back out into the dirt, pacing, panting, begging to leave. "Jesus fucking Christ, what are we waiting for," Gaul, my vehicle's gunner, complains, hopping onto the hood with me.

Rumors spread up the line, Humvee by Humvee, a well-received contagion. Everyone knows First Cavalry Division came into Iraq thinking their balls were bigger and hung lower than ours. They are here to replace us and are damn sure they are going to end the war in a blaze of bullets and medals. But they are still children peeking out from beneath their too-large helmets, eager, reckless, and fucking everything up.

"Colonel Robinson told them not to arrest Sadr's lieutenant," King says, leaning against my Humvee, "but they didn't want to listen."

"Of course they didn't. They just wanna come in here, draw some tick lines on their Kevlars, and go home—treating everyone like the fucking enemy," Gaul adds. For someone who eventually joins Special Forces, he's the least violent man I'll ever meet.

The Iraqis weren't the enemy, and 2nd ACR has spent a year establishing that. The squadron spent more time improving Baghdad than destroying it. Troops were sent into the streets to help build hospitals, schools, train the Iraqi Civil Defense Corps and new police units. They kicked in their fair share of doors on raids, but even insurgents knew when to shoot and when to not—because you don't kill those who come to pass out food and medical supplies. But 1st Cav doesn't know anything about this, and their vehicles are sand beige, a clear distinction between 2nd ACR's foliage green, and 1st Cav will take fire when we don't, because they don't want to help, they want to win.

There is a splatter of AK-47 fire to the backdrop of our conversation, which we ignore, because we have forgotten what life sounds like without it, but the sound lingers as the rumors build. Protesters have set fire to Iraq. Iraqi police officers have been murdered, expelled from their stations. Convoys going in or out of Baghdad International Airport are ambushed with deadly effect. "Your enemy prefers terrorism," says cleric al-Sadr, and the cities ignite.

It's said that 1st Cav sent in a five-ton to retake the police stations, the massive vehicle getting stuck in the dense urban streets, and it's the 2nd ACR with Tenth Mountain Division that swept in to save them.

We hear this in tidbits, bread crumbs of broken stories, some of it true, some of it not.

"We just had to go in and save their asses," says King. We as in Second Armored Calvary Regiment. Not we as in us—we're linguists. We don't do the real shit. "And they got twelve of our guys killed."

It turns out to be eight soldiers dead, fifty-one wounded, but rumors always inflate the numbers.

Gaul sits up sharply, pressing his combat glasses farther up his sharp nose. "Twelve? Fucking *twelve*?"

"Twelve," I repeat as my hands clench my elbows. I don't know the 2nd ACR guys very well but I've met a few of them here and there, and familiar faces tumble past my vision. I wonder if it's anyone I know. I want to be angry. I should want to grab my rifle and burn this shit down. But I'm not. I'm scared. This is the wrong time to suddenly become human.

"We're rolling." Sergeant Daniels appears, as if conjured, slapping the metal roof of my Humvee to get everyone's attention. We start to scramble into our vehicles, the number twelve sitting heavy on our tongues. The monster at the back of my skull wonders if this puts the numbers in my favor—if we've just lost twelve soldiers from our regiment, what are the odds that we'll lose one more? I hate myself.

I follow the convoy into the Regimental Support Squadron based at Al Rasheed airfield. A great weight rises from my shoulders as the gates swing closed behind us; I am convinced we have narrowly escaped a tragedy.

Everyone says we'll only be here a matter of days, but it's not true and we amble around our restricted area, kicking up dust in boredom now that our books have been given away and our games handed off.

Eventually we're packed into a circular theater room made of gray walls and hard benches. The stone structure keeps away some of the heat, but all the bodies squished together begin to reek of sweat, unwashed skin, and body odor. I can bite the air—it's filled with stink and tension.

First Sergeant Bell stands in the middle of the room and drones on about something that doesn't seem very important. Meanwhile, rumors are still slinking through the ranks. Cities have been lost; hostages have been taken.

It's not a good time to be in Iraq.

But we've done our year. The Army can't extend our time frame— there are rules in place against that sort of behavior. It would cost a hundred dollars a day to keep each soldier beyond their twelve-month mark, and there's no way the Army is going to pay that.

So when First Sergeant Bell announces that we'll be moving to Al Najaf, he's received with silence. There is no Q&A; no one gets to ask how long we'll be there, if we'll get paid our due, or, most important, why us?

No one asks when we're going home.

"Al Najaf?" Locke exclaims, joining our tight huddle outside the briefing building. We haven't moved far, our limbs are too heavy. She produces a cigarette and Andres takes it. "That's like the Fallujah of the west. Who the fuck wants to go there?"

I accept the outstretched cigarette even though I don't smoke. Andres lights it for me and I pull the smoke into my mouth, slowly cycling it out my nose so that it looks like I've inhaled. "We're never going home."

I laugh, because it's funny. I wait for the rage, the fear, the protest, from me, from anyone, but there's none. There is nothing. We laugh.

"We're already dead," Andres clarifies with a loud chuckle. "This is actually hell."

"It's certainly hot enough for it," agrees Locke.

"We're all going to die!" I chortle, choking on my smoke, and Locke snorts with me, face flushing red with laughter as she hunches over to hold her stomach. I throw my head back and let out a deep laugh until my ribs ache with the absurdity of it all.

We're allowed a quick call home on the satellite phone, a bulky piece of plastic that hisses and spits down the line. My mom answers on the second ring; her cell phone is now permanently attached to her body.

"Hi, Mom, I can't talk right now but we're not coming home." I spit it out in a rush; enunciating the words would make it too real.

"What?" she calls back, sounding like she's at the far end of a tunnel.

"We got extended so we're moving to another part of Iraq."

"What? For how long? Where are you going? When are you coming home?"

I glance at the person behind me in line, who is waiting, listening, and I'm pressed for time. "I don't know. I love you. I'll call you when I can. Oh, you're going to get a letter from me. Just ignore it."

"Wait, wait!" she exclaims, but I hang up and pass the phone on so that the next person can call his mom and tell her he's not coming home, either.

the ghosts of al kut

WE END UP IN AL KUT instead of Al Najaf. I don't realize we're in a completely different city until someone happens to drop the name one day. It doesn't matter to me. I go where I'm told. Self-agency is a thing of the past.

The 2nd ACR boys went south into Al Najaf, Al Kut, and Diwaniyah to blow shit up and generally kick ass. They're sent there before us—the MI, Supply, and support folk—clearing out the cities in short but brutal battles, then calling us down when it's safe and sound. There's an immense sense of pride at the ferocity of our regiment. Not only did they get it done, they got it done quickly. I feel ineffectual in comparison, standing behind the bloodied warrior and only there to hand him a few passing notes. It might have been different had we been the Intel who cracked the code, located the enemy, and pointed the machine in the right direction, but we weren't. Mission-wise, nothing I do in Iraq matters.

Al Kut is the heart of Iraq, if not literally, then in beauty alone. It's a different sky here, a vast dome hovering over a flat land of muted colors. Night never comes quickly. Day stars burn in a canopy of pink and the moon is a ghost until the last of lavender fades, then glows bright, large, and fat.

I stand on the flat, clay-brick roof of our house, gazing at the show.

The evening air is cooler, tinged with a faint breeze, and gone is the humidity of Baghdad. Instead a small wave of goose bumps sweeps up my arms and across my bare breasts as I bathe on the roof. I feel like Bathsheba, one hand holding the bin to pour water over my head, soap-suds tinged with the dust and dirt of the day. I feel beautiful standing under the ancient sunset, on rooftop architecture that hasn't changed in a millennium. The only kings watching are the Special Forces just across the way, the Gods of War, who similarly sit on their rooftops. Supposedly, if you catch the light just right, you can see the glint off their binoculars.

We had rolled into Al Kut on my twenty-third birthday, after spending the previous day on the dusty road from Baghdad and the night huddled in a circle of Humvees somewhere in the flat desert. The night had been surprisingly cold, as if all the heat had been sucked out by the blackness, and even by morning, when I sat on my cot by my Humvee, there was still a bite in the air. Sergeant Daniels embraced the cliché and shaved with a knife in the vehicle's side mirror behind me. Female King took a picture of me to commemorate my birthday, and I sang "Happy Birthday to Me," softly as I put my gear away. By midafternoon we had swarmed the sprawling camp of Al Kut.

This town isn't what I had anticipated. Coming from Baghdad, I had expected more of the city feel, the stacked sandstone buildings and thick, cloying dust, the wet heat brewed from the Tigris and Euphrates, the continual activity and shooting, shooting, shooting. But Al Kut is silent. Remote. Both larger and less populated than our last camp. Even the wind tastes different.

And this is the beauty of Iraq—it sneaks up on you unexpectedly, unnoticed until it strikes, engraving a deep scar just behind your eyes. It's like the frustratingly uneven chords of a song stuck in your ear, annoying, until one day you notice the layers in the sound and you realize it's a masterpiece. The realization aches, part shame for missing it all in the first place, part unbearable sadness because once you go, you'll never see this savage beauty again.

I like it here. Surprisingly. I like my makeshift shower on the roof, bathing under the sky. I like the new privacy of being placed in a house several buildings down from the top brass. Most of the women from our platoon are back together and in one building, our own little ladies' house. The ten of us carefully clean off blasted debris, sweep away shards of glass and crumbled stones until our hands bleed from blisters. We continuously sweep at the gray dust that storms through the empty windowsills and lays a thick layer on our cots and gear. It's a small price to pay—the top brass doesn't care about the women's house, they don't visit or check up on us and we don't want them to. Sergeant Daniels stops by occasionally, pausing just before the door that doesn't exist, to announce his presence, as if he couldn't see through the gaps in the walls where windows once stood.

Most of the linguists are back together, but analysts are broken up and shipped off to separate camps. Andres is sent somewhere. We can only communicate through letters delivered at the mercy of the supply platoon. I miss him, but not as much as I should. I adjust way too easily.

I bathe in the twilight, then dress, ignoring the dampness of my skin as I pull on a clean uniform, and spend the rest of my time on the roof, headphones stuffed into my ears, dancing in senseless circles because up here there is no one but me.

The houses are all in a line on this side of the camp, much like houses in 1950s suburbia, though they are made of sandstone and floor-to-ceiling windows. We sit at the perimeter, flanked by a minefield that works as a natural barrier. I often stand by the window, squinting at the barren field of sand and clumps of harsh, long grass, imagining the shiny bits of deadly metal sticking out from the dirt. They were protectively laid from a war long before ours.

The entire camp had once been officer housing for Iraqi upper brass and their families. I imagine they left in a hurry—the land had been smashed and flattened by bombs, all the glass broken, and the houses stripped bare.

Almost.

On the walls of our house are flowers drawn in wax crayons. They are low on the walls, green stalks and wide petals imperfect, as if colored with an unsteady hand. A child's hand. Replicas of houses periodically appear between the flowers, and a bright sun sits in one corner, painstakingly colored in stark yellow.

In the front yard and curved around one side of our house, little plastic hands break through the dirt. Dolls, half buried, eyes black and filled with mud, are scattered about the yard in shallow graves. We leave them there in the dirt, occasionally toeing a pink arm. No one mentions how creepy they are. No one mentions them at all.

These are the only remnants of those before us. I tell myself that everyone had been evacuated, and the bombs just fell on empty buildings and deserted roads. No one tells me this, but no one tells me otherwise, and this is what I choose to believe.

Nothing otherwise occurs to me or dissuades this belief, not even when, pacing to my music on the roof one evening, just on the cusp of dusk, a dark figure cuts directly in front of me. It is the size of a toddler, its little arms pumping up and down as it runs; a disproportionately large and deformed head perches on a skinny neck. The shadow rushes off the roof and down the steps, disappearing into the blackness at the bottom of the stone stairs. I freeze, one of my earbuds displaced from my ear and swinging by my jaw, System of a Down screaming through the silence, and my feet are rooted. I want off the roof and yet I can't go down the stairs behind the thing; surely it's waiting there to push me down the already crumbling steps. I've seen this horror movie before. So I wait, motionless, as the sun continues to set, making the roof darker, and I'm stuck for ten minutes that feel like an eternity, hairs at the back of my neck straightened to attention. Finally I press my back against the wall, creeping down the stairs, waiting every moment to be pushed, knowing that *thing* is going to shove me down these fucking stairs and I'm going to break my neck, what a stupid way to die in Iraq, and finally my boots touch the last steps and I'm flying out of the house to stand in the street, spooked.

I see female King just ahead of me as she strolls down the street with one of the mechanics. It's not an unusual sight; lots of the soldiers go for walks as the sun sets and the cooler air comes out to play. I shoulder my M16 and rush over to them, falling in step as I ask, "Do you believe in ghosts?"

The mechanic throws up both hands in the air. "I don't want to hear it! That shit creeps the hell out of me."

King shrugs. "I think there's a lot of stuff out there that we don't know about."

"I'm serious, because I swear to God, I just saw this kid with a stupidly large head in all black just run off the roof and down the stairs." I gesture toward my house. "Swear to God, its little arms were going like this." I copy the pumping movement.

"Nope, nope, nope! Don't want to hear it!" The mechanic picks up his pace, shaking his head. "I am never going to your fucking house ever. That shit is haunted."

I give him a crooked smile because it could be true, or maybe not. We begin a discussion on demons and spirits, the difference between the two, parallel universes and ghosts, because a soldier believes. Maybe not before the war, and possibly not after, but right now, in the middle of it all, we believe.

Oddly, I never connect the child ghost with those drawings on the wall, or the broken dolls in the yard. That's not to say there wasn't just a little bit of evidence of what may have happened before we arrived. In the back of the supply platoon's yard, just before the perimeter of the minefield and beneath a tree with pale-gray bark and wide, green leaves, is the shallow grave of King Tut, a charred corpse that was once hastily buried, one foot peeking out from beneath the dirt and blackened toes pointing toward the sky.

It's the supply platoon that names him King Tut, led by Staff Sergeant T, who is particularly proud of his find, and he draws massive arrows onto the outside of their house, directing foot traffic to the back of the yard, COME SEE KING TUT! The tomb draws a surprising number of visitors. Starre is back from the cigarette factory with her own stories, and we giggle as we follow the arrows, standing not too close to the grave, marveling at the burnt foot, looking for other body parts, and a little disappointed that the famed Tut is not more exciting. I wonder out loud if the rain will wash away the rest of the grave, but the rains never come, and once we've seen it we never bother going back, though we sometimes wave in the direction of the tomb as we pass the signs. If it's callous, it's because we never stop to process what a nameless shallow grave means. That's saved for much later, when you're out of the military and home safe in your own bed. That's when the real ghosts come.

And perhaps there is something, after all, to the idea that Al Kut is haunted. I sit with Starre on our driveway one evening, bare feet planted on either side of a pink bin. I share some laundry detergent with her, pouring the white powder into already black water, scrubbing the rough material of my uniform together until my knuckles are raw. Behind us, camis of yellow and brown hang on a 5-50 cord, flapping in the light breeze. I like the smell of the sun-dried material, sometimes burying my nose into the uniform once I take it off the line, still warm and smelling like wind. Life is simpler here. It should bore me, but it doesn't.

Beyond the dim circle thrown by our battery-powered lanterns, I see it from the corner of my eye—they're always in the periphery—a shifting thing of all black, and I snap my head to the side, trying to catch it. It's gone, of course. The shadow creatures mimic animals, like nature gone perverse, some animal you'd expect but with an extra head, or humped back, or tiny, shrunken limbs. Some of the others say they've seen things similar, not quite the same but always there at the edge of their vision. I've grown used to them by now. It doesn't even bother me the night I'm startled awake by the dog standing half in the room, as if it had just decided to stroll in through the window. I half sit up because this is a real fear; there is nothing to protect our cots from animals that might wander in off the road. The animal is huge, like a desert wolf, large head hung low as it slowly surveys the room. Then I see it has six legs and I groan, rolling over and burying my face into my makeshift pillow of undershirts, promptly falling back to sleep.

People talk about it. No one loves a good ghost story more than a soldier. Al Kut is either haunted or it's a shared hysteria, if that's a thing. Or maybe we're just tired.

The camp is protected by the Ukrainian Ground Forces, part of the thirty-eight countries that contributed to the multinational coalition in Iraq. I continually forget who they are and call them the Norwegians for no real reason. They guard the perimeters of the camp in impossibly tall towers hastily made of wood and barbed wire. I continue to run in Al Kut, the experience far more enjoyable in the coolness of twilight. I'm obsessed with the ritual, still carefully picking through my meals to push away anything carb-related, loading on extra exercise in shame, terrified that I will once again slip back into that fat body. My worth is determined by how low the uniform pants hang on my hips, by the extra space between the fit of my brown undershirt and the frame of my body. Because I am thin, because I am fit, I think this is healthy.

Female King and Starre often run with me. The Ukrainians press against the edges of their towers, waving hands over blond heads, howling an accented "Hello." They say more that we can't understand, and I wave back.

"Don't do that," King huffs, swiping away beads of sweat from the crown of her forehead. "Ignore them."

And if I don't ignore them, will that seem like I'm looking for attention? I've come so far; I have to be vigilant against any old labels that may be applied should I slip up. I press my elbows to my side, staring down at the bumpy road as I run.

Some evenings, long after the camp has gone black and everyone is tucked away in a cot or snuggled up on a hard stone floor, the Ukrainians commence with Operation Scare the Living Shit Out of the Americans. My room suddenly rolls, rocking with a thunderous boom, dirt and bits of stone shifting down from the ceiling as I snap out of my cot.

"Get your gear on! Move, move, move!" I can hear Sergeant Daniels's screaming from one house over. The sky flashes phosphorous white, and the spatter of some unrecognizable gun offsets the boom of the mortars or land mines.

I have just grabbed my M16, woken so suddenly that I'm still not really processing, simply moving, when Sergeant Daniels yells, "Stand down!" The other girls and I stand by our cots, gear half scrambled into, glancing around in the dark, swiping sleep out of our eyes, but no one really says anything.

Sergeant Daniels, already in full gear (perhaps he sleeps in it), strides up our driveway, waving us off. "Go back to bed. It's just the Ukrainians doing some kind of live-fire exercise." He doesn't say more, just turns on a heel and heads back toward the black street.

It's not only the night exercise, though. Sometimes it's simply mindless rifle firing, often bored Ukrainian night guards shooting at coyotes in order to stay awake. Most times it's loud—tremendously loud, like the sky is being cracked open and the entire field of land mines is on fire. I strain in the dark on my cot, waiting to hear Sergeant Daniels's voice, hand wrapped around the muzzle of my M16, counting ascending numbers in the flashes of light, because if no one has responded by now, then it's probably nothing. Then I roll over, tugging my woobie over my head, and mutter, "Fucking Norwegians," before I slip back to sleep.

Locke strolls up the driveway one evening, M16 slung over her shoulder. She looks around the darkened house. "Where is everyone?"

I'm sitting on a nylon chair, straining to read a book under one of the battery lanterns. I glance around, shocked to find the house empty. I shrug. The girls could have dispersed to any number of places—playing cards with the boys in groups of four, or huddled around a six-inch screen to watch a movie on a portable DVD player, or perhaps just strolling from house to house to visit and talk. The lack of electricity has made socialites of most of us.

Locke shrugs back. "Okay. Want to go take a shower?"

I lean back in my chair, thumb holding my place in the book. "I took a bath earlier."

"No, I mean like a real shower. With running water and everything."

I place the book on the ground; now she has my full attention.

Locke points off in the distance, her slender form outlined by the last of the dying light. The sky is still a gauzy gray. "They have milvans on the other side of the camp with showers. Like hot/cold-water shower, and electricity and everything."

"What? Why do they get showers?" I'm not sure who *they* are but I'm outraged by the injustice.

Locke grins, her teeth white against her sandblasted face. "Who cares? They're ours now. Gaul, me, and Frenchie are going. Are you in?"

"Fuck yeah!" I hop up and rush into the house, throwing my hygiene bag into a sack with my PT uniform.

"Get your Kevlar!" Locke calls.

I snag the helmet out from under my cot. "Why do I need my Kevlar?" I ask as I jog over to her.

"Do you really want to walk across the entire camp?"

I scowl, falling into stride beside her. "They told you we can take a Humvee?"

She flashes that smile. "Sure. Let's go with that."

Gaul and Frenchie lean against the stone wall beside Sergeant T's driveway. Gaul holds one finger against his lips, and Frenchie flicks the red cherry of his cigarette into the dark. Locke points to one of the Humvees in the driveway and the boys position themselves in front of the grille. Locke slips into the driver's seat, doesn't turn on the lights, and throws the vehicle in neutral. Gaul and Frenchie lean down low, hands braced against the front as they push the Humvee out of the driveway and into the road.

"Let's go," Locke hisses and Frenchie slips into the passenger seat as Gaul plants a foot onto the tire well and hops into the open back of the truck. I scramble over the tailgate and roll onto the metal floor. Gaul snorts and I grin back from the bottom of the Humvee, fitting my Kevlar into place.

"Are we going to get into trouble for this?" I whisper as the Humvee flares to life with a low growl. Locke still doesn't turn on the lights as we slowly crawl down the road.

"Nah," Gaul says and leans back against the wooden rails, legs leisurely spread out in front of him on the bench. He reclines his head back, one arm latched around the rail to keep him in place. He smiles up at the passing stars. Sweet Gaul, who will eventually achieve his dream of joining the Special Forces, whom I've seen rescue an imprisoned hedgehog from a trap and release a comfortable distance from the house into the desert, Gaul, who will call me still periodically over the next decade, sometimes at three in the morning, sometimes from places far away, and his voice will become a little lower, a little flatter, as if that quick, ready grin has been snuffed out, and I will worry for him, because even gods can die—in fact they do quite often.

The farther we pull away from our unit, the faster Locke drives. Once we turn away from the dark row of lightless houses, she lets out a loud whoop.

Gaul responds with one of his instantaneous, loud laughs, and Frenchie reaches one arm out the window and loudly raps the roof like a drum. Gaul and I yelp in unison as another bump sends us bobbing. "You're going to kill us!" I scream at Locke, a surge of adrenaline curling my toes and causing my skin to burn.

Locke throws back her head and howls and for a second I release my grip on the rails, laughing, raising both fists to the sky, glowing, pulsating, grinning.

I gulp the wind, as if I can't get enough and this is the moment. The moment I'm in love with. The moment where I'm alive, in some part of the world with a landscape of ancient beauty, dazzling skies, stolen Humvees, and secret getaways.

And I like it here.

two miles out

WE ARE IN AL KUT for three months, then shortly to Diwaniyah. I see Andres again. Our time apart has worn us thin. He wrote to me more than I did to him and he knows it. He tries to physically make up for the imbalance, and we have sex in a dark, abandoned room. He's angry at me so I kiss him harder and that seems to work.

When our company leaves Diwaniyah to head for Kuwait, the regiment takes away most of our ammo. It goes to another unit, cutting our supply nearly in half.

"So you're telling me if we get in a firefight, we won't have enough to defend ourselves?" asks Captain Noble, standing at the head of the convoy, his standard-issue Oakleys strapped tight over his eyes. He's exasperated. We all are, as we divide our magazine stacks in half and hand them over.

"Less weight to carry?" I try for optimism. My TA-50 certainly is lighter, but I'm not sure the trade-off is worth it. There is a ripple of a rumor circulating around the convoy, a sort of snarky opinion that an MI unit wouldn't know how to defend itself in a fight anyway. Leave it to the big boys. Give them the ammo and let them do the real work, like they've been doing this whole time. They're better trained, but the reminder still chafes.

Someone starts a prayer circle, no one knows where the chaplain is, but the ring expands one by one, and I trot over, clasping the hands of two other soldiers and adding myself in, head bowed. I don't know who

I'm praying to anymore, what name to use, but we are all feeling a hunger for protection, a desperate desire to place our lives in the hands of something bigger and higher. "Please place a hedge of protection around us," I murmur, words too familiar to cast aside. There is a calm here, in this ring, a little bit of peace, before we break, re-sling weapons over our shoulders, and disperse into the dusty line for our own vehicles.

I'm Starre's driver now and she strings CD player speakers up on the ceiling of our Humvee, the dust-covered boxes dangling between us. Music isn't allowed but since we don't have a radio, it's not like we'll miss hearing anything important. I'll need the music as we head out, rolling out of the camp gates, passing the concertina wires into the flat, long plains of Al Kut. This trip isn't quartered into miles and hours. The mandate that we stop for the night after eight hours of driving is tossed away. We just need to get to Kuwait. We plow onward, following a sun that never seems to set, stopping rarely for quick latrine breaks, which consist of stepping out of your vehicle and pissing beside a smoldering tire.

"Kevlar!" a sergeant screams down the line on one break, annoyed at all of us who have peeled off some part of our gear, tossing our helmets in the hope of a break from the heat. I strip open my flak vest, holding open the heavy flaps, praying for wind to brush up against my wet uniform. The land is flat, a single line of shimmering gray at the horizon, an entire world comprising one singular line. It's neither beautiful nor ugly. It's overpowering in its simplicity.

We drive for nineteen hours straight. The music keeps me awake, even as my forehead occasionally dips and taps the steering wheel. The heat makes me tired, dulls my fear, my reaction time; the windshield is shrouded in a fine layer of dust. And then, just two miles out of Kuwait, we come up on another unit's convoy, one that was a little ahead of us, their entire line sitting on the side of the dirt road, engines cut. One of the five-tons had been pulling a trailer, a trailer that caught at the edge of the road and flipped suddenly, dragging the truck down the ditch, twisting the metal ties until the five-ton also rolled, like some felled beast going belly-up, oily tires pointed to the sky, crushing the two soldiers inside. Just two miles out of Kuwait.

It seems unjust somehow. We can see the Kuwait line, the space that divides war and peace. They're not the first or last soldiers to die in this war, but somehow the nearness makes it feel even more unfair, that they would never leave this place, even when they could see the end. Just two miles out.

Desecration

homecoming

LOCALS FROM AROUND BANGOR, Maine, meet us at the airport gates, holding WELCOME HOME TO AMERICA signs above their heads, passing out cans of soda and bags filled with homemade chocolate chip cookies, shaking our hands as we pass. American Legion and VFW veterans wear their hats, their unit pins, grasp our hands hard, make eye contact hard, looking but not saying, *The hardest is yet to come*. They lead us into a closed-off room with a table full of donated cell phones, letting us call home in a time when day minutes were a thing and it must have cost a fortune. I cry a little, head tucked to the side, because it's kind and unexpected. A woman in a BANGOR sweatshirt wraps an arm around my shoulder and hugs me in a strong, sturdy way. I laugh. She laughs.

I call my dad and tell him I'm here in Maine, of all places. I had called him from our stop in Germany, telling him we might land in Bangor, but also maybe not. Command keeps it vague. Loose lips sink ships, and all that. They only tell us once the plane is up in the air, and they pronounce it wrong so that the men snicker for hours, yelling "Bang her!" back and forth to each other. My dad scrambles, trying to make it to the airport on time, but Maine is a big state and we're back on the plane before he even has a chance.

So I don't really stop to touch American soil until we land in Fort Polk. I clomp down the metal stairs onto the tarmac and pause in the shadow of the plane as the rest of the platoon flashes by. I crouch and press my palm against the hot asphalt.

"What are you doing?" Andres asks, half turned back toward me.

"I don't know, it seems apropos or whatever. First time touching American soil and whatnot."

"You know that's not soil, right?"

Stones and tiny bits of asphalt stick to my palm, and I have to brush it against my leg. The image of kissing homeland is a bit marred but I stand, lean back on my heels, and breathe in the wet Louisiana summer air. "It's good to be home," I say.

He scrunches up his nose. "It fucking reeks." He turns back toward the platoon, shifting his pack higher on his back. And it sort of does, of diesel fuel and smoldering tar, but that's Fort Polk for you.

I'm not the only one touching the ground, though. A few guys copy me, fingertips against the pavement. Several wait until they reach the edge of the tarmac, stooping down to touch the tangled green weeds and blooming dandelions.

There is an otherworldly feeling to walking up the stone steps of the barracks. They take our M16s, pack them away, and now my left shoulder feels too light. They collect our gear and there's nothing on my back. My entire body feels off. There's no guard duty, no walls. The open and unprotected spaces between barracks buildings are startling. I'm home, but not. Something has shifted. I never cared for this place, not after what happened, and now it has changed again, even though the cement blocks are still the same. The floors are still linoleum, the walls are still whitewashed to cover the black mold creeping along the upper corners of the ceiling. It all looks the same but everything feels different.

The 2nd ACR is deactivated, Tenth Mountain takes over, and the entire brigade is moved to Washington State. They have no use for the linguists and are ready to ship us off to Fort Gordon. Except Andres isn't a linguist, which means he stays, I go, and we're handed an expiration date. We break up slowly, bit by bit, in the three months before I leave.

I yell a lot now. I don't know why, except that it feels good. Words bubble up behind my teeth and spill out with a sneer, with a hiss, and it burns as it exits, feeling like power. Andres yells back. We create our own little war.

We try to vacation for a weekend in Lake Charles. In a few days I'm going to Fort Gordon, which is where I always wanted to be posted. I'm happy, Andres is not. We haven't decided what we'll do with this new, physical distance between us. We yell about it. The hotel room shakes with our anger.

"God, see? This is why we can *never* be together," I scream, gesturing sharply between us. "All we do is fight."

Andres stands in the bathroom threshold, stunned into silence, as if his entire body has been struck immobile. He stares at me blankly for a moment, then rounds on his heel. He slams the bathroom door in my face.

I didn't mean to say it like that. I didn't mean to tell him that way, so definitively, that I already know there isn't anything left for us. I don't know how to tell him I'm not feeling much of anything but rage, that only in these brilliant moments of anger do I vibrate with excitement. Here, in this emotion, I feel invincible.

He cries in the bathroom, on his side of the door, privately, because Andres hates naked emotion, hates revealing anything besides anger and general disgruntlement.

You're destroying a good man, I realize. Dismantling him piece by piece, because despite his flaws Andres is a good, kind man, attentive and faithful. I watch myself breaking him. I'm an effective poison. I hate myself on the other side of the door, forehead rested against the wood, and yet I don't tell him to come out. I don't take back the words because I don't know how.

And even still, when I leave Fort Polk, he stands by my car door, holds me tightly against his body, face buried into my hair. We linger there. I etch the span of his shoulders into my memory, the feel of his arms around my back, how mine tuck under his and press around his waist. I carefully fold up the memory of that last kiss, soft and sad, one of his thumbs brushing along my jawline, and I tuck that memory away, somewhere safe where I can't taint it. This, at least, is real.

I love Fort Gordon. I love its green, rolling hills, its massive oak trees, the fact that the base sits fatly in the middle of Augusta, Georgia, a bustling city. I love my platoon, filled with almost all linguists; my command, who have been in the military intelligence field for years; my female commander, who has a way of stopping what she's doing when you talk to her, of making eye contact while you talk, like she's actually listening. I love the smartness, the casual enjoyment people have for intelligence, the appreciation of academic discourse.

I reconnect with Josephine, my Air Force friend from DLI. We friend so hard that the men are baffled by our bond and call us lesbians. She encourages me to continue writing, because I had stopped shortly after I came back from Iraq, when I sat at my desktop and tried to read back my novel in progress. I quickly deleted the thing. I dug through drawers and bags to find any paper copies, gathered them up, and took them outside to the dumpster, disposing of the book without a backward glance. The naïveté of that writer infuriated me. Her staunch view of black and white, as if there were either, was childlike. Josephine encourages me to start from scratch and I write a world of gray.

But mostly, I love that they don't really know me here. Those who transfer over with me, Starre, male and female King, Baum: They say nothing. This command doesn't know who I was or what happened to me. I stroll into the unit with a combat patch on one shoulder, at a time when combat patches are rare, when most of the soldiers at Gordon have been carefully hidden behind computers and top-secret equipment, and I am more than just a novelty. When a guy from Strategic tries to get too mouthy with me I sneer at him, "Suck my dick, kid." He startles and scampers off for less hostile prey. They can't handle me anymore.

I relish the swagger that accompanies a combat patch. We are the few and get to pause when a higher-up attempts to correct us, to glance at their shoulders, to raise our eyebrows when that space is empty, when they have no war to speak of. It's an unspoken hierarchy that is silently enforced, and I get to be right up there at the top. My unit notices.

I'm made squad leader almost immediately, despite only being a Specialist. I'm given soldiers to attend to. Fort Polk never did this. They never gave me responsibility, they never trusted in my abilities. So here I shine. I am given the chance and I shine with all I have. I am offered days to lead PT. When I lead, we run suicides, lunge steps, bear crawls, sprints, destroying our quads so that the next day we can't make it up the stairs and I love it. I love that they schedule me only to lead on Fridays, knowing I'm brutal, knowing the soldiers will need the weekend to recover. Here, they never know I was once fat. They'll never know I failed PT tests, I who run on my off time, around the track at night so that I keep up with our platoon sergeant on long-run days, six miles, right behind him. For the first time ever, I pass the PT test at the male standard.

I cover for the platoon sergeant some days, acting platoon sergeant, three ranks above my own, and this isn't supposed to happen. I'm specifically chosen, this time singled out for the better, sitting in meetings with the commander and First Sergeant, and other platoon sergeants, taking notes, and they take me seriously. *They take me seriously*, turning toward me at the table, asking questions, wanting my take on the situation, how I think our platoon sergeant would act. *Fake it till you make it*, my drill sergeant always said, so I do, and they listen, and they nod, and at some point I actually know what I'm saying. I'm actually in the know.

My First Sergeant selects me for the company Soldier of the Month board, where I'll go before my senior NCOs and officers, display my military knowledge, answer questions about current events or whatever else the board decides to throw at me. It isn't just a matter of skill and knowledge, but professionalism and confidence. Be confident even in your uncertainty. A confident soldier who knows nothing is better than a weak soldier who knows everything. I win.

On my work shifts, I'm still not the best Farsi linguist, but I get by. They task me with learning Dari as well. I manage. NSA selects a few military linguists to help carry their workload and I'm one of them. I love my job.

I receive special training as a range specialist with new sighting equipment, a job that should go to someone well above my pay grade. I train soldiers in ranks above and below me on how to better sight their weapons. The Command Sergeant Major drops in on one of my classes. He lets me show him the new equipment, how to zero the weapons, keys on how to shoot efficiently. He doesn't remember my name but he speaks about me later, at a meeting for the higher-ups, saying, "We even have Specialists doing amazing things well above their rank," and it feels so good to be recognized. It *feels so good* to be here.

After morning formation, a few weeks before my ETS date, I see a video of myself in uniform, a rarity in the days before smartphones, and I'm a little shocked by what stares back at me. The woman on the screen carries a slanted grin, shoulders back, hands in her pockets because it's not allowed and she's a little defiant, legs spread as if to make space for her swinging dick. I want to say, *Who is that girl?* but that's no girl. I'm a little shocked at the visual evidence of the masculinity that slides on with the uniform, the easy vulgarity, the cocksure tilt of the head, that steely confidence. I don't hate him, though. I kind of love him. I love his self-reliance.

A quiet part of me wonders: If I had always been here, if it had happened here and not at Fort Polk, maybe I would've been all right. Maybe I still can be. A doctor at the aid station admires my medical file, looking up at me, at my easy grin and the way I lean confidently against the table, and she says, "It looks like you managed to heal yourself over there. That's really impressive, you know. Most people come back worse and you came back better."

My grin raises a notch, my spine straightens with satisfaction, and I agree with her, I'm fine. I'm good. I'm in love with this Army, with this uniform, and nothing can take this away from me, that which I've earned and fought for. The war, the rape, it didn't really affect me that much at all. I think this even as my relationships end and I fall into random beds, picking men who close their fists around my neck, who bust my lip open while I laugh, blood staining my teeth, high on the sheer violence of it all.

your ending, my beginning

NOTHING REALLY BAD HAPPENED to me so I can't have PTSD, I tell myself, and that makes sense to me. I don't feel amiss when I come home from Iraq. The doctor said it herself. I came back *better*. At Fort Gordon, not only do I reconnect with my old friend Josephine, but I find Jonathan still there, my first lover, the slice of me that once was. Andres and I have parted ways for good, and Jonathan wants to get back together with me. Now, what a pretty war story that is—the soldier returns home to her former love, the flame that never died. We move in together. We even get a dog. Here's your storybook ending, that 1950s post–World War II kind of perfection. Except it's not.

Something is amiss right from the start, but things further deteriorate by the end of the first year. I lie in bed, staring up at the ceiling, tears rolling down my temples, choking on nothing. My eyes trace the lines of these four safe, comfortable walls and I feel nothing. Jonathan's chest rises and falls with each soft snore, his head turned in the opposite direction. I watch that point on his chest steadily going up and down and I feel empty. I sit up, cross my legs, my hair tangled down my back, and I dig. I dig inside my memory, into my chest, trying to resurrect those old feelings I once had for him, that suffocating obsession, the way my heart used to flutter and kick when Jonathan glanced in my direction. I wait for that intense need to hear his voice, the way I used to rest my head against his barracks wall and let him talk for hours, loving the inflections of his voice. I never had that with Andres, the wild desperation of a first love. I thought it was because there was no one like Jonathan, that I would never love anyone else like I did him. But I have him back now and I feel nothing.

There's a hole here in my chest, and this has to be normal, right? This is what happens when you grow up. This is what it means to be an adult. And I turn my head just a little, unintentionally glaring at him, at the way the sheet is tucked around his shoulder and brushing his chin, the way his lower lip hangs open as he sleeps, almost like a child. I have the sudden urge to grab his shoulder and shake him awake. I want him to hug me. I want to look him in the eye and tell him he can't hurt me anymore. He could ignore me or not. Love me, or not. There's nothing here to break. This is ending, we both know it, but I don't know how to drag up the emotion to care.

I slide out of bed, expertly navigating the maze of stacked books and comics on the floor, padding silently out of the room and across the house in the dark. I like the dark. It feels comfortable here where no one can see me. I can't sleep, but I can't tell you why. I don't have nightmares. I dream of nothing. There is so much nothing here.

I open the door to the garage, to where that new dog sleeps. Dorian Gray raises his head, golden-brown eyes wary. I climb down the wooden steps. "Hello, there," I coo, and fold myself onto the dog bed with him. I curl up my legs, tuck my cold feet against each other, and rest my temple against my folded hands.

Dorian watches me, ears folding down in uncertainty. Someone had starved him. Someone had beaten him. We didn't know at first, when we took him home from the shelter, a sweet, visually stunning creature with long, full white-and-gray fur. He's a Siberian husky, German shepherd, something else mix, and looks all wolf. But there's no wildness in him. Beneath all that fur, his spine presses against his skin. His ribs protrude. He cowers when you toss a ball at him. He's tentative and quiet.

I snuggle close and share his air, breathing in his out, my nose just touching his. I reach out and sink my fingers into the thick mane around his neck. He raises one white paw and leaves it on my arm. "I'm going to sleep here with you," I tell him, and he doesn't seem to mind. This, at least, I feel: It's only been a few days, but this dog is mine. The world could burn, but I have my Dorian Gray.

I sigh and he lowers his head a little. "You're going to be okay," I promise him. I loved Dorian before he loved me, but I earn his trust through these quiet moments, through sleeping up against him on his bed in a dark, cold garage. Very soon Dorian Gray will grow back his confidence; he'll shed his reticence. He'll stand strong beside me, leaning against my legs for *my* support, not his. Dorian recovers quickly and marvelously.

I don't.

Things end with Jonathan much as they did with Andres. I don't see the common thread. Instead I bounce again from bed to bed, sprawling out on foreign sheets, blissfully detached, well versed in the worth of a body, in the weight of its limbs and the importance of sacredness, which is nothing at all, we're all a little bit worthless, our bodies flung from here to there with little control or agency. I chase infatuations, then drop them once they're caught, feeling powerful. I can consume everything because there's such a divine freedom in feeling nothing. Liberty hums through my bones, splits my face into a grin; I twist men around my hands, my body fearlessly devouring, because they can't take what I don't have—from the married warrant officer who swears he's separated and maybe he is but probably not, to the beautiful, blond British soldier who sings me "God Save the Queen," naked, one arm slung behind his head while I laugh, a finger pressed against my bleeding lip from where he punched me, to the young civilian who doesn't know what to do with me, a little cowed by my aggressiveness, my clear understanding of exactly what I want.

And through it all, I hear the cast-iron ringing of the words *what if I can never love again*, and I brush it off, because that was uttered by a soldier who saw things, did things, so that can't be me. Nothing that bad really happened to me. I can't have PTSD.

fight me, bitch

I LEAVE ACTIVE DUTY in September 2005 and return to Connecticut. I buy a small apartment in New Haven with my deployment money and live alone, just Dorian and me. My mother picked out the apartment before I even got home, because it was cheap, cute, and exactly six miles from her house. She smiles as she helps paint every room in the place. She would've moved me into her house if I agreed, but I didn't, so this is close enough.

I go up to Maine to visit my father, only to arrive while he's out. The bartender at my father's rustic restaurant tilts his head and stares at me blankly.

"Wait, who are you again?" he asks.

"I'm Pete's daughter," I say.

"I didn't know Pete had a daughter."

My stomach sinks.

"He never mentioned you," says the bartender, and a few of the waitresses laugh.

I glance down at my bag, trying to hide the disappointment that clenches my throat. "Oh," I say simply.

"No, I'm not being serious!" he backpedals, not realizing this is the worst joke he can make. "It's funny because he talks about you *all the time*."

I'm skeptical and it's obvious. He tries to convince me, some of the waitresses and even the cook chime in, but I'm not sure if it's real or pity. The bartender is forced to list my achievements—Japan, Army,

Iraq, languages I speak—before I start to believe him. The idea that my father talks about me so often seems a little too good to believe.

If my father does or doesn't, he gives no indication. He places me in one of the best rooms in his B&B, one with a quiet view of the Dead River, allows Dorian to sit in the restaurant by my feet, and, when I fuck one of his river guides nearly blind, sportively requests that I not break his men.

Back home in Connecticut, I party like a soldier, which is to say hard and repeatedly by civilian standards. I've embraced the femininity of pink and heels and lip gloss, having left my combat boots packed in the back of my closet, but I feel no loss of power. I stride with a purpose, spine straight, eyes direct. The lights of the club pulse blue and white and I twist on the dance floor, arms overhead, the hair at the nape of my neck wet with sweat. I own this floor. I am all high heels, long legs, and short skirt. My gaze doesn't flitter away if you say you want me; I grin, because of course you do. I am a bright, burning star, always looking for *more*, looking for something to push back against me.

I slip easily between people, moving toward the bar, in control of my stride, my shoulders, the steady sway of my hips. I pause at the bar, one hand resting against the wood, and the man beside me slips his hand up the hem of my skirt and presses his palm against my bare ass. He does so with a smirk to the boys behind him. He doesn't even glance at me—I'm not a woman but the punch line of a joke I haven't been invited to.

So I punch him in the nose. My fist makes contact hard. His head snaps back, he stumbles, his hands flash up to his face, and it's magnificent, every second is magnificent as he falls away from me. He looks at me now, stares at me with eyes wide, half his face obscured by his hands, and I grin. I want to hit him again. *Fight me, bitch*, I think, fists clenched, body clenched, hard. This is my rage and I am everything with it.

The man quickly points to the man beside him, to one of his friends, as if to say *he did it, he did it,* but I don't care. I take a step forward because I want to hit him again. Him or his friend, I don't care. I want to see his nose bleed. I want to hear the crack of bone. I can't breathe around my own fire, it burns so hot that I'm blinded.

A friend grabs my elbow, trying to pull me away, but I shake off their grip, stalking toward nothing with a purpose, teeth clenched, shimmering with contained violence. I glare and people give me space, as if they can feel heat rolling off my skin. I wonder what I look like. I imagine I look glorious, like a warhorse dancing across the battlefield.

I'm sexually aggressive. I crook a finger, take a lover home, and flip him off me, us both tumbling off the bed and hitting the floor. I land on top, every time.

"Whoa," he breathes, eyes a little wide, a little startled.

"Yeah," I say, all teeth. "Whoa." One hand is clamped around his throat. I clench, lean down, and tease his lower lip with my teeth, staring, glaring. He likes it. I like it. I like me on top.

I feel no fear anymore, as if the emotion has been sliced out of my brain. I walk at night, late at night, two or three in the morning, headphones brazenly pressed against my ears, following the banner of Dorian Gray's white fluffy tail. I walk shadier sections of New Haven because I can't sleep, my brain running, running, running, never stopping. I like to stretch my legs when everyone else is asleep, when the streets are black and quiet. I like the music loud in my skull. But mostly I like the potential for violence—the slightest edge where something probably won't happen, but *could* happen. I thrive in that possibility. It feels like home.

I imagine an attempted rape while I walk here in the dark, where men think to violate me and I envision each try ending with brutality as I thwart them, again and again, each fantasy a shock of lovely adrenaline, as if I can rewrite my own narrative, begging for it to happen again so I can revise how it ended, give myself the happily ever after. I imagine myself ripping my would-be rapist to bits and pieces and leaving clumps of flesh and body parts on the pavement.

I dream of violence. I imagine being targeted and turning with feral glee. I'd rip at ears, those come off with minimal force; impale eyeballs with thumbs, I hear they pop like grapes. I'd wrap strong legs around a waist and bury teeth into the neck, into the carotid artery. The power in the human jaw is truly something amazing—265 pounds of force. The body, when committed, can offer such remarkable viciousness. It's a beautiful bit of machinery. I feel rage in my hands; they want raw violence, not the kind behind a gun but with fingers and nails and muscles. I want to break bones and feel them crack under my palms.

There's no place for this kind of rage in civilian life. I expected it to stay behind in Iraq, or unpeel from my skin when the time came, along with the uniform. Civilian life is quiet. Mundane. I have nothing to be angry at, but I'm still angry. The boredom and safety enrage me. I'm part of the stereotype—the angry soldier, standing over a body outside some bar, knuckles white and red, mouth black with a wordless scream. I should mind it, I know something has to be wrong, except everything *feels* right, like I'm perpetually high, brain-devouring endorphins making my body tingle. It's a potent emotion—feeling in power instead of out of it. The only problem is my dreams aren't listening to the rest of me. They're not empty anymore. They've morphed into nightmares and they disturb what little sleep I manage.

I'm in the sand, huddled against a thorny bush, hands dragging through the silt, nails digging into the rock bed as mortars sing and crash overhead, but I can't find my M16, hands grasping at nothing, heart pounding. I'm crawling through the dirt, cringing with each explosion, screaming, calling my weapon by name, as if it will respond and come home, but I can't find my fucking M16, and when I wake, gripping sheets soaked with sweat, I still can't find it. My hands are still empty. And it hurts.

Or there is the recurrent dream where I am both soldier and insurgent, two bodies at once, staring down the barrel of an M16, staring up the barrel of an M16, huddled against a stone wall, feeling trapped and helpless at one end of the rifle, and also standing, rifle tucked into the shoulder and with the superiority of holding metal and gunpowder in my hands. There's the fear of dying on one side, the fear of killing on the other, one of us hisses, "Die," the other screams, "No!," the crack of a shot and we both live and die, the sensation of life draining from the body, while also being simultaneously victorious, standing over the dead me, finally having done what I am trained to do. They say you can't die in your dreams, but I've done it over and over again, felt that death, the terror of staring up into the black hole of a muzzle. That narrow little barrel becomes my entire existence, too large to escape from, impossible to look away.

I think I can ignore the nightmares, or the inability to fall asleep, or to stay asleep. I can do this. When I do finally sleep, I doze late into the morning, into the afternoon, and it seems like a reasonable trade. I can write late into the evenings anyway, shifting everything around. It's okay. I can do this.

the warworn's battle cry

IT'S NOT LIKE I haven't heard of PTSD. But there's a hierarchy to these things, a level of justifiability, and I don't match up. I didn't kick down doors; I didn't put bodies back together, or count the missing parts. I didn't huddle down in firefights, my Humvee never exploded. I'm not deserving of PTSD. So it's a kind of betrayal the first time I hit the deck at a loud noise.

I'm newly home and at a Memorial Day parade, asked to march with the local American Legion in my hometown. It's surreal to march down the streets I grew up on, past buildings I once ran through as a child, seeing young faces stare up at me. Am I now to them what those soldiers in Haiti were to me then? I wave big and wide.

I march with older soldiers, real soldiers who saw real war, veterans of World War II and Vietnam and Korea, some slightly shriveled and bent with age, but brilliant and hard underneath. I am small and inconsequential in their shadows, a peripheral figure, a member of the new wars, those absent of trenches and napalm and overgrown jungles. I march with them, feeling a little out of place, a whole lot of unworthy, just me, the only Iraqi War veteran, the only woman, and when they shake my hand and pat my back, I know I'm a fraud. They give me such attention because I'm young and new and female, and I bow beneath its burden.

At the end of the parade, as I'm stepping out of formation, a man presents his hand to me. He is graying at the temples but has sharp, intelligent eyes. "Thank you for your service." His handshake is firm, strong, and I grin back.

"Thank you for yours," I start to say, seeing his black hat with the Vietnam insignia.

A cannon goes off. The crowd claps but I hit the ground, flat on my ass, legs spread inelegantly, and with no recollection of how I got here. I'm dazed for a moment, surrounded only by legs, slowly realizing what I've done: I've hit the deck in front of all the crowd, in front of all these veterans who've seen worse things, violent, bloody things, and I'm the only one who flinched.

Then hands clamp onto my upper arms and pull me to my feet. "You can always tell the ones who went over." The Vietnam veteran holds me up, his grip firm and comforting as if he can will his strength down his arms and into my body, his gaze resilient, daring me to look back at him and be all right. I want to sink into that stronghold, that embrace, the commonality that might bridge that chasm I always feel between everyone else and me. I'm so tired and I want to rest.

But I haven't earned this PTSD. I glance around, avoiding his eyes, ashamed. The girl dropped to the ground, of course it was the girl. So instead of accepting his kindness I flash him a quick smile. "Thank you, I'm fine," I say hurriedly, not really looking at him, pulling out of his grasp. And the skin is already crawling at the back of my neck, every muscle tightening, tensing for the next impending explosion. I already know I'll hit the ground again, in front of them all, so I escape quickly. Not running but fast, get out before the next blast, get into the car where no one can see you cry, and I have to remember to breathe, to let out a hiss of air between clenched teeth, red-faced, shamed, because nothing that bad happened to me, so why am I like this?

The veteran calls after me, saying, "It's okay, don't be embarrassed," but I'm out of there before he can finish his sentence. It must have resonated with him somehow, because he writes a few paragraphs in the local newspaper a few days later, to the Iraqi female veteran. And he wants to tell me that it's okay, to never be sorry for the things I've seen; that he wants me to hold my head up high, and that he gets it. He gets it. And I should've written back somehow, to thank him for those few words, those short seconds, but I'm still too ashamed, because what did I see? What really happened to me? So little, so very little in comparison. And so I pull my PTSD close against my chest, afraid to let anyone see, lest they ask me why, why, and what can I say? I have nothing to say.

I join the Connecticut National Guard in 2005. I'm not ready to be separated yet, to be cut off from that thing which is bigger than me. I need the uniform and the purpose that comes with its sharp lines.

I see war on the news and I ache. There is no draft anymore, and service members are devoured by the machine, crunched between gears and spit back out, accumulating years of war, accumulating PTSD, and TBI, and broken bones and shattered limbs, redeploying and redeploying, silently marching forward again and again and it should be me. My fifteen months are short, I feel useless here in the civilian world, sitting behind a desk as a mechanic shop office manager, guilty, as soldiers line up for yet another deployment, backs bowing slightly more with each rotation, and *it should be me*. I wear my civilian life with scarlet shame and guilt. I don't want to go back, I never want to go back, but how can I not when everyone else is?

So I join the National Guard as a journalist. I don't want to return to Iraq, but I'm soothed by the possibility that I *could* go, that I'm still doing my part. If I don't go, it's not my fault, I didn't hide; blame my unit for not sending me. But for now I'm safe on parade detail on the streets of Hartford. Right now, my biggest concern is that this Veterans Day parade runs smoothly. No one knows my secrets here in this little unit far removed from active-duty life. I preen before the crowd in my uniform, still in love with the sandy colors and the combat patch over my shoulder. The national anthem plays and I salute, pride closing my throat and causing my vision to blur.

Boom. A cannon explodes, a sound of celebration, and I'm on the pavement again, gravel digging into my palms. People stare, every head turned, eyes black and watching. I scramble to my feet, the anticipation of another boom strangling me. I feel the second explosion in my gut, and I crumble, pushing off the pavement with fingertips, clinging to the brick wall for stability. I never reacted this way in Iraq: Mortar, IED, and EOD explosions were par for the course. So why now? When there is no real danger, why must I react now?

I push through bodies, ignoring the way they swivel to watch. I escape down an alley, radio cracking to life as I gasp that someone needs to take my post. At the next boom my knees buckle and I'm hyperventilating, slapping my hands against a locked glass door, desperate to get inside, as if that will somehow soften the blow.

A police officer finds me curled in the brick doorway, pressed against the glass with fingers twisted in my hair, covering my ears as I dig my heels against the pavement. "Come in here," he coaxes, opening the door to his squad car.

"I'm sorry, I'm sorry," I mumble, frantically pushing away tears. "I'm so stupid," I confess.

"It's all right, it's perfectly normal." He turns up the music to drown out the next cannon cry.

I don't think this is normal.

Then there is the aftermath, standing ashamed in front of my sergeant's desk. "I don't think you should re-enlist," he confides, with what seems like genuine concern. "We could be deployed and this"—he gestures toward me—"could only get worse."

I hold on to the edge of my uniform as he speaks, as if by gripping it tight enough, I can ensure that it can't be taken away from me.

But it can. And it is.

No one really explained the dusky film that settles over civilian life, how the safety breeds a mind-numbing boredom, how everything feels a little dead. *I'm not meant for this*, I think, watching everyone content in the endless movement from A to B, as if only partially aware of the feeling of life. I ache maybe not so much for Iraq, but perhaps the uniform, the power behind the M16, the comradery in misery, the space that is *mine*. I have no place here, I think. The words that escape from my mouth are too quick, too brutal, and civilians cringe a little when I talk. I'm other, an oddity, all the more rare for being a woman in this masculine identity, the Veteran.

I'm not meant for this. I stare down at my office keyboard, deeply entrenched in civilian life. The computer screen is filled with numbers and columns, and there's a bitter taste in my mouth. I shift in my seat, skin twitching. The four half-section walls of my cubicle are suffocating me. Looking at their blue padding I have the sudden urge to claw up over them, to stare down at my blind, fish-eyed co-workers and hiss "You're all dead," feeling trapped and cornered by the onward march of the mundane, the ringing phones and mechanical grins and incessant typing, everyone doing something that is nothing.

Then there is the car accident on a rainy afternoon, when the Subaru skids across the highway, elegantly hydroplaning, rear end swinging around to the front, a ballerina twirl until the tires slam into the hard ditch on the edge of the double lanes, having crossed traffic and misplaced itself in the wrong direction.

No one screams. There is quiet horror as we spin, and a moment of silence after the vehicle finally stops. Four people in the car and three of them exhale. The driver is clinging to the steering wheel; the college girl in the back, a tiny blond swimming in her gray university sweatshirt, is trembling.

I'm in the passenger seat, one hand lightly touching the seat belt, and in the dead silence of the car I tilt my head back, crack open my mouth, and laugh. I remember this feeling! I laugh from the gut, with my whole body, because *I remember this*. It reminds me of the time in Iraq, during my first R&R, when Delta forces traded volleys of mortars with insurgents over the river, and a stray mortar soared over our stone wall, crashed into our compound, sliced a tree in two, but didn't detonate. If it had, we all would've been dead. We crowded around the dud shell, marveling at the shattered wood, the way it planted itself deep into the soil but never exploded, and commented on the kill radius, which expanded way beyond us in our little stone bunker.

"How was R&R?" Sergeant Baum asked when I returned.

"A mortar hit our compound thirty feet away from us but didn't explode," I gushed. "We almost died." Because almost dying is bragging rights.

I laughed, he laughed, so now I laugh.

The driver turns to me, appalled, jaw a little slack. "Are you okay?"

"I'm fine," I giggle, fist pressed against my lips as I try to swallow my laughter.

"She's in shock," says the guy in the back, and that almost puts a damper on my mood.

I swing around toward him. "I'm not in shock," I snap. I know what shock is, and this is not it.

"We almost died," the little blond whispers.

I'm back to smiling again. "But we didn't die. That's why it's funny."

"It's not funny," she says back softly.

But I think it is. They're reminded of death, but I'm reminded of feeling alive, brain synapses lighting up like fireworks, remembering that delightful space right at the cusp of life, so I laugh, and finally realize there's probably something wrong with me.

After that the crying starts.

I'm standing at the edge of a festival in my hometown, my mother and brother deep somewhere inside the crowd, but I'm walking the outskirts, for some reason unable to dive into the throng. I take a few steps in, then instinctively find myself back out, as if pushed by some invisible barrier. Each time I stop, Dorian Gray leans against me, his weight pressed against my legs, face tilted up at me, watching my face.

An older woman pauses and touches my wrist, causing me to visibly startle. "Are you okay, honey?"

"What?" I blink at her. For some reason my vision is blurred. "I'm fine," I say. But when I touch my cheek, my fingertips are wet. "What the fuck?" I brush the heel of my palm across my eyes, realizing I'm leaking.

"I'm sorry," I mumble, pulling away, dashing for my car with my head down, one fist digging into my stomach, as if to hold my insides in. I coil around Dorian in the car, wet cheeks buried into his fur, and he sits quiet, holding up my weight with his perpetual calm. I have no idea why I'm crying, and that in and of itself seems absurd.

And so I begin to cry randomly and inexplicably. No emotion is too small—happy or sad, frustrated or delighted, I regulate nothing. It's the worst kind of punishment for the once-soldier who prided herself on the impression of strength and masculinity. Soldiers don't cry. At least not where everyone can see them.

I make a tally of my symptoms, a little checklist that is startling—nightmares, jumping at loud noises, hypervigilance, difficulty sleeping, rage, inability to regulate emotions—and realize that maybe, just perhaps, I have some post-traumatic stress. I silently wonder if any of the others got it, as if it's some contagious disease, or if I'm the only one who got infected. Does female King have trouble sleeping at night? Does Sergeant Daniels think of the mortars, the IEDs, the bullets? Does Locke dwell on her time in the turret seat, lost beneath a Kevlar and a flak vest? Am I the only one, the weakest link, fracturing while everyone else stayed whole? Will everyone snicker, just softly, beneath their breath, when they hear that I've caught the disease, and say to themselves, to each other, "Of course it would be Dostie. It wouldn't be anyone else but Dostie." I don't ask because I'm afraid of the answer.

I call the Veterans Affairs hospital for guidance and somehow end up at Compensation and Pension. "We'll send you paperwork," says a woman on the line, who isn't nasty, but isn't friendly, either. A robot would be just as effective. "Are you going for therapy?"

I pause, sitting on my couch and drawing one knee up to my chin. "No."

"You should," she says curtly, "if you want to get paid."

"If I want to get paid?"

"You'll get a higher rating if you're going to therapy," she tones, voice flat, as if her attention is elsewhere.

"I'm not looking for a disability rating," I respond. I'm looking to stop crying.

"Sure." She doesn't sound like she believes me. But she sends the paperwork regardless, and I shift through the lines and questions, filling out each block accordingly, until I get to 3E: DESCRIPTION OF THE INCIDENT. It provides a sizable box of space that somehow is both too large and too small. Dread fills my stomach. I tap my pen against the paper, stand, walk across the room, then come back. The box stares up at me, empty and fat. Describe the incident. Write it here because it should be that easy.

Never mind that writing down the event will later be the basis of my fourteen-week cognitive behavioral therapy. Never mind that I will fear each session, standing at the door of my apartment, one hand on the doorknob, and sob, because I won't want to go, I won't want to talk about it, and I certainly won't want to commit it to paper, where someone else could read it and judge for themselves. It will take years of therapy before I can scratch out "the incident" for an undergraduate thesis, and more therapy mixed with bottles of benzodiazepines and selective serotonin reuptake inhibitors before I can fully commit, can wholly describe it, hunched over a laptop in a local coffee shop, punching out each letter, jumping up periodically and pacing around the shop, wasting time, procrastinating until I force myself to sit, hunch, write the next sentence, repeat, a herculean effort as laborious as birth but not nearly as beautiful.

So I don't provide a description of the incident then. I jam the half-finished form into its manila folder and toss it in the mail, counting on my records to show *something*. Except I've forgotten that Fort Polk has lost any and all of it.

We were always told to keep copies of any military document for our own records, just in case. Before I out-process from Fort Polk, I dash over to the hospital to stand awkwardly in line at the information desk. When it's finally my turn, I shuffle up to the desk and lean over the hard linoleum counter. "I need a copy of my rape kit report," I whisper to the man on the other side.

He blinks at me, freezing in mid-place, one hand still clenching a file. "Your what?"

"The rape kit report?" I lean further so that I don't have to say it any louder.

The soldier is young, probably just some clerk hardly past his teens. He flushes red and fumbles with the computer. "I don't...do we have that here?"

His embarrassment rubs off on me, and I turn crimson. "I was told you would." I don't make eye contact. Not that he does either, of course.

"I don't think we would have that here," he says again, and I stare down at my hands as he punches in my information. "No," he mutters. "No, I don't see that."

"Where would I get it?" I want to be done with this conversation.

"I don't know..." He clicks some keys but I have the feeling he's doing it randomly, not really looking for anything. "I guess if we had it, it would be here?" he finally admits, voice lilting at the end, as if questioning himself. "But I don't have anything under your name—"

I can't take another minute so I wave one hand. "Thanks, that's fine, I'm good." I dart out of the hospital door and don't look back.

A little over a year later, Fort Gordon doesn't fare much better when I try to out-process from them and active duty altogether. My palms itch as I wait on the other side of the counter on the ninth floor of Mental Health. I wipe my palms against my DCU bottoms. I'm *this* close to holding the report again and I might be sick. I breathe out, simultaneously hot and cold. I'm not sure if I'll try to finish reading it this time. I shove around the thought, focus instead on how I'll have it in my hands because maybe I'll need proof of what happened one day.

"Hmm," muses the clerk, finger on the mouse and scrolling down. "I don't have anything right now."

"What do you mean?"

He shrugs. "I mean that Fort Polk never sent over your records."

"What?" I blink at him, stunned. I don't want the report, don't want to have to touch it or read it or even know it is in my proximity, but I at least want to know it *exists*.

"I can request for it, though," he adds.

"Oh," I mumble. "Okay, that's good. How long will it take?"

He shrugs again. "Few weeks. Maybe months."

"But I'm out-processing *now*." My voice rises a little and sounds suspiciously like whining. I clear my throat gruffly.

"I can forward it to you once it gets here," he offers. "Just give me a forwarding address." I write down my mother's address back in Connecticut and he smiles politely, as if just registering I'm there and I'm human. "We'll send it over to you."

He never does. The report goes missing or lost or whatever happens to reports that no one wants to see or be seen. It is hiding somewhere out there with my rape kit.

So when the VA goes to process my claim, I have no evidence, even though it should all be there. Nothing remains from Fort Polk, as if it were a black smudge so easily wiped away. Yet they award me 10 percent because although Fort Polk lost the rape report, although they lost the rape kit, there is a single piece of paper in my files, one tiny report where I once went catatonic in Iraq, after the death of Avery, when I happened to mention to a doctor that I was raped, and she just so happened to write it down, the only lasting evidence of what took place, preserved entirely by accident but at least just enough for them to know it happened.

just say the word

THE VETERANS AFFAIRS HOSPITAL decides fourteen weeks of cognitive behavioral therapy is the best option for me.

It's ghastly.

The therapist sits across from me, one leg casually slung over the other, her shoe dangling off one foot as she bobs it up and down in time to music only she can hear. "Why don't you tell me a little more about it."

It indeed. We're walking circles around the word *rape*. I find colorful ways to get there. *What Happened at Fort Polk*, or *The Thing That Happened*, but mostly simply *It*. I hate the word. It's a very concise word, no room for error, no ability to wiggle to the side and misunderstand or misconstrue. It's brutally succinct. *Sexual assault* is softer. No one jerks in shock when they hear it. Instead their bodies melt forward, eyebrows drawn down, shoulders rolled kindly, sympathetically patting a hand. But *rape* jars people. They resent the reality laid bare. You have to have manners about this sort of thing. That's what I tell myself.

"After It happened—" I start, but she interrupts me.

"You're doing really well, Ryan. You are. But we've talked about what happened after the rape—"

I flinch.

"—I want you to talk more about the rape itself."

Goddamn it, woman, stop using that word! I sigh, cross my arms, look away. "Avoidance behavior," she calls it. All of it. The inability to make eye contact when I speak about It, the inability to say the word at all. I'll talk about my shame for sleeping with Andres so soon afterward. I'll talk about how it felt standing in that formation, my commander sneering at me from the front. But not It. There's nothing to say about It.

I automatically reach down, fingers searching for Dorian's mane, then I remember she wouldn't let me bring him here. I have to do this "on my own," and without a crutch. The empty space by my feet is cold.

She tilts her head, her dark bobbed hair swinging around her chin. She's young and pretty and kind. She doesn't push me. "So for your homework," she says, changing the subject, "I want you to write about the rape itself. You need to get this out, Ryan. You have to let it out into the air somehow."

Fuck that. I clamp down hard, fingers wrapped around the bottom of my chair seat. I don't have to do shit.

She's persistent. I'm stubborn. We dance for weeks.

"It's not your fault," she says firmly. "You couldn't consent. You didn't consent."

I scrub my face with both hands. "But I don't know. I didn't say the word *no* exactly."

"You let him know in *every way possible* that you weren't okay with what he was doing."

"But if I hadn't been drinking..."

"You're allowed to drink, Ryan. You're allowed to drink and get drunk without being raped."

"I know that, but...I should've just been sober."

"No. You shouldn't have been raped."

"Yeah, well, I was." I angrily fling my hands up in the air.

"You were *what*, Ryan?"

"I was—*you know*. And if I hadn't been drinking, I could've fought him off. Or my command would've believed me. And they wouldn't have just said I regretted it afterward or I was just embarrassed or I just made a bad decision while drunk or any of that shit. If I hadn't drunk that night, *none* of it would have happened. Or it would've all ended *very* differently." I feel the rage and the hurt and the helplessness burn at the back of my throat, like I want to scream and shake her and shake the whole fucking world because it's so unfair.

She leans forward, elbows on her knees, like she can taste a break-through. "But that's on them. Your command. That's their inability to understand rape, or face the reality of rape. That doesn't change the fact that *you* were raped, Ryan. And no one has the right to take advantage of someone in a vulnerable situation. He targeted you for being drunk. He preyed on your inability to consent. He raped you. You know that."

"I know," I hiss, teeth clenched, glaring out the window, tears streaking down my cheeks.

"Just say the word, Ryan."

I glare at her then, resentful, grateful; this terrible, curative therapy. "I was raped." My eyelashes flutter, my shoulders sag. My voice cracks. "I was raped and it's not fair."

"No. It's not."

But there's nothing any of us can do about that, is there?

So I'll say the word. I might dance around a little, twist my wrist round and round in a circle, gesturing for you to catch up and get the gist of the thing, but I'll say rape. Cognitive behavioral therapy gives me this. It gives me back my mouth and my tongue and restores my glorious rage. I have a story that is a sword and I can wield it, cutting outward, not inward.

interim

AFTER THERAPY, COLLEGE IS an easy transition for me. *Sergeant* is traded for *Professor*, a simple exchanging of ranks. I'm comfortable with the hierarchy. I do what I'm asked; I follow orders well, I keep in my lane. I relish the order of the academic world.

I enroll into Southern Connecticut State University in 2006, taking advantage of its free tuition for veterans, despite the fact this is the very college I tried to avoid a lifetime ago. But the classes are small, the professors serious and knowledgeable. I think I'm going to be an archaeologist, to dig down into the ancient world, stand in modern-day Iraq and find the veins of older things beneath the earth. I can't shake that part of the world. But archaeology involves a lot of osteology, biology, and -ology in general, so I switch to history, because it's the final product that I love the most anyway.

One day my regular Western Civ professor is ill, and a different professor covers for him. This man's lectures transform me; he plucks historical factoids from the air, spinning ancient history into a breathing thing, a fantastical creature that brushes up against this side of our modern world, relevant and alive. I fill page after page of notes until my fingers ache. Here I read *Epic of Gilgamesh* and the tale of Utnapishtim, the precursor of Noah, the story so similar, but older, so much older that how can one be true and not the other? And once again my axis tilts. What started in the streets of Iraq comes full circle in a history class about the ancient streets of Iraq. The last clinging bits of my Christianity are shattered; I'm more fascinated than I am dismayed.

My professor also talks of Inanna/Ishtar, the Sumerian/Babylonian goddess of war and sex. Her very existence rings through me. She should be contradictory—a woman at the helm of war, a war goddess who wears sex like a virtue. How had I not understood that war and sex were so tightly bound? How have we forgotten that these two entities are so deeply entwined, both turning us fierce and wild and alive? How could War be anything but a woman, for all her power and powerlessness?

I tattoo her eight-pointed star on the inside of my wrist to remind myself of her duality, of both my parts: sex and war. I wear her as if I can claim both, not yet realizing that I'm still conflating sex with trauma, and that one has dramatically complicated the other. I think I am triumphant, embracing the icon of a goddess who is more similar to me than any god, and not realizing that indeed the worst is yet to come.

It's easy for me to enjoy college, sitting among students who are mostly younger and a little less experienced. In one of my first English classes, the professor asks us to introduce ourselves with three interesting facts. I listen to the kids just out of high school talk about their majors and hobbies; when it gets to me I lean back, embracing my masculine persona with one foot resting on the other knee, arm flung over the back of the chair, and say, "I was a Persian-Farsi linguist, with a proficiency in Japanese, and I was in Military Intelligence for the Army. I was deployed during the initial invasion into Iraq."

"Jesus," one of the students breathes. "This is literally like one of those National Guard commercials where everyone is like blah, blah, and then there's you."

I raise my eyebrows at him, smug.

"I guess I won't be talking about politics anymore," the professor laughs nervously, obviously regretting her earlier anti-Bush rant. I shrug and smile.

In another English class, I sit next to a girl in a hijab. She's from Baghdad, she says.

"Oh, I've been there!" I say with delight, thrusting out my hand to shake hers. "I was there with the Army. Operation Iraqi Freedom I and II." I grin, so enthused for this connection, expecting her to brighten, smile, embrace me.

Instead her dark brow curls and she stares at my hand. "So I'm supposed to be happy you're one of the ones who invaded my country?" She turns back toward the professor, shoulder pressed against the table, body tilted away so all that I can see of her is her straight spine.

Well, fuck you, too, I inwardly snarl, deflating, dropping my hand into my lap. What does she know, I sniff, crossing my arms aggressively over my chest. She's here in pretty America, what does she know? The truth is I should have asked, because maybe she knew a lot. It was so easy to be proud then, though.

"You don't know what the fuck you're talking about," I snap at another student on campus, getting in his face at his own rally, standing closer than he'd like, and he leans back just slightly, the sign he's holding overhead flagging. "I was there when grown men dropped to their knees, sobbing with joy, when Saddam was captured. They *begged* to hang him. I was there when his sons were killed. I *saw* how they celebrated in the streets." I quiver with fury. "I know the stories of what Saddam did to his people. I heard them firsthand." And I had. I'd heard the stories of what his sons did to women in the streets, of the kidnappings and the murder, the torture of citizens, how citizens feared bullets in the head for something as inoffensive as having the wrong accent. It was so easy to be proud then, when we helped stop all that. "So don't *you* tell *me* we're over there slaughtering innocent people, that we're killing women and children, because you don't know what the fuck you're talking about. It's the insurgents killing all those people."

The student scoffs. "Why would they kill their own people?"

I'm stunned into momentary silence. "Are you—seriously, do you not—Shi'ite versus Sunni? Civil war? Do you have no idea what's happen—no, no, fuck you." I turn dramatically on one heel. "Just fuck you." Because they're fucking kids behind computers who have no idea what they're talking about—

"I've read the accounts of soldiers who were *there*—" he calls after me.

"*I* was there." I turn back. I don't know if he can't believe me because I'm wearing a skirt and heels, or because I'm here and not there, but it's really starting to piss me off.

"—and they said it happened all the time, where soldiers killed civilians. It happens *all* the time!"

"I'm telling you firsthand experience, not something from something you read somewhere!"

He shakes his head at me and I flip him the bird before storming off. Of course, there was that one time when a group of Marines raped those two Iraqi teenagers, one literally to death, and the other was later honor-killed by her family, but that doesn't occur to me until several steps later and I'm not about to go back and tell *him* that.

Then there are the young women who look at me strangely, in awe or horror, as if they don't know how to process me. I stand outside their boxes. They can't decide if I've bravely defied the machine or if I've been cowed and indoctrinated by it. "Is it even anyplace for a woman?" some ask. "Would you suggest I join?" ask others. One particular woman stands before me, face open and bright, staring up at me as she says, "I'm thinking of joining the Army. Like becoming an officer. What do you think?"

I think I feel old as I look at her, she who is young in more than just physical years. I open my mouth but nothing comes out. How do I answer this? Whom am I loyal to? Do I side with the pride of the uniform, the love for the service, for those years that made me hard but strong? With the love of flag and country and the brothers and sisters I stood and fought beside? Or should I be loyal to my sex? Should I tell her about the darker side of being a woman in that uniform while standing with those brothers and sisters? Should I warn her about what the love of flag and country will cost her?

Instead I stutter, "It'll either be the greatest thing you ever do, or the worst." Which isn't an answer at all, and the girl knows it. She tilts her head at me, frowning. "It's...hard," I clarify lamely.

"I don't mind hard," she shoots back, lifting her chin in defiance.

"You have to be able to handle a joke and you can't be sensitive." I'm already subconsciously training her on how to conform. "Like not at all."

She practically rolls her eyes at me. "Obviously. I grew up with three brothers. I'm used to hanging around guys."

Which isn't the same at all, but suddenly I don't want to scare her away. "Honestly?" I say with a sigh, deflating. "I loved it."

Because I did. Overall, by and large, I loved it. And knowing what I know now, if I could go back to the girl I was and stand over her shoulder as she leaned over a contract, readying to sign her name, I don't think I could whisper in her ear, *Don't do it.* I don't think I would take it all away. I'd lose running along the beaches in Monterey, flutter kicks in the tall grass of Soldier's Field, my drill sergeant finally smiling at me, the one night in the Iraqi desert as it grew colder and colder and the sky was a blanket of unadulterated stars, all the good and all the bad. I'm not so sure I could change me.

She grins because it's what she wants to hear. I'm just here as her confirmation bias.

As she walks away, I feel a little guilty. I don't think I properly prepared her. I feel like I lied somehow. But the Army needs good women. It needs strong women. It needs those of us who have no interest in white picket fences and traditional domesticity. We have been around for thousands of years, us women who don't want to conform, and they need to get used to us being there. We're not going away. We're not going to let them win this one.

It was so easy to be proud and cocksure then. But that was years ago. That was before we broke a region, like a toddler playing with a delicate toy, growing uninterested in the shattered bits when they don't work anymore. Ask me now, "Are you proud of your service over there," and I'm not so young and arrogant.

I'm proud of my intentions, at least, of the hope I had that we would all watch Iraq rise from the ashes and flames. I had dreamed of returning one day with my daughter or son, to see a bustling metropolis, rich with both history and innovation. I envisioned it thriving like any world center, with us standing under the Gate of Ishtar or burying our feet in Babylonian soil. I wanted to crouch down and whisper in my future child's ear, "I helped make this," a dream I recognize now as so terribly naive and arrogant. I was proud of the desire to better this world, of wanting to end a dictatorship that only terrorized and murdered. But can I still be proud if nothing is left to speak over, just a nation plunged into further civil war? What have we done for Iraq? What has been left now, as the region deteriorates, as ISIS slips in, stealing what was once meant to be great? What did we kill for? What did we die for? I don't know. The individual soldiers, those of us in the bottom ranks who sacrificed the most, at least our intentions were pure, though.

tubthumping

I MEET ROMAN, the former Marine infantryman, in early 2006, a year into civilian life, when I'm so goddamn *functional* that I think I must be normal now. I'm at a local karaoke bar, where the DJ welcomes me home from the Army, and one of Roman's friends grabs my arm, pushing us together, because here is a former Marine, and don't we have so much in common? And we do. He's studying US history and wants to teach. I want to be an ancient history professor, in love with the world beneath the streets of Baghdad, with the idea of Babylon, infatuated with the soil still embedded beneath my nails.

We sing Chumbawamba's "Tubthumping," a throwback for both of us, and I laugh into the mike, dancing in knee-high suede boots, ignoring the hem of my jean skirt that lifts and flashes upper thigh. The Marine sings loudly, off-key but with enthusiasm, and I like it. I stare him straight in the eyes, those beautiful, sea-green hazel eyes, and expect him to look away first. He doesn't. I don't intimidate him, which I find bewitching.

Roman is tall and broad across the chest. He's a man's man. He wears work boots, drinks beer, and has long, dark chops that make him look like a young Elvis. When he smiles, his cheeks round slightly and he's both boyish and mischievous. He's a fun kind of trouble. The kind that makes you laugh, not the kind that burns.

When I leave the bar that night, he shakes my hand, a firm grip, and slips a napkin into my palm. I look down at it, his number written in dark pen, and when I glance up, he's gone. I smile. Very James Bond.

I hold off a little on calling him, because I like men who are a little mean to me and who ignore my calls. I don't know what to do with a man who seems to enjoy my company, who sits for hours in a restaurant booth while we talk, as if he's actually listening to what I'm saying. I've always found being pursued so boring. I prefer to hunt rather than be hunted.

Yet there is something different about Roman—there is no desperation here. He's interested, but not enough to make a fool of himself. His self-assurance makes me think of an iron ship in the middle of a storm. He takes no shit. He rises to meet me, not intimidated by my crassness, not embarrassed by the masculinity that peeks from behind my spiked heels and short skirts. I can't rattle him. I find this fascinating.

I fall in love with Roman the Marine over baklava and a Turkish coffee in the heart of New Haven, in a Middle Eastern restaurant he specifically picks out because he knows what I like. Somewhere along the way, he falls in love with me, too, and that makes sense to me then. How easy I must have been to love then, when I had such dreams, such independence. I am top of my class, straight A's, on track to get into some grand graduate school, to be a history professor, financially stable, already owning my own place, my own space sliced out of the world. I have everyone by the balls, and, oh, what promises I make to myself and to the man who loves me.

Who would I have been, had that girl been allowed to grow? She had a little rage, didn't like crowds or loud, sudden noises, but she was fierce and optimistic. Where would she be now? I wonder. Perhaps the rage would have destroyed her, too. Maybe her recklessness would have taken apart her world, brick by brick. Maybe she would have destroyed everyone around her, burned too hot, turned her world to ash. I wonder if either way I was destined for desecration.

But I don't know this yet. I'm still twirling around in delight, feeling, truly feeling, realizing I *can* love, I *do* love, that Iraq and the incident did not cost me my humanity. I'm grinning like a mad hatter, running full tilt into love, because that's pretty much how I do everything anyway. I wait the three dates, the arbitrarily specified amount of time a good woman waits before sex, because damn, he's the type of boy you take home to your mother. I say things like, "I don't normally move this quickly," with a little internal chuckle, although I don't think he would have cared either way. He certainly doesn't offer any excuses for moving too quickly, but then again, men never do.

And things go well. We plan for movie dates but miss the times, sitting instead for hours in some Thai or Indian or Ethiopian restaurant, lost in ourselves, in our conversations, fingers interlaced under the table. I like his hands, large palms, long fingers, which so easily wrap around mine. I feel delicate against him, yet I don't have to be—I'm a hybrid of feminine and masculine, as if I'm wearing two skins that fit equally as well, and he's okay with that. We hang out with fellow veterans, and this feels a little like home. We spend summer nights on the West Haven beach, my feet buried in cold sand, body warmed by the bonfire flames. Roman wraps one arm around my shoulders, holding me close against the line of his body, his cheeks a little flushed from alcohol, and I glance up, staring at that face, with its strong Eastern European lines, at the way his mouth tilts when he grins, and in that moment of warmth and contentment, I realize I have something to lose.

The realization is earth moving. A sudden anxiety sets in, breathing life into the dead thing in my chest, into the space that once had no feeling at all. I quickly try to bury the fear, the sudden nausea, the way my heart hammers hard for no reason. I brush aside the panic with a few gulps of cold air, not realizing this is the small spot of rot taking root, that it will one day spread, devour parts of my brain, eat holes into my sanity. I instead think it's nothing. Maybe there are too many people here, I think, scanning the dark beach, noting each body at the party, where they stand, what's in their hands, where they're looking. I down the rest of my wine, wait for the alcohol to run a light hand over the anxiety, to lull it back to sleep, and I slowly unlock my muscles.

It's nothing, I think. But as I look up again, there is a new, dark voice in the back of my skull, one that sneers with such clarity: *You know you're going to fuck this up, right? You dirty little whore.*

belletristic

WHAT IS PERHAPS my last lucid moment comes in the summer of 2010, when I'm spending eight weeks in Ireland, studying ancient Greek at University College Cork. Over the past four years, Roman and I have moved in together, gotten a dog—a rambunctious Alaskan malamute puppy who adores Dorian Gray—sold my apartment, and bought a house in a quaint town outside New Haven. In December 2009 Roman proposed in Rockefeller Center, just beneath the Christmas tree. This is the dream of domesticity, though I haven't exactly been able to tame my restlessness. And the rot hasn't begun to spread yet.

I'm here in Ireland for an eight-week language intensive course that's supposed to prep me for my ancient history studies in the years to come. Two summers ago I studied French at Université de Bourgogne in Dijon, France, and I've taken both opportunities to backpack through Europe with Josephine, my fellow wayfarer sister, who understands that wanderlust burns in the gut. We've stretched our fingers up toward the Nordic sun, bathed topless in the Aegean Sea, followed the slopes and dips of Paris cobblestone streets, sleeping in old, haunted castles in the Highlands of Scotland, cramming all our limbs into tiny hotel rooms in London, Rome, and Brussels, because neither of us knows how to stay still.

But Ireland is mine.

Foilhommerum Bay is to my left and Bray Head directly in front. I've been traveling the entirety of the island by circling the coasts and, much as I miss Roman and Dorian Gray, there's something brilliant in this solitude. There's an old, wind-battered tower near the summit of this cliff and I lean in, hands reaching out to grasp fat clumps of long grass as I climb, calves aching.

The path is empty, there's no one here but wandering cows and sheep. I reach the tower, a little winded, and step forward, craning my neck, to stare down the sheer cliffs below me.

Thundering waves smash against the rocks; the emerald-green grass juts out over the black stones. There's the distant, consistent roar of the ocean meeting the land, mist gathering up, mixing with low-hanging clouds, twisting and twirling overhead, before plummeting back down the side of the bluff. I stand transfixed. I sigh, breathe in the wet air, straighten up. Behind me is the highest cliff, the very tip of the island. To climb it in this wind could be reckless. So I do.

Heart pounding, I tackle the steep incline, body stooped forward, fingers touching the ground for balance. The wind tears at my hair, my eyes, whipping my light jacket violently around my body. I have to bow my head, cradling it against the inside of my arm as the wind tries to remove me from the hillside. If I'm ripped away from the earth, how long until someone finds my body? I taste the fear, swirl it around in my mouth. "You're a dumb-ass," I mutter to myself and push upward.

When I reach the tip, a small, jutted peak of thick green grass, I sit down in the center. The wind quiets. I dig my fingers down into the soil. There's nothing here but the ocean, the earth, the sky. Off the coast, the heavy mists part, revealing the purple outlines of the Skellig Islands haunting the coast. They burn in precision for a moment before being swallowed whole, as if they had never been there at all.

Exhilarated, I weep. I weep and I laugh, head flung back, the sun warm on my cheeks. There's such clarity here. I feel a tie with the earth beneath me, the wide expanse of the ocean before me. I'm home. I've never belonged anywhere but here, in the middle of nowhere, the road less traveled. My chest opens up, my arms ache to hold and cradle this intangible space. I *want* the indefinable. You find your gods in your churches and synagogues and mosques—but here is my god, my goddess, my gods, and my goddesses.

But this moment on the mountaintop is perhaps the final time I am fully me, the powerful me who climbs slippery slopes in foreign countries, who drives on the wrong side of the road, radio on full blast. This is the last time she will exist in all her brashness and fearlessness and violence. And I miss her. Oh, let me be her again. Let me have ambition and fire and daring. Let my only want be the unattainable space of skies rarely seen. I want her back, this better version of me.

Things go wrong in a way I never could have seen coming, one evening at an Irish bar. It's been a hard week for me; I've been in language intensive courses before, but classical Greek beats me bloody. I'm in a perpetual haze of declensions, future and past infinitives, lost somewhere in the multiple forms of third-person imperative (indicative or middle). I'm supposed to be good at languages. This should be easy for me. This is my thing.

"Maybe you're not naturally good at languages," says one of my classmates. "Maybe you've just worked so hard in the past that you just think you are." He's a British kid from Oxford with a bowl cut and a young face that would be much improved by a fist in the middle of it, but only because his intelligence is so easy and unburdened. Here I'm surrounded by students from Brown, Oxford, Yale, casual intellectuals who chat in courtyards in beautiful, crisp accents, with cutting wit. I still have German to learn, and add to that Latin and perfecting my French if I want to be competitive for graduate schools. These are the peers I'm up against. I'm used to being one of the smarter people in the room, but here I'm reminded that I am most certainly not.

So instead, I party. I'm not like the clever little Oxford boy, who barely glances up from his books while we all plan a night out. Maybe there's a reason he's top of the class. It would be smart to stay in and study. But I guess I'm not very smart.

We head down to the local bar, where, surrounded by tart hard ciders and thick, bitter Guinness, a man sits down next to me, a Bostonian with a thick accent, and I smile, because that's awfully close to home. When he places his hand on my knee, I press my knees together and swivel the barstool to the side, casually displacing his palm but continuing the small talk, the flirting. He raises his glass, asking for another beer, pushing his shoulder against mine. I'm lonely. I miss Roman, the smell of him, his warmth, his solid self. But I also miss the feeling of a man's gaze on me and so I smile again, resting my chin on my hand, and gaze back at the Bostonian. He's good-looking and I'm flattered.

Then he puts his hand on my leg. I'm wearing a short skirt and maybe I shouldn't be. He slides it up, gripping the meatier part of my upper thigh, and my hand slams down on top of his to stop its crawl.

"Hey now," I say, pushing his hand back. "I'm engaged." I hold up my left hand, flashing the diamond at him.

"Yeah? I notice you didn't lead with that." I feel the accusation in my gut and I gulp down the rest of my drink. "Where's he at?" He swivels in his barstool, scanning the bar.

That's always the most annoying question—like I need to keep my man chained to my hip to prove his realness and relevancy. "He's back at home," I say shortly.

"Well, that's okay then." He brightens and leans in suddenly, adding, "It doesn't count if you're in different countries."

I turn my head just in time and he catches the side of my mouth, his wet tongue swiping the edge of my lips and part of my cheek.

"Okay, I'm done." I rub off the saliva with the back of my hand, hopping off the barstool. I totter uncertainly on my heels for just a moment, then move out of reach, making a beeline for some of my classmates at a table. "That dude just tried to kiss me," I inform the table.

Like a herd, they all turn to look back at the bar. "Cute," said one of the girls.

"Not when he's licking your chin, he's not." I rub my mouth again.

Another wrinkles her nose. "Why'd you let him get that close then?"

I feel that gut punch, too, and fall into a seat, fingers scrubbing the side of my lips. They still feel wet. "I don't know," I say, a little cowed.

As the conversation shifts to lighter topics, I breathe, sip my cider, sit up straighter, and it all begins to seem funny and certainly not that big of a deal. I mean, what woman hasn't had to deal with something like this?

the thing in my vagina

I WAKE EARLY the next morning with a creature sitting on my chest. Its weight closes my throat, like a beast has a foot wedged against my windpipe. I sit up, taking half breaths, palm pressed over my heart, trying to dislodge this invisible thing. I can feel my chest caving, my rib cage twisting inward; there's a sunken hole where my breastplate should be. I try placing my head between my knees but that cuts off what little air I have. I stand, hands interlaced on the top of my head, back arched, head thrown back. *What the fuck, what the fuck, what the actual fuck.* I bow forward, burying one hand in my stomach, trying to rip out the panic.

And so begins my dance with two fatal little words: What If.

What if that guy had some disease? What if he passed it on to me, right there at my upper thigh? I imagine the disease at the tip of his fingers, an arthropod skittering up my thigh, wiggling under my panties, crawling up into the vaginal canal, rooting, rotting, festering on the inside of me, and I think I'm going to be sick. I stare at my open thighs, like I can see the trail there, or a burn mark where his hand had touched, and I can feel the thing inside me.

No one's going to believe me.

The realization burns, claws its way up into my jaw, into my temples, and I blink against the pain. I'm going to have some sexually transmitted disease from that guy's hand and *no one* is going to believe me because that's not how it happens. That's not how STDs happen. I turn my head to listen to that thought, to try to grasp on to it. That's not how it happens but *what if* this time it did? I am the minute possibility, the one in a million. It's never happened before until now.

And my mouth. My hands rush there, tugging at the lower lip as if to remove it. His mouth touched my mouth, I remember his saliva there, wet and smelling of old beer. Can you get HIV like that? The thought had never occurred to me before but now I can't dislodge it, no matter how I try to dig up the roots.

No one's going to believe me. Jesus Christ, *I* wouldn't believe me.

I wait for the rage. I wait to be filled with that hot heat, the anger, the steely confidence to sneer, *Fuck that guy. Fuck anyone who doesn't believe me. Fuck them all.* I want it, I *need* it, except it doesn't come. I call it by name but there's nothing there but an empty echo. I didn't use it when I should have, I didn't punch him or slap him or sneer at him, and now my rage is punishing me. It's abandoned me. I'm huddled naked and bare without it.

The anxiety sticks to my heels as I walk to class. I stare down at my notebook, at pages filled with Greek, and am blinded by the high-pitched scream inside my skull—a singular loop that never needs to take a breath of air, the same thoughts going round and round and round.

I told you, sneers a voice. *You're a whore. A dirty little attention-seeking whore.* There's a creature at my ear, its serpentine body wrapped around my torso, flexing its coils until my ribs crack. *Now everyone's going to know*, it says, with its long snout brushed up against my ear. *Everyone's going to know what kind of whore you really are.*

Roman is going to leave me. *Of course he is.* He's never going to believe me. *No one's going to believe you.* I see it all playing out, Roman staring at me with shocked, hurt eyes, slamming the door behind him, his friends who will glare at me sideways, at the lying bitch.

I can't concentrate. I barely can read but let's be honest, I was never going to pass this course anyway. I stare at blank pages for two weeks, for the final time of the course, barely able to collect nouns and verb endings. Not that it matters. *Nothing matters. You're dying and everyone is going to find out why. None of this matters.*

I fly back home in a daze, my entire body electrified with terror. I think that when I get to Roman it'll be okay, it'll all melt away, and I can lose this demon.

I half jog my way toward baggage claim, but when I see Roman I'm doused in icy water, cold from head to toe. I carve a smile on to my face, open my arms, pray they hold steady, and bury my head into his chest. I hear his heart, the steady beat that I hope will lure me back to sanity. I glance up and stare at his face, at the hazel-green eyes, the sideways grin. He looks like a man in love. The scream inside my head continues, rising in volume.

Roman takes me home, to bed, where we reunite, having been denied eight weeks of each other's bodies, and I try to find joy in him. *You don't deserve this.* I want to whisper in his ear, *Tell me I'm not a slut. Tell me I'm a good person.* But I can't unwire my own jaw to ask. *You don't deserve him.* I know that! I know that. I'm choking on terror and self-loathing. I never deserved him, I know this now, and knowing scorches.

But I smile. I'm astonished by my own acting abilities.

A few hours afterward, at dinner, I feel something low in my stomach. It presses against my lower back and distends my abdomen. I groan and fold in half.

"What's wrong?" Roman asks, resting one hand on my back.

I'm dying and I'm taking you with me.

"I don't know," I whisper. I take a sip of water, trying to wash away the bitterness in my mouth. "Maybe it's a UTI?" Maybe. I haven't had sex in eight weeks and doesn't that happen when you suddenly up and have it again? *Stupid bitch, you know what this is. Think about it. About his hand right there on your thigh, about his tongue at your mouth. You did this.* I did this.

Roman drives me to the local VA hospital, where the doctor tells me I don't have a UTI. I should be relieved but I'm not. My anxiety spikes. Roman rubs my back absently with one hand. I wonder if he can see me screaming. He says nothing.

The ER doctor tells me to make an appointment with my primary if the pain doesn't go away, so I do. I feel something rotting low in my stomach. I want to slice off the entire lower half of my body. I'll lose the legs but at least the vagina will be gone.

The doctor meets with me. Then a psychiatrist joins us. "This isn't how these things happen," they say. "You did nothing wrong," they add with brows flexed in mild confusion. I did, I did, I did. I am complicit in my own punishment.

"But we can do tests just to give you peace of mind," they say. Yes, let's do that. "And give you medication for your anxiety." Yes, please. Please. Please. "And you'll need to continue weekly therapy." Yes, sure. Twice a week. Three times a week. Anything to dislodge this demon.

But it will not budge.

I have to go back to life with it still wrapped around my body, slowly splintering me from the inside. I have to go back to college classes filled with white noise. All my energy goes into the mask: a light smile, a bounce in my step. But my grades are slipping. There goes summa cum laude to my left. I'll never get into my grad schools with just magna. *What does it matter?* What the fuck does it matter. I balk, twist, and smash my dreams onto the floor.

My favorite history professor tries to talk me out of it. "Don't let the Greek scare you away," he says. We sit in his office as I change my career plans, shelving my academic pursuits. He sees great things for me. I see nothing now.

"No, it's okay," I lie. "I'll still be in history, I'll just be a high school teacher. And it'll give me more time to write. That's what I really want to do anyway." I try to console myself. Being a teacher would give me a lot more time to work on my fiction career, wouldn't it?

He leans back in his chair and for a brief moment he looks defeated.

"Well," he says with a sigh. "Don't lose your love for the ancient world." It's a dismissal. I can leave now.

I step out of the office and into an empty, dark room, and bow my head to cry. My heart is broken. I'm broken. I don't see the point in putting myself back together again.

Sometimes, when I'm driving, the median looks very enticing to me. I could smash my car into it. It would be really easy and probably quick. I don't think about the pain. I don't want to die. I want silence. I dream of the afterward, of lying in a white, sterile hospital bed, alone, of white curtains and quiet beeping machines, and it seems so peaceful. It doesn't occur to me that it'll hurt. Possibly dying is secondary, an afterthought. A car jets in front of me on I-95 and I contemplate not hitting the brakes. It doesn't occur to me that I could hurt another, too. I press the brakes more out of habit than need. I expect a rush of fear at the close miss, like the time the Subaru hydroplaned across the highway, or even the sudden relief at surviving a near accident, but there isn't anything, especially not silence.

interim ii

AND THEN, ONE SINGULAR, unparticular day, I sit up in bed and for the first time in over three months, I can breathe. The terror has dissipated. I hear nothing. I feel silence. I blink at the morning sunlight. Just like that, I'm me. No rhyme or reason, no trigger or indicator, nothing I'd be able to replicate or control. I float down the stairs, hover in the kitchen. I'd forgotten what normal feels like. No heavy knot in the stomach, no tense muscles, no jittery fingers and hands and feet. I stand in stillness. My chest expands.

I'm me. Mostly. There's a tiny quiver at the very bottom of me, a fear that it will come back and that if it does, I have no idea how to duplicate this sudden restoration. But overall, if I ignore that glaring detail, I'm restored. I smile. Genuinely. I smile so deeply my cheeks hurt.

As I move forward, though, the world tastes different. The air lacks a certain bite. I'm still me, but I've grown a little less bright, like a gas lamp turned low. Since I'm no longer aiming for Ivy League grad school, I flag. I lose my pursuit and direction. No one really notices. That's okay; I don't want them to. I have an extra year of school now, a fifth year of undergrad as I finish some English credit classes. There's no need for history teachers in Connecticut; I'm rerouted toward becoming an English teacher. Fine.

I need a challenge, though. I knock tentatively on my creative writing professor's door. I had taken a creative writing course with him once, my first year of college, and written a short story about a futurist American civil war, the protagonist an infantry woman, because women in combat arms seemed like science fiction in 2006.

"The heart of this," Tim had said in workshop, "is really about a woman in this massively male-dominated world, and her struggling with themes of masculinity and fitting in."

I snorted. "Sounds like the story of my life." The class stared at me. I waved off my explanation with one hand. "I was in the Army and Iraq and all that."

"Oh my God." He firmly planted one finger on the manuscript. "That's what this is. That's what this needs to be. Write that!"

I took his advice and wrote a short piece involving a military rape victim forced to work with her rapist. The class didn't know what to do with it, a silent workshop, a handful of undergrads refusing to make eye contact with me as they shuffled the papers. But Tim knew.

"You really should do a creative thesis for the English Department," he told me way back then, and I made a face, laughed it off. I had to be serious about my academic pursuits in history then. Writing was my dream, but I needed to be financially stable first. Writing doesn't keep the lights on.

But here I am now, hands clenched around my book-bag strap, nervously shifting weight from one foot to the other, because I need direction. He is thrilled that I'm finally interested and together we make something raw and ugly and simple, but it's mine. It somehow feels good to get it out there into the air. It makes my reality something to mull over, to casually and openly deliberate over words like *rape* and *trauma*. There's no place to hide here and, to my surprise, there's a comfort in that.

Tim tries to encourage me to keep writing, to apply to the university's MFA program, but I'm too afraid to take that jump off the stern cliff of financial stability. No. I'll be an English teacher and write on the side. I'll squirrel away moments in dark hours of night to flesh out fiction characters and plots, when everyone else is sleeping. This is a plan, right? That's sort of a future. I feel no flutter of excitement, though. No joy anymore. But I assume that happens to all adults, when their dreams skulk off to die in a forgotten corner somewhere.

And on an early October morning in 2011, I wear a white dress, a feminine full-skirt, off-the-shoulder gown, my long hair curled and coiled to one side. I clutch a bouquet, stare down the long aisle to the man by the altar, his hands clasped nervously in front of him. His smile grows. I barely feel my feet as I walk, eyes locked with his, and I forget everyone else in the room, the church, the world. My heart swells. I blink back tears and reach out my hand to touch him, my Roman. And when we kiss, now husband and wife, he slips me a little tongue just because he knows it'll surprise and delight me. I break away with an unruly laugh, head thrown back, and I'm happy. Perhaps I'll never be so happy again.

the bat

LESS THAN A YEAR later that interim of sanity ends. In the late summer of 2012, a bat breaks into my bedroom and I have a mental breakdown. It happens a month after Dorian Gray dies at age eleven. The VA says those events are not connected, but I think they are. Dorian has always been there. When I thought I was okay, everything fine, fine, fine, but then not, there was always Dorian, soft and sturdy, his body against my legs. The more nervous I became, the more relaxed he grew, a vigilant sentinel of long white fur and dark eyes, watching everything so I didn't have to.

But then there was the cancer, sudden and devastating, and our last day was the same as our first, me lying on the dog bed beside him, resting my face close to his, so that our breaths intermingled, so he would know I was there. He passed there in the living room, quiet as he always was, forever the gentleman, now forever gone.

So when one month later, a bat breaks into my bedroom, I go crazy.

It's not instantaneous. I wake to the sound of thumping and half turn, one hand drifting down to the side of the bed to brush Dorian's fur, then remember he's not there. Freya, our Alaskan malamute puppy all grown up, is standing in the middle of the room, hopping up into the air at odd intervals. In the dark a thing zooms by her, swoops over the bed, loops around, and dives for the other side of the room. Freya jumps up, jaws open, trying to snatch it out of the air. I push Roman's shoulder, trying to rouse him. "What the hell is a bird doing in here?"

Roman rolls over, rubs his eyes, and leans back against his mountain of pillows, observing the scene. "That's not a bird," he says at last. "That's a bat."

"What?" I squawk and hunch down on the bed, clutching a pillow over my head. "Get it out! Get it out!"

He shrugs, a lot less concerned about this than I am. As if waking with bats doing aerial laps around the room is a perfectly normal thing. "Let Freya get it."

"She can't! She'll get rabies!"

"She's had her shots," he reminds me.

"That doesn't mean she still can't get rabies!"

"That's sort of exactly what it means," he says drily.

I'm clutching another pillow against my body, making a soft, downy fortress. "It could bite her and take out an eye!" I glare from the inside of my fort until he sighs dramatically, rolling out of bed. I follow him to the kitchen, half dragging Freya down the stairs. She's the only one reluctant to leave.

I hunker down on the kitchen floor, as if being closer to the ground will make me less of a target, even one floor down. I clutch Freya to me like a fur barrier. Roman comes up from the basement dressed in a camo jacket, hood up, string tied tight under his chin, and pulling on old gardening gloves. He holds a broom at the ready, bristle-side up. "Go to my mom's. I'll call you when it's done."

And off he goes to hunt the bat, calling one of his friends for backup, and they ransack the house looking for the little creature or its friends or a nest, none of which they find, because the bat went out the same way it came in—through a tiny hole in the AC unit.

Which is all kind of funny in the light of day as I tell my peers in my Alternate Route to Teacher Certification Program. It's a good story, quirkier because I even snapped a picture of Roman decked out in his hunting gear. I pass around the phone with the picture and we laugh, until one of the students sits back in his chair, crosses one ankle over his knee, and says, "So did you go get a rabies shot?"

I pocket my phone, smile flagging. "No. It didn't bite us."

He shrugs. "That you know of. Their fangs are so small that they can bite you and you wouldn't wake up or even know. That's what the doctors told my uncle when they found a rabid bat in his house. Like over half of all bats have rabies, you know. Or maybe higher."

And just like that, I have rabies.

Like my terror of HIV in Ireland, it is an all-consuming, irrational fear, an instantaneous anxiety that seizes my brain. It breeds nervous energy, forcing me to stay perpetually in motion, as if I can move away from the fear, physically separate myself from the terror.

I convince Roman to go to the doctor with me, perversely comforted by the fact that he's in this with me, he could be infected, too, but he lacks the same sense of urgency. As does the doctor, who tilts his head at me, concern pulling his brows together, but it's not the right kind of worry. He doesn't see the need for the vaccine, he says.

Roman and the doctor watch me from across the little clinic room, as if in silent agreement, wholly aware of something I'm not, exchanging sideways glances and excluding me as they shift their weight, glance over my head.

I squirm in the examination chair, the paper sheet crackling, and finally admit, "I've had anxiety before." This is an understatement. I remember the unwavering terror that devoured my every waking moment for those three months in 2010. I taste a metallic tang at the back of my throat and know it's panic. Not so much of rabies, but of those three months, because I don't think I can weather it again.

"I used to take lorazepam for the anxiety," I say and the doctor nods, as if he's already a step ahead of me. It's the best I can ask for. I can't push for the vaccine because I know I'm crazy. I can feel the irrational thoughts wiggling around in my brain, taste their off-ness, but the ability to decipher their illogicality is only made more frustrating by the inability to fight them.

I shuffle out of the doctor's office, humiliation sprawled across the back of my neck. Roman drives us straight to the pharmacy because I demand it, because I'm hoping to cut off the growing madness before it fully starts. I stand in the Walgreens line, my hands already dancing, fingers bouncing. Roman wraps an arm around my waist, pulling me against his chest as we wait, trying to craft his body into a weapon of comfort, but my muscles are already clenching, growing rigid, and I ache for the medicine, for the white fog of oblivion, anything to cut off what I know is coming.

The pharmacist finally hands me the bottle and I crack open the top, taking two pills right there at the counter, checking the time, knowing how long it will take to settle in. There is a sense of relief at the chalky taste on my tongue. I've got this under control, I think. I can stop this.

But I can't.

dirty little whore

I USED TO LOVE male attention. I adored my breasts, the expensive bras that would push them up out of a shirt, straining against a blouse. I loved the validation that came with the male gaze, the way men turned in their chairs to notice me, to grin at me, to catcall, to seek my attention. Being sexy felt powerful.

Until it didn't.

Like a light switch flipped, suddenly I despise sexy. Propelled by an anxiety awoken after the encounter with that random bat, the irrational fear happens abruptly, overnight, and suddenly I feel that gaze like an accusatory finger pointed in my face. Grins are now sneers, catcalls send me into a tailspin, and it all makes me uneasy; I'm suffocating and it's my own fault. They can lift their noses like dogs and sniff out the dirty on me. I think of the night at a casino when the man next to me leaned in and I felt his skin touch mine, the sweat of his palm settling against my lower back, and I wanted to rip off all my skin then, ball it up and throw it away in the trash. I twisted away, mumbled something, but I wanted to scream, *Don't touch me!* Why do you keep touching me? Brushing, stroking, converging, *touching*, as if I am a thing to be handled, examined, cracked open.

The thought of my breasts now makes me queasy. CrossFit adds tight muscles to my chest and reduces their swell. I revel in the loss. I begin to wear bralettes, ones that bind my breasts close to my body until they're nonexistent. I change my wardrobe, going Bohemian-chic, my slender frame swallowed by fabric, the curves drowned out, well hidden, and I turn women's heads, who love the fashion, the edginess.

I obsess over my diet, carefully restricted and regimented, giving up sugar for months on end, whittling down to a size two and loving it. I love the sense of power that comes with the discipline—the inflexibility that makes me thinner and thinner and this is mine to control. I devote myself to CrossFit and develop squared shoulders, trapezius muscles visible under a shirt neckline, a waist that thickens with muscle, my quads round and hard. "Men don't want their women to look like that," people whisper to me. "Men don't like women who are too muscular," they say. Well, good.

I read in a magazine that men don't like short hair so I shave half my head. Women stop me to compliment it, to comment on my entire look, and I've found a way to be pretty, to be fashion-forward but also slip under the radar, because most men don't notice the muscular girl with the flat chest and shaved hair, and fucking good. That's the point.

"Oh," Roman will say, when he sees the new haircut. "It's short." But that's the most he'll say about any of it, and the entire thing makes me feel *safer*. Safe from other men's gaze, but still valued in Roman's, because if he hates the hair or the clothes or the flattened body, he never lets on. Which is lucky because in my obsession to disappear from other men's view, I never did consider his.

The exam table paper crinkles as I shift my weight. I don't look the doctor in the eyes. "So you think you have HIV?" There is heavy skepticism in his voice.

"See, feel here?" I say, my shaking fingers pressing to my throat. "Swollen lymph nodes. And my throat is sore and I have a fever—"

"A very mild fever."

"Yeah, but it can just start with flu-like symptoms." That's me, WebMD PhD.

"But you're not having casual sex?"

"I'm not, I'm monogamous but..."

But. But men looking. Men touching.

"If you would wait here for just one moment," says the young doctor, trying to be cheery although I don't know why, because doesn't he know I'm dying? And no one is going to believe me when I say I got it from a guy who touched my skin in the bar, they're all going to say I'm lying, and Roman is going to leave me, because of course he is, and they're going to say this little story of mine is just a way to hide that I'm a *dirty little whore*. All the same fears circulated on repeat.

My fingers flutter up against my throat, behind my ears, and in the time allotted I examine my nails, check if they're strong, then roll forefinger against thumb, checking the dexterity of my fingers to make sure I don't have ALS. The doctor comes back mid-ritual. I didn't even get to check my balance yet. I'm annoyed at the interruption, file the habit away at the back of my brain to finish later, so I can feel well and hopeful for a few minutes, like I always do once a ritual is successfully completed.

The doctor stands to the side to let someone else pass, and an older woman strides into the room. She looks at me in my thin hospital gown. She sighs. I sigh. We know each other well. She's the head psychiatrist of the women's clinic, who had sat there with a slightly tilted head, listening to me cry over fears of rabies from a bat bite. Then when a puppy's tooth had scratched my hand in passing and I didn't ask the owner if it had its shots because I knew how crazy that sounded, and I thought I could handle it, but then I couldn't. And she had sat me down eventually, after there had been the MS fears and the ALS terror incident, and said, "I think you need to be on medication."

I had blinked at her, taken aback. I knew what kind of medication she was talking about: SSRIs, antidepressants, which are an intensely different beast from the anxiety-reducing benzodiazepines that don't seem to be working for me anymore. "For how long?"

"Maybe forever," she said as she collected her stuff and walked out the room, passing on that information to my regular psychiatrist.

I know she's going to say this now, with that same tilt to her head, clinically sympathetic, and I don't want to have to say that I'm a writer, that writers can't be on SSRIs, or have to remind her that I've done my Google research and artists say it kills the craft, the need to create, and if I'm going to be a mindless zombie who can't write, I'd much rather be dead. Let it kill me then.

We've had this conversation before, round and round we've gone, so she sighs. I sigh. Then I leave.

I know what PTSD is supposed to look like, and I don't think it's supposed to be like this. It should be a textbook response. Boom. React; hit the floor. I've seen it a hundred times in movies. I understand that, even when I don't think it's mine to have, a fear I didn't earn. Standing in a bar, the press of people causing me to spiral inward, gripping my drink too hard, marking the exits over the masses of heads and bodies and hands and eyes, taking an extra swig of that drink because it makes it a little better: that I understand, too. They show this in the movies, on the television screen. This is what they talk about, when they display PTSD. But I don't have this kind of PTSD, not exclusively. Mine has bred into something different, something far more insidious, and if I'm going to have PTSD, then goddamn it, I want normal-grade PTSD, the Hollywood version, not this batshit-crazy variety that has no lines running back to combat. It makes no sense to be terrified of bats and rabies, or MS and ALS. I was the girl who once dropped a cookie in Iraq, then quickly scooped it out of the dirt, dusted it off, and popped it into my mouth, sand and all. "A girl after my own heart," one of the sergeants said with a wink, and I grinned, because it's just dirt.

It's just dirt, and now I can't even run my hand down a banister without fear of contamination. The fears don't add up. None of this can be PTSD, because I don't see how it can be traced back to Iraq or the rape. Maybe I was always predestined to go crazy. Maybe when I was first formed, God scratched out the word *insanity* on a Post-it and stuck it to my forehead. I feel like a fake, sitting in the VA hospital women's clinic office, recounting to a psychiatrist terrors that have nothing to do with the military. Fucking Dostie, soaking up tax dollars with a grade of crazy that was all her own to begin with.

And so I don't like to show my crazy. If you saw it, you wouldn't call it PTSD, so it's better that you don't see at all.

I graduate from the teaching certification program week the summer of 2012, the summer of my mental breakdown. I start work as a long-term substitute English teacher in New Haven. I expect this to be like the infamous mental break of 2010—three months and done. I can buckle down and take this for three months, I think, even as I pace rooms in the dark, twisting, twitching, decomposing. But it's not months. It's *years*. There's no interim, no moment to gasp for breath, a perpetual scream lodged at the back of my throat and I see no end to it, every day on repeat, everything on repeat, like a score permanently on loop and if I want silence, I think I'm going to have to kill myself.

I long for the fight in me, the rage that once made me so invincible. This fear has gutted me, chipping away at who I am, bit by bit, and I'm haunted by the terrifying awareness that silence can be bought with the Kel-Tec .380 handgun in the nightstand, nestled comfortably against loose pens and forgotten books—and the thoughts scare me. It's too tempting. I don't know how I avoided this in Iraq when here at home the thought trails behind me like a steadfast puppy.

I gobble down two milligrams of lorazepam—one prescribed, one extra just in case. I lie on the couch, curled on one side, hand dangling down onto the floor. If I could, I would muster the strength to run fingers through Freya's fur. A little drool creeps out the corner of my lips.

My dreams are dead. I see nothing behind my eyelids as I sleep. I'm comatose but it passes the time. That's all I want—for the time to pass.

I am in purgatory, this place in between, and maybe if enough time passes I'll finally make it to hell or heaven.

Roman comes home, accompanied by a cold blast of outside air and smelling of fireman gear. He takes one look at my mismatched stare, hears my words heavy and halting, then he goes into the kitchen to cook dinner.

My incompetence burns.

The lorazepam slows the whirling reel in my head, and I can sit on the couch, I can half focus, half see. I can eat, even though I don't want to, I can speak, even though I have nothing to say. And when I go to bed, I down another milligram, knowing that it will block out the nightmares. I slice another pill in half, licking the white powder off my thumb with a dry tongue.

I bob and weave my way up to the bedroom. I don't have to look for sleep; it slams into me like a sledgehammer.

The VA eventually gives me a 70 percent disability rating for PTSD, after all. Congratulations! You are *this* fucked up. It's a victory and, also, most certainly not.

"It's possible," my psychiatrist says slowly, "that you might not be able to work full-time right now."

I'm cracked in half, fingers digging into my eyes, elbows on knees. I groan.

"Stress both brings on and exacerbates PTSD symptoms," he's saying and I've heard this all before. My brain is no longer wired like everyone else. A few cords have popped free and overlapped, shoved back into the wrong places so that now simple stressors become overwhelming. I get how it works but can I not even do *this*? I've gone from ancient history professor to English teacher to...what now? I'm dragging myself across a crumbling road, reaching up for handholds and only getting fistfuls of loose brick and mortar dust.

the breaking point

ONE NIGHT, when I come home after a few martinis with my cousin at dinner, Roman pauses in the kitchen, tilting his head at me as I laugh at Freya. "Did you drive like that?" he asks.

"Like what?" I say. "I'm not drunk." I knew I'd be driving, so I was careful to keep my stomach full, to evenly space my drinks.

"You definitely had something to drink," he accuses.

"Yeah, but I waited to drive," I shoot back, angry that he's killing my buzz.

"Okay, whatever." He holds up his hands and retreats.

And—much like the American in the Irish bar, the bat, or the man's hand on my back at the casino—that should be the end of it. Instead I wake up in the morning with a familiar sense of dread. What if. What if I *did* drink too much? What if I blacked out and I didn't know it and during that blackout, what if I hit someone? What if I killed someone?

I scoop up my phone, immediately searching local news for any information about a hit-and-run. There's nothing. But maybe the news hasn't gotten the story yet. I run outside to my car, barefoot. I crouch in front of the bumper. Not a bump, not a scratch. I painstakingly examine the front, the side, the grille, underneath, for clothing, or blood, or bits of hair. Could you hit someone and not have any mark on your car? That's possible, right? It's not *im*possible, surely.

I scour my brain for any time missing, for any holes, and I can't find any but would I remember if I had blacked out? I hop into the car, still barefoot, and drive the route, from house to restaurant, then back again. Nothing. And yet... I grill my husband on how I looked when I came home.

"You were a little flushed is all," he says, as I follow him around the house, stuck to his heels. "You didn't seem that bad."

What is *that* bad? Can "bad" be broken down into fractions? Isn't any bad bad? If I was bad at all, shouldn't I be punished? Shouldn't I be in prison for the rest of my life? How much worse would it be that I couldn't remember something so monumental, so horrific? I'd have to kill myself, I realize, with sudden clarity. I accidentally killed an innocent person and now I have to kill myself.

All roads lead to suicide.

Even if I can't prove I killed anyone with my car, right now I know for sure I've been raped and I don't remember it. I think I'm pregnant but Roman and I have been so careful, so clearly the next logical step is to assume that I've been raped by some guy and I just don't remember. I momentarily glance down to check my jeans, as if I'll find them unbuttoned or torn. Everything is perfectly in place but I'm convinced somewhere between breakfast and now, I was raped. I just don't know it yet. I try to trace back time, find any moment where I could have had a blackout. But I drink less now. Can you black out while sober? Is that a thing that happens? I agonize over the possibility that I'll bring home a disease, infect Roman, and no one will believe the truth because *I'm a dirty little whore*—the same anxieties that have churned through me for years, since that first night in Ireland, with only slight variations.

But at last, *at last*, I understand this. There is a focus here I can finally grasp, casually pointed out to me by my psychiatrist and how had I not seen it earlier? I can pull at these strings and follow them back to one event, years prior, to a rape followed by a command who refused to believe me. *This* is PTSD, not insanity, not something I was born with. *This* isn't hypochondria or OCD, it is a result, not a cause. I don't know why it took a decade to catch up to me. I'd managed to outrun it for a while, somehow staying just ahead until suddenly I couldn't. And the realization is good, it brings a sort of comfort to know my own mind, but I'll still require an extra push before I'll do anything about it—a final straw needed to break the camel's back.

They call them delusions, but I don't think of them like that. They seem too probable; too absolute. So one day it suddenly seems both probable and absolute that my husband is cheating on me. I've never caught Roman so much as look at another woman. He doesn't get any strange text messages or late phone calls. He doesn't work more or later. In fact, his behavior hasn't changed at all, except I'm certain he's cheating on me.

Roman is in the shower. I sit on the couch in the dark, because the sun set without me noticing, stuck here, staring into nothing, listening to the delusion go round and round and round again in my brain, to other delusions, to things I've never said out loud, not to anyone, because I know how they sound and I won't admit them here, not even for you.

I scuttle off the couch and half crawl across the hardwood floor to where his phone sits on the table. One ear trained on the shower, I tap the screen. The phone comes alive. I know his password. That's how open he is, how unafraid, and yet I'm flipping through his text messages, pausing to read some, even under men's names, because come on, that's where it would be if you're going to keep your mistress's number in your phone. But there's nothing here—why is there nothing here? Must be in the emails. Or browser history. I've never done this before. Not in all the years we've been together. Roman has never given me reason before, and it's only when I find nothing, when I carefully lock the phone and place it back where I found it, that I realize he's not given me any reason now.

I slump back against the leg of the table. This is how marriages end. I know the difficulties of living with someone who has PTSD. I've heard the stories of marriages disintegrating, decaying from the inside until they split open and spill out lines of rotten bonds. I had always assumed it was from fighting, one soldier screaming at the other in a fit of rage, lost in anger and war. But this is a silent killer. I realize it will creep up on me like this, breaking down his trust, his ability to deal with my moodiness, my irrationality, the way I interrogate him when he takes the dog for a walk or sits in the car too long. This is how it will end.

I move back to the couch, both hollow and heavy with realization. I open my laptop and email my psychiatrist, telling him I'm ready to start antidepressant medication. It's an immediate decision. I can't do this anymore. This isn't normal. And maybe these pills will kill my creativity, my writing career, but goddamn it, I can't let my marriage go down like this.

interim iii

I STRETCH OUT on the truck hood, staring up at a blanket of stars, a silver flask of Spanish liqueur resting near my mouth. I wind one arm under my head and abandon myself to the quiet music of the desert night.

"This is the life," I sigh. It's the summer of 2014. Josephine leans over and plucks the flask from my mouth and takes a gulp, the sharp scent of orange and alcohol lingering between us. Our white, waterlogged bare feet swing together, rubbed raw at the edges from eight hours in The Narrows of Zion National Park. We had hiked miles in the Virgin River, shaded by the high gorge walls, sometimes holding our bags up over our heads as the cold water hit our chests, pushed our thighs, demanded we retreat, but we didn't. My muscles already ache, the arches of my feet screaming from slamming into wet stones and rolling rocks.

She hogs the drink. "You're already living the life, remember? You're getting paid to write." She pauses to take a sip. "Living the dream."

I wrestle the flask away from her fingers and grin. "Yeah, and I only had to go crazy to live it."

She softens slightly. "You're not crazy, hon."

"Dude, I'm fucking nuts."

She snorts and leans back, her profile slowly dwindling as the last of the daylight drains away. "If you're crazy, then so am I."

"Sisters in madness," I joke. The military has left its mark on Josephine as well, prying apart her brain and searing its brand somewhere deep inside the nodes and synapses. Maybe that's all our stories.

But right now, I don't feel mad. Right now I feel good and whole and bright. This is what the medication has given me—quietness and lucidity. The SSRI jump-started my brain and there is silence in here now. I'm doing well in the MFA program that Tim Parrish helped me get accepted into. I can still write; creativity still burns inside me. I'm almost high on the excitement of normalcy. I feel that shiver there in my chest, the delightful wings of ambition. I feel good.

She drains the last of the liqueur and then yawns, heavy with sleep and alcohol. Her yawn is contagious. "I needed this," I add.

"I know." Solidarity in two words.

I prop my head on her shoulder and close my eyes, heavy and happy and calm.

This is what the medication does: It hands me these weightless moments, the ability to enjoy. I grin because I can. I feel normal.

I'm terrified that will change. I remember that dark self and she scares me. I want nothing to do with her. It never occurs to me that one day I'll have to stop taking my medication. That one day I will pee on a stick that will show two blue lines instead of one and the decision will be made for me.

I sit in the doctor's office chair, staring at the woman behind the desk, my fingers interwoven with Roman's as he grins at her, grins at everything and everyone, and I'm fighting the bubble of anxiety in my chest, remembering the me who was dangerous to herself, the feeling of being stretched to the point of fracturing. How far down the rabbit hole will I tumble this time? Will this finally be the time I *don't* make it? The fear keeps me taking that pill every day, even though we have to go for extra ultrasounds, Roman gripping my hand as they probe deeper, checking for holes in our daughter's tiny little heart. I feel the shame of this danger, the weight of it, mine alone to bear, but I'm so afraid.

So I ask Roman to hide the handgun, just before my third trimester, because that's the time I *have* to get off the medication, by every doctor's suggestion. "Just put it somewhere else," I say, one hand rested on my swollen stomach, cupping the underbelly of my pregnancy. "Somewhere where I won't find it."

Roman nods, but the gun never moves from its drawer. I only know because I checked once, just to know if it was there.

But in the summer of 2015, after the first time I hold my daughter against my chest, both of us bloody and panting and dazzled, I know in that moment there will be parts of me I will never fear again. There will never be another suicide scare. As long as she is here, I'll never worry about the gun in the drawer or hitting a wall on the freeway. I can be re-formed here with a squirming baby resting against my bare chest. Her tiny toes press into the suppleness of my stomach, my body softens, my heart softens, as I stare down at this tiny thing, the girl with the deep-gray eyes and wet wisps of golden curls. I run one finger against the curve of her cheek and am saved. I can't be on medication while breastfeeding and I don't need it. I curl that little girl in my arms, enchanted, singing a soft song into her ear, tears dripping off my chin. It doesn't matter how different I am from everyone else. I can still love wholly, with all of me, and that's all that matters here.

"You'll be my greatest adventure," I whisper to her, a clichéd line I saw on some chalk-painted wooden board in Hobby Lobby, but it rings true for me. Adeline rewires my brain in a way no prescription ever could.

closing

DOES THAT MEAN THIS is my happy ending? Of course not. The demons aren't gone forever. That's not how this works.

Sometimes I'm convinced Roman doesn't love me anymore. He meets this accusation with a baffled stare, or a roll of his eyes, and, "I love you, babe. It's all in your head," but how can he? What is there left to love here? I am the woman who once spoke six languages, who climbed Mount Fuji, Le Mont-Saint-Michel, and Skellig Michael, but for whom now getting off the couch to wash a sink full of dishes is too hard.

PTSD is a sneaky motherfucker. I would have been prepared for the anxiety, the irrational thoughts, the OCD and health fears. I know what those are, know my triggers, know when to seek help because I can recognize when I'm sinking. But the depression sneaks up on me. It's subtle and quiet. I don't realize it's there until I've sunk most of the way down, sobbing over the kitchen sink, rubbing my eyes with the back of my hands as my daughter asks from her high chair, in her tiny, high voice, "What wrong, Momma? What wrong?"

I don't know how to tell her that I don't love me anymore. I was once something great and vicious and now I'm flat and dull. I don't know how to describe that loss to her, that she'll never meet the great woman I once was. "It's okay, baby. Mommy's just sad but you make me happy."

She brightens, her cheeks curl just like her father's, and she pipes back, "Make Momma happy!"

"You do," I gasp, cupping one hand around her cheek. I smile with tears streaking down my face. "You make me happy."

In a few days the episode will pass. I won't cry all day. When Roman comes home, I'll hold up my face for a kiss, smile and feel it. He won't seem distant to me, his hugs the perfect duration of time and effort. So what the fuck? What the fuck is this?

This is a different kind of demon. This creature sits on my shoulders and drags me down. And then the thing lifts off, dissipates suddenly, giving me just enough time to stand up, straighten, blink the haze from my eyes, to feel good. Then it returns again. Rinse and repeat.

"It may be time to think about going back on medication," my psychiatrist suggests. It's not something he says lightly.

"But I don't want to!" I don't want to have to get off it again for the next child, if we have one. I don't want to go through the vertigo and the nausea and the headaches, the weight gain. What I want is to be *fine*. I want to just be better already. I want to be over it by now.

I want the impossible. Doesn't everyone?

I'm always looking for closure. If I can find the proper ending, will I be able to move on then? Just close the book on my trauma and put it behind me? In the summer before Adeline is born, I think I can find closure in Sergeant Pelton, whose abandonment had been the biggest betrayal. The sergeant I had trusted the most for protection, who had turned on me. *I just need to hear the right words*, I think, *and then I can move on*.

Before Josephine and I embark on our summer cross-country trip from California to Texas, we agree to meet up in our old stomping grounds, beautiful, old Monterey, for a picnic with some other linguists. Josephine is still enlisted and in a Farsi refresher course, where she met Sergeant Pelton for the first time, whom she then befriended, long after Fort Polk, so long after that none of it should matter anymore. But it does. Every photo of him on her Facebook page turns in my gut. There he is laughing, diving off a boat into the ocean. There they are, drinks in hand, lounging by the beach. I don't know how to say, *You can't be friends with him*, so I say nothing.

So I bury my toes into the cold sand, fortifying myself with one arm wrapped around my waist, the other clutching a hard cider bottle. *Don't hug me, don't hug me*, I internally hiss, seeing Sergeant Pelton's bald head turn in my direction, watching his face brighten, the excitement reaching his vivid blue eyes.

"Ryan!" he crows, opening his arms, and stomps through the shifting sand, his flip-flops kicking up dirt behind him. He engulfs me then holds me out at arm's length, hands planted on my upper arms.

I flex. I'm thinner then, hard from years of CrossFit, from obsessing over what I eat, even if the medication has forced me up a size. But I'm still all lean muscle, and so I flex, because the last time he saw me was before Iraq, right before he left for another post, back when I was fat, what the Army labels *a shitbag soldier*: anyone who doesn't make weight or breaks tape. Back then I was still writhing down in the dirt, begging for a scrap of attention, for someone to validate me.

"You look great," he says. He seems genuine. Instead of my confronting him, rejecting him, we dig a bonfire pit together, taking turns with the small shovel, throwing cold, dark sand onto the beach.

The sun sets and I down another hard cider, feeling the alcohol settle down in my stomach and warm my limbs. I stare at the bonfire, the flames reaching up and casting shadows against the bluffs behind us. I press my cheek against the cool bottle, and I ask him.

Sergeant Pelton sits beside me. "I don't remember," he says of it all. I stare at him, with his head tilted just so, as if he is sympathetic, and I'm not satisfied.

"There are huge holes in my memory from my time there at Fort Polk," he says, and he then tells me why, the trauma that disrupted his life and his memory, and it's his story to share, not mine, but I'm still not satisfied.

"You don't remember me going to those CID appointments?" He shakes his head no. "The time I crawled under your desk before formation and just cried?"

He arches his eyebrows. "No, not at all."

"The report? You *read* the report."

"No. I don't remember."

"You kicked me out of your platoon," I accuse.

He shook his head again. "No, I didn't. You got moved for some reason. I don't remember why."

I hate that he's so convincing. I hate that his story makes sense. I hate that he has a perfectly good reason and that I don't get to have my day, my moment of anger, I don't get to stand here and rage at him. I hate that my trauma, my pain, the events that shaped my whole adult life haven't been worth remembering to those who had once meant the most to me.

He can't apologize, or explain why he did it, why he failed me, and that doesn't seem fair at all. And mostly I hate that I still like him, and that maybe I still want him to like me. I should have grown beyond this, yet sometimes I'm still the little girl who wants her daddy to turn around and notice her, struggling to keep up with him on the stony path. So I don't tell him to go fuck himself. I don't tell him that it's not okay. I don't get my closure from him.

The rest have moved on. Social media has tightened our world and I see our faces in little flashes from inside timelines. Female King has remarried, Locke is traveling the world with her own backpack, Sergeant Daniels has children. I sit behind a computer and type in a name, chest tight in apprehension, squinting at thumbnail pictures as I scroll down, examining all the Kevin Hales out there in the world, looking for the one I know. I don't find him. I wonder if I remember the spelling of his last name correctly. Was there an s maybe? An odd y? I squirm in my seat, scrolling down, hating that I'm looking, morbidly entangled because I don't want to see his face (would I remember his face?). I don't want to find him looking back out at me (would I know if he was?). And yet I look. I want to know where he is, so I can place a pin in that part of the map and avoid it. I picture him in the Midwest. I don't know why. Perhaps someone had once said he was from there. If he's out there somewhere, I'll never see him then. I'll never accidentally stumble into him on the street; he'll never walk into my CrossFit box, or one of my university classes. But I can't know for sure because I never find him on social media, no mutual friends, no familiar face. I'm relieved. I'm not relieved. There is no closure here, either.

"He's from Wyoming," my dad says suddenly, during my most recent visit to Maine.

I blink at him. "What? How do you know that?"

"What do you mean, how do I know? His name is ▮▮▮▮ and he's from Wyoming."

My father says Kevin Hale's real name, a name I haven't heard in decades, the name I haven't said in just as long. I stare at him, mouth open. "How . . . how do you even remember that?"

"Ryan." He stills, levels an unflinching stare at me. "That's not something you forget."

Maybe, all this time, I was looking for validation in all the wrong places. My father is the only one of my family to remember his name. It's somehow a well-preserved thing between just the two of us that I didn't know we shared until this moment.

"His unit hated him, you know. They wanted nothing to do with him."

I shake my head, baffled. "What are you, the FBI? How do you know all of this?"

He does that short laugh of his—one part at himself, the other part at the world. "I just did a little digging. You know what kind of dirtbag you need to be for your unit to hate you that much? They couldn't wait to get rid of him. He's gotta be behind bars now."

"Is he?" I exclaim.

"Or he's dead. Someone like that, you don't live in normal society. Dirtbags like that do that sort of thing again and they get caught or they get killed. He's taken care of." There's such conviction in the way he says that. I'm not sure I agree. I always thought he was out there somewhere, married with children, living a perfectly normal life, telling everyone about that one time some crazy bitch tried to cry rape against him. It never occurred to me that there was another possibility—I like my father's version better. It's idealistic and pretty and maybe even possible. Wouldn't that be nice?

Maybe there isn't closure for this sort of thing. Maybe this is closure enough. Maybe you never actually get over rape or war—you just have to carry it always, and it sits inside you, filling in the places where other things are lost and gone. I'm not okay. I'm not all better. I never tied myself back up and became like everyone else. But I have moments of vivid lucidity. I have flare-ups of exhilaration and ambition and delight. Sometimes, I laugh fully. I still open my arms up to the sky, spinning on a single foot to make my daughter laugh and to laugh with her. I dance like a horse, leap like a deer, twirl around with her in my arms, and I see a future here. For me, and for her. I see her finding love, her first heartbreak, the first time she'll rise up from the ground, dust herself off, and push forward.

I survive the demons and live in the interims. I'm not better, but I'm not broken, either.

Acknowledgments

I was never sure I'd actually get here, the last page of a published book, the one now sitting in your hands. I had hoped (and wrote), and dreamed (and wrote), and despaired (and wrote), and now here we are. My grandest dream has come true, and this most certainly is not an accomplishment I did on my own. First, I'd like to thank my brilliant editor, Millicent Bennett, who took something raw, scattered, and probably a bit melodramatic, and made it sleek, structured, and—let's face it—comprehensible. Millicent, this book would not be what it is today without your unending dedication and hard work. You've managed to edit while always making me feel confident and supported, which was essential, because I'm *such* a needy writer. Thank you for listening, collaborating, and turning my story into more than I ever could've imagined.

I also would not be here if not for my agent, Eve Attermann. Eve, I can't thank you enough for taking a chance on me based on nothing more than a few pages of work. You've supported and encouraged me, and probably had to hold my hand a lot more than most authors, and for that, thank you. You always, *always*, have my back. You make for the best battle buddy ever. Thank you also to Siobhan O'Neill and Svetlana Katz, who are fighting hard to, literally, get my book out there in the world.

Jake Halpern: How can I ever adequately thank you? You took the time to read the work of some random girl from the gym, then encouraged her and passed that work along. It may not have seemed like a big deal to you, but to me, it was everything. I can only hope that I'll one day be able to pay it forward for someone else, just like you've done for me.

It goes (almost) without saying that I'm deeply grateful to my mother, Linda Taylor. Thank you for always being my number one fan and supporting me in everything I've ever done. The woman I am today is only because of your endless love and support. To my father, Peter Dostie, I'm thankful for your quiet and steadfast love. Thank you for supporting me, even when I didn't realize or recognize it. You always let me be exactly who I am, and I think it's you who understands me the most. To my family—David, Jesse, and too many more to name here— and to my many friends, all those at CrossFit New Haven, all my fellow writers at SCSU, to everyone who has uplifted and cheered me on, you all know who you are, and you are loved.

Pamela Brodman, you're practically my soulmate. It's an under-statement to say you've always been there for me. Thank you for having seen the worst of my crazy and still come back for more. Thank you for reading everything I've written twelve times and still agreeing to read it once more. You nurture my writer's heart, which is to say you nurture me. Thank you for all of it and so much more.

Dr. Joseph Erdos, there is no question that your years of commitment have literally saved my life. There would be no book without you because if not for you, there'd be no me. Thank you for talking me through every variety of my insanity. You once told me to write just to make it through another day, and look where we are now.

Which leads me to Tim Parrish. Tim, everyone else helped me along this journey, but you're the one who started it all. You encouraged me to tell my story and made me feel like I had something worth saying. Thank you for withstanding every panicked email, text message, and frantic meeting. You took someone very green and somehow managed to turn her into, dare I say it, an actual writer. My entire craft I owe to you, and to Southern Connecticut State University's MFA program.

I also have to thank those people with whom I served (some of whom may or may not be very happy with me at the moment). I couldn't include everything and everyone in this memoir, but I was lucky to serve with some of the bravest women and men I've ever met, and whose own stories could shake the world should they ever tell them.

And of course my deepest gratitude goes to my husband, Mark Roman Osenko. Mark, you've put up with more than any husband should ever have to. You've seen me at my lowest and loved me anyway. You've weathered through things that would make lesser men run and carried burdens you should never have been forced to carry. You've done it all without complaint and, frankly, I don't know how you do it. Thank you for helping me pursue my dream and never once trying to dissuade me. I love you. Also, you're stuck with me now because I put you in a book.

Last, but perhaps most important, I need to thank all those who made *Formation* physically possible. Before this, I never realized the massive team that goes into creating and publishing a book. I sort of stumbled forward with a manuscript in hand, saying "Here. I wrote a thing," and the following people took that raw, fractured thing and helped turn it into the beautiful book you see now. My deepest gratitude to both Michael Pietsch and Ben Sevier, publisher of Grand Central, who saw enough promise in my early draft to let Millicent take a chance on me. Thank you to Karen Kosztolnyik, who has been a huge supporter of this book from the very beginning. To Matthew Ballast, Brian McLendon, and Beth deGuzman, thank you all for your support at acquisition, and all your hard work since. Thank you, Albert Tang, for working hard on getting us the very best jacket. Also to Liz Connor, who tirelessly produced endless different jacket comps so that we could find the perfect design, and who also is the very first person to gift this book to someone else, which is the greatest show of support any author can ask for. To my publicists, Linda Duggins and Kamrun Nesa, I'm so grateful to you for being a huge advocate for *Formation*, and for being willing to pull a James Bond move when necessary to help get it attention. A special thank you to Amanda Pritzker, Andrew Duncan, Alana Spendley, and Morgan Swift for all your creative marketing efforts and for diligently striving to get the word out there to readers. Which leads me to the sales department, where Alison Lazarus, Chris Murphy, Karen Torres, Rachel Hairston, and Ali Cutrone have bent over backward to help get *Formation* onto shelves and into readers' hands. Thank you, Bob Castillo, for helping to make sure the book is flawless on every practical level. Also to Laura Jorstad, my copyeditor, who caught my one hundred and one "shrugged one shoulder"s and overall saved me from being appallingly redundant. Thomas Louie came up with the kickass interior design. Thank you to Marilyn Dahl at Shelf Awareness for the wonderful writeup for *Glow*. Finally, thank you to assistants Meriam Metoui and WME's Haley Heidemann for the million and one things you do in between all this. You both are the vital supply lines to this army. Thank you all for going above and beyond the call of duty.

As a debut author, I'm aware that not every author is lucky enough to have such an amazing and enthusiastic team. I'm humbled and appreciative for all your hard work and especially the faith you've placed in me. I can only hope that I will prove worthy of such blood, sweat, and tears.

About the Author

RYAN LEIGH DOSTIE was an Army Persian-Farsi/Dari Linguist in Military Intelligence and was deployed to Iraq during Operation Iraqi Freedom. She holds an MFA from Southern Connecticut State University. She lives in New Haven, Connecticut, with her husband, her wondrously wild daughter, and one very large Alaskan Malamute.